The Boss's Survival Guide

The Boss's Survival Guide

Bob Rosner
Syndicated Columnist, *Working Wounded*

Allan Halcrow

Alan Levins
Attorney, Littler Mendelson

McGraw-Hill
New York   Chicago   San Francisco   Lisbon
London   Madrid   Mexico City   Milan   New Delhi
San Juan   Seoul   Singapore   Sydney   Toronto

Library of Congress Cataloging-in-Publication Data

Rosner, Bob.
  The boss's survival guide / by Bob Rosner, Allan Halcrow, Alan Levins.
    p. cm.
  ISBN 0-07-136273-8
  1. Supervision of employees. 2. Corporate culture. 3. Management. I. Title: Survival guide.
II. Halcrow, Allan. III. Levins, Alan. IV. Title.

HF5549.12.R67 2001
658-dc21   2001030969

McGraw-Hill

A Division of The McGraw·Hill Companies

5 6 7 8 9 0 DOC/DOC 0 9 8 7 6 5 4 3 2 1

ISBN 0-07-136273-8

This book was set in Times New Roman by MacAllister Publishing Services.

Printed and bound by R. R. Donnelley & Sons Company.

McGraw-Hill books are available at special quantity discounts to use as premiums and sales promotions, or for use in corporate training programs. For more information, please write to the Director of Special Sales, Professional Publishing, McGraw-Hill, Two Penn Plaza, New York, NY 10121-2298. Or contact your local bookstore.

 This book is printed on recycled, acid-free paper containing a minimum of 50% recycled, de-inked fiber.

For every boss who doesn't want to give Dilbert any more fuel.

To Robin, who lost far too many evenings working on her beloved novel to contribute to this manuscript. To my daughter Hallie, who I hope will avoid some of the bad managing that I had to experience in my career.

—BR

For Brian, for reasons beyond words.

—AH

To my wonderful wife, Sharon, and my daughters, Emily and Amy Levins. You are my daily inspiration, and the reason I have gone down the "road" that I did.

—AL

Contents

Acknowledgments

Thanks to everyone who has written to me through the years or has contributed to WorkingWounded.com. You are the real motivation and spirit behind this book.

—BR

Many thanks to Bob, Robin, and Daniel, who gave me a crash course in Books 101, and to Billie Cummings, who taught me the basics. This book was written during a very difficult year. My heartfelt thanks to my father, Douglas Halcrow, and his wife, Eileen, for being there. To the great, treasured friends who helped me through it: Scott Bartchy, Nancy Breuer, Shari Caudron, Lynne Gabriel, Juanita Odin, and Charlene Solomon—I am forever grateful. To my nieces, Marie and Nathalie, who inspire me to focus on the future. And my thanks to all the people who contributed stories—the book is richer because of you.

—AH

To the attorneys and staff at Littler Mendelson, the National Labor and Employment Law Firm, where any "boss" can be confident that questions regarding labor and employment law will be answered quickly, accurately, and in a commonsense way that will help him or her through what could otherwise be a difficult situation.

—AL

Authors' Notes:

All the material in this book reflects the views of the authors. It should not be construed as legal advice.

In the interest of improving readability, we decided not to use the cumbersome "he or she" and "his or hers" construction of sentences when we are not referring to specific people. We also chose not to break the rules of grammar and use "they" when referring to a single person. Instead, we've used "he" or "she" throughout the book. The choice of which we used in any given place is entirely random, and should not be construed as a political statement. Really.

1

Welcome to the Swatch World: How the Workforce Has Changed and What You Need to Know to Manage It

It's not your father's management job.

That's the first and most important thing to know, whether you're a new boss, a veteran boss, the boss's boss, or a boss to be.

Yes, Dad may have trudged eight miles in the snow to get to work, but when he got there, he could depend on seeing the same faces he'd left the night before and that he'd see the next day, the next month, the next year. By and large, they did what they were told, reliably. Employees gathered at the water cooler to share jokes they thought were funny. If someone brought a briefcase, it was to carry paperwork and slide rules. And Dad was always right—at least that's what everyone said to his face.

But that corporate Camelot was a distant moon ago. Now you'll pray through the morning rush hour that your best people haven't scored a better deal overnight. People giggle nervously at jokes, worried they're not politically correct. You hope that security checks briefcases for cocaine and guns, and you go to parties wondering whether your peers will be talking about their new severance packages. Riding the economy offers more thrills than a roller coaster. Your labor lawyer is a speed-dial button on your cell phone, and a kid half your age is apt to look right at you and ask, "How do I know you won't screw it up?"

It's easy to be nostalgic for the good old days. "When I started out, the boss had all the power and all the perks," says Tom, a middle manager at a manufacturing firm who just celebrated the Big 4-0. "We did what we were told, and waited until the day we could be the boss. Now I am the boss, and no one will do anything unless they want to. I have to cater to *them* or they leave. When is it *my* time?"

Well, Tom, believe it or not, your time is *now.* It's true you've missed out on three-martini lunches, power suits, and insincere fawning. But you've also missed being a cog with no real power or influence. You've been spared doing the same damn thing every day for 30 years just to get a gold watch. You've also been entrusted with a job that *matters* in a way that managers' jobs have never mattered before, because your actions, more than any other factor, will make your best employees stay or go.

Your mission, should you choose to accept it, is to be a bolder, better boss: A boss with a strategic impact on the success or failure of your organization.

Of course, back when they tapped you, they never said that being a boss was easy. It's not. There's an alphabet soup of laws and regulations to worry about—ADA, FLMA, I-9. There's the challenge of trying to "do more with less" (if only your employees knew you're as tired saying it as they are of hearing it). The nature of work itself has been forever changed by technology and a global economy. In many ways, you're being measured against tougher standards than any boss before you.

But those changes pale in comparison to changes in the workforce. Those reliable, 9-to-5, pin-striped employees of the past have morphed into workers with a way of thinking and behaving all their own. Their needs, their values, and their concerns mean they need to be managed in a wholly different way.

And to make matters even more challenging, there aren't enough of them.

Let's step back for a moment to put your workforce into perspective.

GOODBYE GOLD-WATCH WORKERS, HELLO SWATCH WORKERS

Until the 1980s, employee loyalty meant punching the same time clock from diploma to grave. Whether the boss was a kindly father figure or an antacid-swilling S.O.B. didn't matter. People shrugged it off and kept plugging away until they earned that nifty gold watch.

No more! Today's employees have attention spans the length of an MTV video. They don't *want* your gold watch. They're Swatch employees; watches and jobs are of the moment, not for a lifetime. No wonder the average job tenure is now 3.5 years and shrinking.

But don't dismiss this Swatch mindset as youthful rebellion and wait for GenXers to just "grow up." The Swatch attitude cuts across all age groups, and it has nothing to with being raised by Big Bird. To understand it, think back to the mid-'80s when hundreds of thousands of employees at America's biggest companies were axed —often with little or no regard for their contributions, longevity, or dignity. The message to employees was clear: You're only valuable until we have a bad quarter and shareholders scream, at which point you're expendable. And although we like to think of mass layoffs as part of our unenlightened past, they're not. Record layoffs in 1999 and 2000 didn't make headlines only because the economy absorbed the shock.

　　Swatch workers have actually accepted this new economy, but they aren't stupid and they *do* have mortgages to pay. So they're ever ready to go where they can get the best deal: the best job challenges, the best compensation package, and, yes, the best boss.

Yes, Virginia, There Is a Labor Shortage

As if the Swatch mindset isn't enough of a challenge, the problem is compounded by demographics. We'll save you the expense of therapy and tell you right now that you can blame Mom and Dad for that. They didn't have enough kids! You can do the math:

> 　76 million Americans in the baby boom generation are beginning to retire.
>
> − 　44 million Generation Xers are left in the workforce. That means there are
>
> 　32 million fewer workers to fill America's jobs.

　　And over the next 15 years the problem's going to get worse. Workers will be aging and retiring. The supply of 35 to 45 year olds will *decline* by 15 percent, but even according to the most conservative estimates, the demand for workers will continue to *increase*. You don't need a calculator to see the problem. It won't begin to get better until 2010 when the kids behind GenX enter the workforce. That's a long time to wait.

Labor and Talent Are Not the Same Thing

OK, but suppose you're some sort of cockeyed optimist and you think the boom times of the late '90s were a freak occurrence and economic downturn will free up all that labor. Sorry. Even that won't solve your problem, because *labor* and *talent* are not the same thing. If they were, the Rangers would have help wanted ads at DFW and Alex Rodriguez wouldn't be earning $170,000 a game for the next decade.

For most of the '90s we had a labor shortage *and* a talent shortage. But when companies downsize, guess who they'll send packing? Not the best workers. It'll be the people who couldn't get interviews before the boom times!

In fact, if anything, the talent shortage will grow *faster* than the labor shortage because of the changing nature of our economy. As we shift increasingly from a manufacturing to a knowledge economy, more jobs require people to think, conceptualize, and create than ever before. Not everyone can do those things, or at least not well. (And even if the Gen Xers are right and they *are* disproportionately smarter than all other generations, there are fewer of them, so fewer still who can be superstars!)

Nope. The shortage is real, serious, and long-term. Accept it.

Let Them Be Paid Cake

Of course, some companies feel like they've already got the situation under control. When the manager at a Silicon Valley company recently pointed out to his boss that many experienced workers were leaving the company, the boss gave him the Marie Antoinette wave. "Oh, just throw a few more baubles at them," she said. Problem solved. Or was it?

Well . . . she had the right idea. With quality workers in short supply, she knew she had to make her current ones stay. She knew *retention* is the name of the game. What she was missing, though, was an effective solution.

And, of course, she wasn't alone. Most companies trying to cope with dwindling talent have developed equally ineffective retention strategies. They practice the three Os:

- Options (they bribe people to stay)
- Overtime (they force the remaining people to work longer hours)
- Offshore (they send jobs overseas to make up for the lack of workers here)

(Then there are the companies that use the fourth O: Ostrich. They simply refuse to see the problem.)

Of course, none of these strategies is effective for the long term. They're expensive, complicated, and stress-inducing. They also do little to resolve the underlying problems that encourage good employees to leave. Fortunately, there *is* a solution to the talent shortage that is long-term, inexpensive, and readily available. So readily available, in fact, that it's usually overlooked. That solution is *you*: the boss.

We Have Met the Solution, and It Is You

You are the solution to the talent shortage because you, more than any other factor, make your best people want to stay or go. Think about your own career. Has a boss ever driven you out of a job? Have you ever had enough of being manipulated, of soothing a fragile ego, of being discredited, lied to, or ignored?

Perhaps you've been fortunate. Have you ever been challenged, encouraged, and rewarded? Been treated with respect and compassion? Found talent you didn't know was there, grown beyond your expectations, and made a real contribution? In short, have you stayed in a job because of your boss?

If you answered yes to either question, you aren't alone. In a 2000 Lou Harris poll, 40 percent of people who rate their boss "poor" said they would look for a new job within the year. Only 11 percent who rated their boss "excellent" said the same thing. Clearly, the boss isn't the only factor people consider when making a job change. But think about those numbers another way. If 11 percent of your people left instead of 30 percent or 40 percent, wouldn't your company show its appreciation with a nice bonus check?

Middle management isn't the disease; middle management is the cure!

"I Would Not Work for Me."

Too bad it's so darn difficult. Being a boss these days is kind of like being in an SUV. You sit there, high in your "command position," powering down the road. Then suddenly you come to a bump or a sudden turn and BLAM! It's all you can do to keep from overturning.

And the bumps and turns are everywhere! Just look at your to-do list:

- Yesterday's Problems to solve
- Today's Production to maintain

- Next quarter's Profits to make
- The Parallel universe (in which your own boss lives) that you have to contend with
- The Politics of the organization
- The Policies you have to enforce
- The Personal stuff (like dentist appointments, dinner plans, and the like) that encroach from outside the company's walls
- And then there's your *People*

We say that people are our greatest asset, but they usually wind up toward the bottom of the list. We get to them at 4:45 when we're tired and our best has been used. We don't set out to do that, but our performance is judged more on production and profits. Besides, the people will be there tomorrow. They'll understand . . . won't they?

No wonder even the best-intentioned bosses find managing well is hard. We said the solution was simple. We didn't say it was easy. Mike J. sent an email to WorkingWounded.com: "I tried to take all the bad qualities of every boss I had and throw them out the window. The problem was, I developed some original bad habits of my own. In my own opinion, I would not work for me!"

Their Way or the Highway

The toughest part may be letting go of outdated management styles. We cling to the way we were managed earlier in our careers, but it doesn't make any more sense than dealing with Russia as if it's still a communist superpower. Swatch employees need a new kind of management:

- *They want to be trained*: They know they may be job-hunting tomorrow, so maintaining and growing their skills is vital.

- *They want to be coached*: They don't need a manager who'll walk to the plate with them, hold the bat, swing, and run. They do need a manager who will show them how to be better hitters, strategize their next at bat, and show them how to beat the opposing team.

- *They want flexibility*: Families and personal lives are their top priorities, and they need flexibility to be able to manage those parts of their lives.

- *They want the truth*: They're savvy enough to accept mergers, downsizings, and massive change as part of life. They can cope with anything, but they want to know what they're coping with.

- *They want to belong*: They want to believe in what the organization is all about, and they want to know they're making a contribution.

Managers who can't provide these things lose their talent. It's that simple. Too many other jobs are out there where the bossing may be better. The old days of "my way or the highway" are gone. Now it's *their* way or the highway.

We're Not Managing Chickens

An awful lot of us put huge amounts of time and expense into finding the smart, skilled, talented people for our jobs—and then we manage them as if they haven't enough sense to come in out of the rain. Fortunately, we're trainable. With a little thought and attention, you can become the kind of boss even the most fickle employee will want to work for.

12 STEPS TO BETTER BOSSING

1. Don't have a feast attitude during a famine

Suppose that you went in to work tomorrow and discovered that a computer worth $5,000 was missing. What would happen? Someone would call the police. There would be an investigation in which people were interviewed, evidence examined, and routines questioned. Ultimately, you might adopt new security procedures or buy security equipment.

Now, suppose that you went in to work tomorrow and a key employee quit. What would happen? Although replacing the employee will cost far more than $5,000, odds are there would be no investigation. No one would see the situation as a crisis. No one would find out why the employee was leaving, and there probably wouldn't be any changes made to make it more likely people would stay. Retention guru Beverly Kaye suggests there should be.

We are in the midst of a labor and talent shortage. Don't be cavalier about people. Treat them as precious resources, and take it seriously if you lose one.

2. Don't recruit like you used to recruit

It used to be (until just a few years ago) that applicants came to the job market as sellers and companies came as buyers. Companies posted their jobs and applicants came touting their skills, hoping to impress the companies into buying. But times have changed. Today, it's the company that has to do the selling, impressing the best candidates so they will come to *them* instead of going with a competitor. One 20-something actually did look at E-Trade's CEO and ask, "How do I know you won't screw it up?" So change that old recruiting mindset: Think of recruiting as a time to "sell" your job—its challenges and opportunities—to the buyer. Share your vision; then lay out a plan for how he can help make it happen.

3. Don't abuse employees

If you abuse employees, they won't take it out on the dog—they'll take it out on customers.

Sam Walton claimed that his highest priority was treating employees well because happy employees would be better with customers, who in turn would buy more. Walton started out in a small town in Arkansas and built the biggest retail company on Earth. Perhaps he was on to something.

4. Don't be a "ready, fire, aim" boss

Recently, the pace of the workplace has become so accelerated that managers have been valued for the *speed* with which they act. That may be good for developing campaigns, implementing strategies, and establishing sales and production targets, but it's *not* OK for working with *people*. One employee complained that her boss spent so little time with her that he couldn't pick her out of a police line-up. If he didn't know who she was, how could he possibly know how to deploy her talents? He couldn't—he was too busy solving problems without all his resources.

Employees need *time*. Time for you to get to know them, time for you to coax out all they have to offer, time for you to make them

feel appreciated. When they come to you with problems, don't save 10 minutes by telling them the answer. Ask what they've already tried, what else they can think of doing. Turn their questions into learning opportunities for you both. It's fine to be a type A personality when it comes to your assignments, but when it comes to people, adopt type B behaviors. Sometimes inefficiency is more efficient in the long run.

5. Don't follow the Golden Rule

We all learn as children to do unto others as we would have them do unto us. But following the Golden Rule assumes that others want what you want, and that may not be true.

Ask what employees want. And then do it unto them.

6. Get out of the way

If you know anything about Ebay or instant messaging, you know that peer-to-peer relationships are where it's at. When two or more people have data or merchandise to trade, going through a central hub or up a hierarchical ladder only slows things down. The same is true at work. Employees who are unencumbered by their bosses can achieve enormous gains if they're given the latitude to work together and make decisions without having to clear everything through the boss.

So don't discourage employees from networking and tackling problems on their own. Don't see them as a threat to your power. Accept that how things get done in your group may bear little resemblance to the organizational chart. If anything, learn who the catalysts are in these informal "self-organizing communities" and then support their efforts.

Sure, there's a risk in stepping back and giving your people freedom, but if you want employees with initiative and creativity, you've got to give them room to exercise them.

Bonnie, a mid-level manager at a health insurance company, required every one of her 50 direct reports to check in with her every morning. How much time, and how much morale, was lost as people waited in line to report to Mama? Don't be a Bonnie. Get out of your employees' way.

7. Be customer focused

We all know that the customer is always right. If we do what customers want, they'll keep buying. Former Sun Microsystems executive Jim Moore observes that bosses have customers, too: their employees. And just like the customers of your business, they can go elsewhere if they're unhappy.

So give those employee customers what they want. That doesn't mean honor every request for a raise, a vacation, and a bonus. It means tailor a working environment for them that meets their individual needs: their need for recognition, the kinds of challenges they respond to, the degree of attention versus independence they require, and so on.

Pavel Brun, artistic director at Cirque du Soleil, has learned that clowns do their best work when put into an ordinary environment, because they look for humor in the familiar. Gymnasts, on the other hand, often do their best work in exotic environments because it encourages them to use their technical expertise in creative ways. That's why he has developed an individually tailored plan for each of his 160 performers. Do you have a specific plan for each of the customers of your bossing?

8. Measure, evaluate, reward

Would Marion Jones have taken the gold in the Sydney Olympics if she'd never set goals or measured her progress? Of course not. In the sprints and marathons of your workplace, your employees need goals and measurements too. They need to know clearly and measurably what you expect of them. They need regular progress reports so they know if they're on target. And like Marion, they need medals when they succeed.

But measuring and evaluating aren't just for employees anymore. Bosses need those things, too. If you're going to be the kind of boss that people want to work for, you need to hear from your employees how you can help them. You need to hear from them how you're doing. And, like Marion, you need kudos from them when you succeed. You need a system (formal, informal, written, or verbal; the specifics don't really matter) that will let your employees give you the same kind of feedback you give them. Create such a system and use it. Listen carefully and act on the information. It's the only way you'll earn the gold.

9. Reveal your waterline

WL Gore is a successful manufacturer with an entrenched and unusual corporate culture. Among other things, they encourage employees to make decisions themselves. Only decisions *below the waterline* are reserved for managers. What's the waterline? It's the point at which a decision can have major ramifications for the company. Think icebergs meeting the hull. A client with $1,000 in sales? Let the employees decide. A client with $1 million in sales? Get the manager involved. Of course, that means that all Gore employees and managers know the company's waterline. Do you and your employees know yours?

10. Ask, "What will it take to keep you?"

Retention guru Beverly Kaye notes that bosses almost never ask what it will take to keep someone. They fear they won't be able to fill the request. But Kaye says that many requests are filled more easily than bosses think, and even if an employee's top request isn't possible, numbers two and three might be. Simply asking the question lets employees know they're important.

Still don't believe us? Then think about how you'd feel if your boss asked *you* this question.

11. E=M(C)²: Energy = Mission x Cash x Congratulations

Do you want your employees to bring more energy to work each day? Then follow the simple formula that Ken Blanchard adapted from Einstein's original formula for the creation of energy. First, create a compelling vision for your people. Even the most mundane widget maker can help his employees see the benefits their widgets bring by reporting glowing stories from the customers. Second, although contributing to a mission is important, it won't have nearly the impact if employees' wallets are empty. So make sure you recognize their efforts with appropriate pay scales, bonuses, and raises. Third, although contributing to a mission and receiving cash rewards are critical, nothing gooses energy on a *daily* basis like genuine pats on the back. So be generous with your praises.

Most people think good bossing is an art, and it is. But in this case, it's also a science.

12. Be their mother flame

For each Olympic games, the Olympic torch is run across the host country, passed from one runner to the next. The process is symbolic of Olympics past, and it allows many people to be involved. Sometimes, however, the torch goes out. That's why a small truck drives alongside the runners. Inside the truck is the mother flame, ready to relight the torch when needed.

Employees need a mother flame too. They get tired and discouraged; their flames and their passions go out. When that happens, they need to come to you to relight them.

One sales manager could sense when one of her best performers was fading and would call the employee into her office for the "Yes, we believe!" speech. It was a mini-pep rally that assured the employee that the manager still believed in the product, the process, and in her. Other managers make it clear that when an employee needs to talk they will put down what they're doing and make themselves available to simply *listen*.

The forms that mother flames take are endless: a few minutes of problem-solving, an encouraging word, a shoulder to lean on or to cry on. Find something that works for you. You'll be surprised. It takes remarkably little to rekindle an employee's flame if the gesture is timely and genuine.

DO THE RIGHT THING

This book is jammed with hundreds of ideas you can use to save time, solve problems, and stay out of jail. It's also designed to help you maximize your strengths as a leader. What is a leader? Someone with a fancy office and a title? Someone with a wall full of awards?

Someone who is constantly called by headhunters? No, we take a simpler view. A leader is someone with followers, and this book is dedicated to giving you the tools and insight to keep your followers.

This book aims to give you something else as well. It aims to give you the tools to create a more humane workplace for your people. There are many reasons to do that. Do it to keep your best people. Do it to attract other stars. Do it to ensure the success of your own career. But most of all, do it because it's the right thing to do.

If you succeed, and you can, you'll earn the genuine respect of your staff. You'll find strengths you didn't know you had. You'll make a significant difference in the lives of your employees and in your company. Imagine what it will do for your career.

2

A Short Course in Management

In the end, the Allied victory in World War II came down to a single event: the Normandy Invasion. The attack was so audacious, so brilliantly planned, and so superbly executed that it was enough to stop the enemy and ultimately end the war in Europe.

There's a lesson in that for all of us. Although a thousand demands are placed on us every day, from "Have you seen the stapler?" to "I'm being sexually harassed," we can't be everywhere at once, and we can't give all our competing priorities equal attention.

So if you have to focus your efforts, which are the beachheads that *really* demand your attention? Here are your battle plans. Follow them to stay out of jail and hang on to your best people. That's not to say the rest of what you do doesn't matter, but at the end of the war, it's how you fought the toughest battles that matter most.

TOP 10 THINGS TO DO TO STAY OUT OF JAIL

Literally thousands of Federal, state, and local laws regulate workplace interactions in some way. Keeping on top of them is a challenge. These are the areas in which managers are most likely to get into trouble.

10. Make sure your offer letter lays out all of the ground rules from the start, and the applicant acknowledges receipt and acceptance of the handbook before officially being hired. (Chapter 7, page 152)

9. Give employees the time and support they're entitled to when they face medical issues and disabilities. (Chapter 12, page 386 and Chapter 8, page 225)

8. Make certain that your exempt employees really are exempt. (Chapter 3, page 48)

7. Respect employee privacy. (Chapter 12, page 382)

6. Give employees, including managers, the training they need. (Chapter 9, page 298)

5. Do everything you can to prevent sexual harassment. If it happens, take action immediately. (Chapter 12, page 368)

4. Make employment decisions based on work-related factors; ignore irrelevancies (such as race and gender). (Chapter 8)

3. Write effective termination letters. (Chapter 10, page 331)

2. Impose effective discipline. (Chapter 10, page 310)

1. Take performance reviews seriously. Be accurate and honest. (Chapter 9, page 277)

TOP 10 THINGS TO DO TO KEEP YOUR BEST PEOPLE

Remember, you're managing Swatch workers, and what worked before may not work for them. Here's how to focus your attention to hang on to your best people.

10. Hone your listening skills. (Chapter 11, page 340)

9. Respect cultural values. (Chapter 8, page 188)

8. Manage to get the best results. (Chapter 9, page 251)

7. Recognize the value of emotional intelligence. (Chapter 8, page 191)

6. Don't underestimate the value of informal recognition. (Chapter 9, page 259)

5. Keep employees in the loop. (Chapter 11, page 346)

4. Vary your leadership style. (Chapter 9, page 244)

3. Manage within the context of your organization's culture. (Chapter 3, page 24)

2. Share your expectations for employee behavior. (Chapter 3, page 50)

1. Walk the talk. (Chapter 11, page 351)

3

Getting Started

For most of us, the flight experience begins when we rush to the gate like bargain hunters at an after-Christmas sale and push our way aboard so that we can take our seats and be whacked by the carry-on luggage of every passenger behind us. But for the pilot, the flight experience begins long before that. He physically inspectes the plane, checks the fuel and instruments, reviews the weather report, and much more. This happens because the pilot has responsibility for the flight, and before take off he must have a thorough understanding of the context in which he is flying.

Although you don't have to fly a 747 safely from Los Angeles to Sydney, you still need to follow the pilot's example before you start managing anything. Get a clear sense of the organization you're working in, the rules you need to enforce, and the resources you have. Then determine your expectations for the people you supervise. If you don't take the time now to determine these things before you even interview a candidate or make an assignment, you can expect turbulence, and you won't be able to blame your problems on the weather.

ORGANIZATIONAL CULTURE: HOW TO MANAGE IN SYNCH WITH YOUR COMPANY'S VALUES

Know the Issue

Close your eyes and imagine going to work for Tiffany & Co. How are you interacting with people? What's the office environment like? What are you wearing? Now close your eyes and imagine going to work for Jamba Juice. Ask yourself the same questions. Are the answers the same? What if the two organizations were Citibank and Cirque du Soleil? Or the Florida State Supreme Court and *Playboy*?

You don't have to have worked for any of these companies to know that working for them offers very different experiences. So why is it that so many people assume that a manager's job is a manager's job is a manager's job? The truth is that management jobs are *very* different from one company to another. Your success or failure will be measured in terms of your work within the context of your organization's culture. An action that earned you a bonus at one company could get you fired from another.

So before you start setting goals and coaching employees, take a hard look at how decisions are made and what behavior is rewarded. The more familiar you are with your organization's culture, the greater the odds that you'll triumph.

Take Action

- *Look at the big picture.* Defining the myriad elements of your company's culture will help you know how to succeed.

- *Success*: How is success defined in your organization? Success may be measured only by revenue or profit, but it may also be measured by meeting goals, learning, maintaining certain standards, customer rankings, or other measures. How does *your* company define winning?

- *Time*: Is your organization focused on the next quarter or the next five years? If you fail next quarter but win over the long-term is that all right? How much time is given for an effort to succeed before the plug is pulled? What is the organization's attention span?

- *Mistakes*: We all make mistakes. How are they handled? Are people who err punished or celebrated? (One company gives bonuses to the people who make the most mistakes based on the theory that they are attempting more.) Do people rally to fix a mistake or step back and point fingers? Does the company learn from its mistakes or make the same ones repeatedly?

- *Decisions*: How are decisions made? Are decisions made at the top and work their way down, or is consensus important? Are decisions respected or second-guessed? Is rethinking a decision in light of new information encouraged or frowned upon? Are decisions explained or defended?

- *Risk*: How is risk tolerated? Is the organization prone to bet the farm (as Boeing did on the 747 and Disney did on Disneyland) or are bets hedged? If you climb out on a limb will people stand below with a net or saw off the limb?

- *Ethics*: How important are ethics in making decisions? Does the company volunteer the truth or wait to be asked? Does the company's public relations department deal with crises head-on (as Johnson and Johnson did after some doses of Tylenol were tampered with), or resort to denial and euphemisms? Does the company consider human rights or environmental issues when making business decisions?

- *Trust*: Do employees trust each other or are you advised to watch your back? Do people trust what they hear from management?

- *Formality*: Do employees interact with top management directly? Do meetings follow Robert's Rule of Order or are they free flowing? Do you have casual dress or is everyone in a blue suit? Does every office space look unique, or does the place look like a spread in *Office Beautiful*?

- *Employees*: Does the company really believe that employees are its greatest asset or are they seen as an expense? Do managers fight for employees or against them? Does management treat employees with respect until they do something to lose that respect, or does management disrespect employees until they "earn" respect?

  There are no right or wrong cultures, but every culture has right and wrong ways of doing things.

- *Listen.* If you've worked for your company for any time, you probably can answer those questions easily and cite examples to make your case. If you're new, you can learn over time and possibly make job-ending mistakes along the way, or you can ask questions—lots of questions.

  This doesn't mean that you should don a fedora and move through the office like Sam Spade, Super Sleuth. But it does mean you should ask people questions during meetings, over lunch, and at the water cooler. Pose the questions as a request for advice ("This project I'm working on could go like gang-busters or really tank. What do you think?") as opposed to a challenge ("Why doesn't anyone around here seem to care about employees?"). Listen without judging and take in the information. Is the feedback that you're hearing consistent, or does everyone seem to have a different take?

- *Observe.* Pay attention to how things are done. Does everyone seem to be using the same playbook, or are they running into each other in a frantic attempt to control the ball? Are words and actions consistent, or do people say one thing and do another? Pay particular attention to how people behave under stress. Let's say you've been told that employees are the company's greatest asset. When numbers are down, do you spend time at a meeting talking about how to downsize or does the idea never come up?

- *Create a matrix for yourself.* Most cultures are not clearly articulated. To make it easy for you to see the culture you're working in, spend 10 or 15 minutes creating a grid for yourself. In one column, list the areas we discussed above. Then, add the following in columns beside each area:

  - Use a few words to describe the prevailing culture ("encourages taking risks").

  - List examples.

  - Note people in the company who are known to have these qualities and are admired for them.

When you're done, you should have a good idea of your environment, and a handy cheat sheet to review when you make decisions. (You'll have people to go to for advice and a precedent you can follow.)

- *Embrace the culture or leave.* Once you've identified the culture, live by it or get out. Any culture is bigger than you are, and you won't be able to change it. Remember, you can't teach a pig to sing; it will frustrate you and annoy the pig.

A proviso: if the culture isn't clear (it has no consensus) or it's schizophrenic (the culture values learning but discourages taking risks), it's hard to win. The best companies have strong cultures that give you clear parameters for making decisions.

Stay Out of Jail

- *If you choose to work in a company that doesn't value employees, beware!* Subverting the law, cutting corners on documentation, discriminating against employees in any group, and other tactics designed to show employees "who's boss" *will* get you in legal trouble—it's just a matter of time. Even if you act with the tacit or overt approval of the company, understand that you could spend a lot of time in court defending your actions. You may find it difficult to find another job if you're seen as playing fast and loose with common sense. And you could even end up charged in a lawsuit *yourself.*

Manage Up

When you're sizing up the culture, pay particular attention to what your boss says and does. Don't get caught in the crossfire of a culture war.

ORGANIZATIONAL STRUCTURE: HOW TO MANEUVER THROUGH THE *REAL* POWER GRID

Know the Issue

The Winchester Mystery House in San Jose, California, was under construction every day for 38 years. It has 160 rooms, stairs leading nowhere, blind closets, secret passageways, and, possibly, a ghost. How the Victorian mansion got that way is a complex story of widowhood, eccentricity, curses, and a spiritual medium.

Fallingwater, Frank Lloyd Wright's masterpiece in Bear Run, Pennsylvania, was built in four years. It's a marvel of design and engineering, straddling a waterfall to blend into its natural surroundings with unprecedented élan. It's the apotheosis of Wright's considerable experience and genius.

The two buildings have just three things in common: they are among the best-known private homes built during the last century, they are popular tourist attractions, and they are also metaphors for many corporate structures.

Some companies are Winchester-like puzzles of layers, chains of command that may go nowhere and secret alliances. Others are models of streamlined efficiency and clear authority. Which do you work in? This matters because the structure—spoken or otherwise—will shape how you get things done and how you are evaluated. So walk the halls and draw yourself a floor plan. You'll need it.

Take Action

- *Find an organization (org) chart.* Somewhere is a document that charts how the organization is *supposed* to work. It probably shows the president or CEO at the top, with branches below that lead to other senior executives and their departments. The org chart can provide valuable insight into how your company works, such as

- Are all departments on the same level of hierarchy, or are some closer to the top than others? Generally, the closer to the top of the chart a department is, the more clout it has. Where does your department fall?

- How many layers are between the top and the bottom? Two? Six? Twenty-three? The greater the number of layers, the more bureaucracy you'll find, and the greater the distance between the top and the bottom, the more likely senior management is out of touch.

- Does the top human resources exec report directly to the top? If so, employees have a better chance of being valued and having the company invest in them and in you. If HR reports to finance, every decision is likely to come down to money. If HR reports to administration or operations, you can expect a flailing bureaucracy.

- *Find out who's not on the chart.* Many people may wield a lot of power in the company and not appear on the org chart.

  In publicly held firms, shareholders and the Board of Directors are other groups to consider. Review an annual report to get a sense of how the Board votes. What's their agenda? Have shareholders generally supported the Board, or is there a lot of dissension present? You'll have better luck selling an idea in an organization with cohesion at the top. You can also forget selling any idea that's at odds with what the Board wants.

If your company is a subsidiary of a corporate monolith, it may be pretty much left alone or it may be micro-managed by the big guys. You can find out which is the case by reading the annual report, asking around in the investor relations department, and reading news accounts of company business.

Even in a privately held company, the boss may not really be her own boss. Are family members behind the scenes? Perhaps they're quite visible even if they aren't on the org chart. Investors might also be calling some shots.

- *Take politics into account.* No matter what the org chart says, politics is an issue; how much of an issue varies from one company to another. Even if all departments are theoretically equal, does the CEO favor one department? Did the CEO and the CFO belong to the same fraternity in college? Have two department heads formed an alliance to get things done? Is it a friendly or hostile alliance? Does a politically savvy underling have more power than her boss? To find out, invite the co-workers who have been around longest to lunch and ask. Pay attention at meetings. And watch how your boss interacts with other employees in the company.

- *Figure out how decisions are made.* Once you know the structure, it's easier to figure out how decisions are made. Which decisions can you make, and which do you need to run by your boss? Which decisions can your boss approve, and which will get bounced up another level or three? How many layers of approval are there? Who in the chain of command can veto a decision?

- *Use your knowledge of the structure.* You may uncover enough intrigue to fill several episodes of "General Hospital," but the information offers more than entertainment value. Use the information to get things done:

- *If the decision-making process has many layers, allow enough time to get a decision.* Don't procrastinate until the last minute, and don't make every decision a crisis.

- *Once you know who the stakeholders are, lobby them.* Don't make your boss do all the work. Visit the stakeholders and sell them on the value of your idea. Keep your boss in the loop so it's evident you're still acting as a team. Remember that lobbying for support and doing an end run around your boss are different. (Don't lobby for ideas your boss has already said no to, for example.)

- *Find allies.* Some people always have more political clout than others. Find one or two individuals who share your values, and woo them. Draw on their expertise and ask for their support of your agenda. Then offer the same in return.

- *Be visible.* If investors, family members, or others play a role, make the effort to meet them. Say hello when you see them, ask about the kids, and send holiday cards.

- *Have the ammunition you need.* If the CFO has to buy off on your idea, have the financial data she'll want. If another stakeholder likes information in bullet points, present it that way. Do what you can to make it easier for people to say yes.

- *Avoid butting in and making suggestions for how others should run* their *departments.* If you try it, watch your support network evaporate.

Manage Up

Respect your boss's position. Publicly support her decisions and policies. Don't go over your boss's head if you're unhappy. Don't act as your boss's agent (by sharing information or making decisions) without her permission.

THE HANDBOOK: HOW TO USE THE RULES TO YOUR ADVANTAGE

Know the Issue

In the beginning, there were the 10 Commandments. All 10 of them include just 179 words, and they seem pretty all-inclusive. But that hasn't stopped people from coming up with more rules. The rules have become more complicated, too. The U.S. government uses 26,911 words to outline regulations on the sale of cabbage. Presumably, nothing nefarious stands between our coleslaw and us.

If we need 26,911 words to control cabbage commerce, how many words does it take to define the rules in our companies? It depends on our corporate culture. At Nordstrom, the employee handbook is printed on an 8" x 5" card and has just 75 words. (Even Moses couldn't do that!) Even at that, there is room for some niceties ("We're glad to have you with our company") around the real meat of the handbook: "Rule #1: Use your good judgment in all situations. There will be no additional rules."

Most companies are a bit more loquacious. At Continental Airlines, the handbook became so unwieldy that management launched a turnaround by torching it and replacing it with a slimmer, trimmer version.

On your grumpy days, you may have been tempted to burn your own handbook. The rules can seem overbearing, arbitrary, silly, or even counterproductive. But don't do it. Whether brief or voluminous, elegant or imperfect, the handbook is your friend. It enables you to be consistent, to treat people equitably, to avoid managing on a whim, and to keep out of court. Yeah, rules can be a pain, but imagine the Bible without the Commandments.

Take Action

- *Know the handbook.* Read the handbook. Then read it again. Know it as close to word-for-word as possible. The handbook is a communication tool that spells out the relationship between the company and its employees. That's a relationship you should understand. And you can bet if your employee wants a particular outcome and the existing handbook supports his position, he'll be able to quote it chapter and verse.

- *Understand the rationale.* Some statements in the handbook may seem arbitrary, but they probably aren't. If you don't understand the reason for a policy, go to HR or the CEO and find out. It's important to be able to enforce the spirit as well as the letter of the rules.

Stay Out of Jail

- *Comply with the handbook—even if you don't agree with everything in it.* Disgruntled employees have won many lawsuits because the policies outlined in the handbook weren't followed. A handbook is a communication tool and a reference guide, but it's also a legal document. This means that ignoring it is about as risky as drinking and driving. Ignorance of the manual is no excuse; if you aren't sure what it says, look it up.

Manage Up

If you spot things in the handbook that are inaccurate, outdated, or not being enforced, bring them to your boss's attention—nicely.

WORKING WITH HR: HOW HUMAN RESOURCES CAN HELP YOU GET THE MOST OUT OF YOUR TEAM

Know the Issue

Using a popularity scale of one to 10 with 10 being wildly popular (Mickey Mouse, a free lunch, and after-Christmas sales) and one being wildly unpopular (telemarketers, Congress, and rush-hour grid-lock), where would you place human resources?

Many people who have been working more than 10 years would rate HR a two—right in there with the IRS and members of the American Dental Association. Those people remember when HR worshipped the rules and their favorite word was "No." They have learned to work around HR if they think about it at all.

Newer entrants to the workforce are more enlightened. They know that in many places, the paper-pushing, picnic-planning policy police of yore have gone the way of the T-Rex and the Dodo bird. That's because as business has changed, HR has changed, too. Today's HR still respects the rules, but they jump right in to help solve problems and now their favorite word is "Yes." No wonder today's employees are more likely to rate HR an eight or nine.

Of course, a few holdouts of the old guard are lurking out there and giving HR a bad name. How do you know whether your HR department is friend or foe? Here is a simple test: do they understand your part of the business? If no one in HR can tell you your department's turnover rate, how long it takes (on average) to fill a job in your department, how much your department contributes to the bottom line, or what your best performers actually *do* all day, then they are probably a foe. We encourage you to ignore them—except when it comes to legal matters, or if you think you have a chance to turn them into a friend.

Today's HR pros are business-focused. They help engineer ways to make the business better, and to do this they have to understand the business and all its components. This means that someone in HR can offer you much more than just accurate information about the vacation plan. She could help you redesign jobs, create an incentive plan to drive up profits, or find an assessment tool to improve your hiring success. If someone from HR asks about your business, is willing to hear about your business, or (best of all) works alongside you in your part of the business, you've just found a valuable partner.

The trick is then getting the most out of that partnership. As with any successful relationship, it demands give and take. But if you invest in a partnership with HR (assuming you have an HR function where you work), you're sure to reap sizeable dividends.

Take Action

- *Identify your resources.* Start by figuring out how HR is structured. In some cases, a central HR function serves the entire organization. The department has specialists in each discipline of HR, such as staffing, compensation, and benefits. In other organizations, each business unit or department has its own HR function; they are usually staffed by HR generalists who have broad knowledge in all areas of HR. Some large companies have a hybrid of these two models.

None of these is the "right" approach. The only thing that matters is that you know who to go to for help. The ideal is to bond with an HR generalist who can either work with you directly or connect you with the appropriate specialist. That person can also advocate for you within HR. If you can't identify a single person to work with, find a handful of specialists and build relationships with them.

- *Teach a crash course.* For anyone in HR to really help, they need to understand your part of the business and understand it almost as well as you do. Offer to take your HR contact to lunch once a week and spend the time teaching. Be willing to invest some serious time because your course needs to be thorough:
  - What do you see as the primary purpose of your department?
  - How is your department's success measured?
  - Where is your department excelling and where is it failing? Why?
  - Who are your star performers? What sets them apart?
  - Who are your poorest performers? What sets them apart?
  - What are your biggest frustrations and challenges?
  - What do you see as your key strengths?

- Where would you like the department to be in a year? Why? How do you plan to get there?
- What happens in your department every day? What are your production schedules, budgets, deadlines, productivity goals, and so forth?

  Be honest. Painting an artificially rosy picture won't get you the help you need.

- *Take a crash course.* Invest some time learning about HR, too. Listen to what your contact tells you about his job. And if you don't know, ask the following questions:
  - How does HR function every day? How are priorities set?
  - What expertise does HR have to offer?
  - Who do they see as HR's key customers?
  - What makes them say yes or no?
  - How is HR's performance measured? How do they win or lose?
  - Which HR programs or initiatives do they think are working best? Why?
  - What challenges does HR face? (Budgetary? Staffing HR? Time?)
  - How do HR initiatives in your company (pay rates, benefits, employee development) compare to those of your competitors? How do they compare to the average company in your area?

- *Put your cards on the table.* This relationship—like any other —demands honesty. Share how you *really* feel about HR, pro and con. Explain where those feelings come from. Are they based on bad experiences, successes, or hearsay? Talk about what you appreciate about HR and what drives you crazy. Bring up HR efforts in other companies that you've heard about and like or don't like. Then ask HR for the same feedback about you and your department.

- *Keep HR in the loop.* Once HR has a solid understanding of your department, they need to stay current. The more they know, the better, and the more they can observe firsthand, the better. There are lots of ways to do that:
  - Invite your contact to shadow you for a day or parts of days —let them watch you and your department in action.
  - Invite HR to sit in on your staff meetings.
  - Send HR copies of key memos, status reports, and other information tied to department milestones.
  - Plan regular lunches or meetings with your HR contact.

- *Choose your battles.* Don't drop 15 problems in HR's lap and expect equal attention to them all. Other departments need help, too! Identify your top concern and work with HR to resolve it. Getting one thing done will give you a sense of accomplishment and boost everyone's credibility.

- *Don't jump to conclusions.* It's great to go to HR with ideas, but don't get too invested into a single course of action. Your HR partner may see other options. Managers often request a training program, for example, when they face a challenge. But changes in hiring practices or even job design may ultimately be the better solution. Respect HR's expertise.

- *Be willing to be a guinea pig.* Perhaps you read about a cool HR effort in the *Wall Street Journal.* Or perhaps you had a great idea yourself. If you find yourself wondering, "Why don't we . . . ," consider volunteering to pilot a program. You can team up with HR to develop a program, and then test it in your department. Together you can work out the kinks. If it works, you'll get the benefits and you can enjoy the acclaim as the program is rolled out through the rest of the company.

Stay Out of Jail

- *If you have an HR function, you should always consult with them about*
  - Hiring
  - Discipline
  - Termination
  - Employee leave
  - Workers' compensation
  - Employee complaints (such as sexual harassment and discrimination)

  Check with HR *before* you take action.
- *No matter how great your partnership is, HR will sometimes say no.* It doesn't mean they don't like you. Remember that one of HR's greatest responsibilities is to protect the company from lawsuits. (As one HR executive observed, "The better we do our job, the less visible we become.") Employment law is complex; trust HR's counsel.

Real Life Examples

How would you like to have a binder on your desk that walked you through every stage of employee development for every employee you manage? A binder that includes job descriptions, required competencies, aptitude tests, specific interview questions, tailored performance appraisal forms, and more? A binder that gave you enough information that you could focus on day-to-day operations and helping employees solve problems?

If you worked at Valspar Corporation, you'd have one. That's because HR has created those binders for every one of the company's more than 3,800 jobs. The effort started as a small-scale attempt to identify core competencies in the manufacturing department and spread from there.

Salespeople at Buckman Laboratories International, Inc. make big sales pitches—pitches in which million of dollars in revenue are at stake. But how can a salesperson in Thailand get the information she needs to close a sale if the home office is closed?

At Buckman, the salesperson can get the information anytime, from anywhere in the world. That's because HR has worked with managers to promote knowledge sharing. The idea is to take the axiom "two heads are better than one" and turbo-charge it with technology. Thanks to online forums, connected knowledge bases, electronic bulletin boards, and virtual conference rooms, employees can tap into each other's knowledge and experience like nowhere else.

At one time, Continental Airlines was the laughingstock of the airline industry. The carrier had been through two bankruptcies and there was a revolving door in the executive suite. Passengers could expect poor service, late arrivals, and lost bags. No wonder employees tore the company patches off their uniforms at the end of the day; they didn't want anyone to know where they worked.

Then management teamed up with HR and took the airline from worst to first. An incentive pay program, streamlined policies (to replace the policy manual that management publicly burned), and aggressive communication improved every area of performance. Today, employees keep the patches on their uniforms and share in the airline's newfound profits.

Employee teams setting goals and measurements for themselves? Employees teams managing *themselves* while managers act as coaches? Believe it. It's a profit-driving reality at GE Fanuc Automation of North America, Inc. More than 40 work teams are proving it can be done and the best coaches are the managers earning the greatest rewards. It works because HR partners with managers in the coaching process; an HR staffer is part of every department.

Get More Information

Human Resource Champions: The Next Agenda for Adding Value and Delivering Results, Dave Ulrich, Harvard Business School Press, 1997.

Human Resources Kit for Dummies, Max Messmer, IDG Books Worldwide, 1999.

www.workforce.com

JOB DESCRIPTIONS: HOW TO DRAFT BLUEPRINTS FOR RESULTS

Know the Issue

Many of us don't read the manual. We just plunge ahead believing that trial-by-error learning will get our new VCR working. Only later, when we find that our tape of the season finale of "The West Wing" has no sound, do we resort to reading the instructions.

This aversion may explain why in many organizations job descriptions are sitting in files and are about as familiar to the rank and file as the schematic for the building's electrical system.

But job descriptions should be vital documents that you and your staff refer to often. Without them, the consequences are much greater than a silent TV episode. Jobs are harder to fill, employees often under-perform, and you face greater risk of legal problems.

Take Action

- *Begin with the basics whether you're writing a job description or revising an existing one*:
  - Job title
  - Department
  - Position to which the job reports
  - *Fair Labor Standards Act* (FLSA) status (exempt or non-exempt; please see "FLSA Status: A Primer," page 48.)
  - Date the description was written
- *State the job's primary purpose*. This is not rocket science. We're talking about a sentence or two to summarize why the job exists in the organization. The statement should help you and the employee focus on what's most important. Some sample statements are
  - Serve food and beverages to customers.
  - Process reservations and ticketing for passengers.
  - Provide non-invasive patient care as prescribed or requested.
  - Monitor and maintain product inventory.

- Sell cars.

- Write articles.

- *Outline the duties and responsibilities that support the overall goal.* This is where you get into details. For example, we all know from personal experience that car salespeople swoop like vultures on hapless shoppers and trail customers with a resolve matching that of the CIA. Their job description might not include verbs like *swoop* or *browbeat* ("greet potential customers" is a touch more dignified), but you get the idea. Keep in mind that the goal is to list responsibilities (for example, "make sure that tables have complete place settings" for food servers), *not* every task that the employee might ever do ("fill salt shakers"). As you write, consider which tasks are essential job functions, and which are a business necessity. (See below for examples.)

- *Define job requirements.* The books are filled with laws to protect employees (and job candidates) from discrimination. In addition, the *Americans with Disabilities Act* (ADA) protects disabled people and requires employers to make "reasonable accommodations" (see "The ADA: A Primer," page 230) to permit disabled people to fulfill the essential functions of a job. Stating your expectations and requirements clearly in your job descriptions will show that all candidates and employees are assessed against a uniform set of standards. Include the following:

  - *Education and experience*: Does the job require a college degree? An advanced degree? Particular certification, such as an RN? Is special training a requirement? How much on-the-job experience is necessary?

- *Language skills*: Take nothing for granted. If jobholders need to be able to read safety warnings or instruction manuals, say so. If they are expected to be able to write business letters or memos, say so. Also make note of any less-common job requirements, such as public speaking or fluency in a second language.

- *Math skills*: Most jobs require people to use basic addition, subtraction, multiplication and division skills. Others require more advanced math skills. Either way, spell it out.

- *Physical demands*: It's almost impossible to be too specific when outlining what employees must be able to do. Will they be required to sit for extended periods? To do any lifting? To walk? Focus on unusual requirements, but the description should be specific enough so that potential employees with disabilities (visible or otherwise) can decide for themselves whether they are able to fulfill the requirements of the job.

- *Work environment*: Finally, talk about the work environment itself. Address noise, light, stairs, walking distance, and so forth.

- *Have your organization's HR department review any job description before you make it public.* If you don't have an HR department, hiring a labor attorney to review it would be a worthwhile investment.

- *Revisit and, if necessary, update job descriptions.* Look at them every time:
  - Job tasks are reassigned from one employee to another.
  - Job tasks are added to someone's job.

- Job tasks are deleted from someone's job.
- An employee is promoted or demoted.
- An employee completes his or her introductory period.
- The organization is downsized.
- The organization is restructured, reengineered, or otherwise changed.
- The organization merges or is acquired (unless your department is unaffected).
- *Encourage employees to keep tabs on their activities and to let you know if they feel their job is changing.* Employees are very aware of how they spend their time, and discussing changes as they happen will avoid confusion or disagreements when it comes time to do performance reviews. But be sure to discuss things; don't let employees change job descriptions on their own.

Stay Out of Jail

Because job descriptions define a job, they can be carefully scrutinized when a legal dispute arises. The courts want to be sure that some sort of discrimination hasn't been built into the job. To protect yourself, address the following two key areas.

The first idea is that each job has *essential functions*. The essential job functions are those job responsibilities that make the job what it is. For example, the essential job function of a waiter is to serve food. He may also have to climb stairs to get condiments out of storage, or use the telephone or a broom, but those duties probably would not be considered essential or core functions. Therefore, you could not refuse to hire someone for the waiter job if the only reason for your refusal was that, due to a protected disability, he could not climb, telephone, or sweep. On the other hand, if the waiter could not serve food even with the help of a reasonable accommodation, then you wouldn't be discriminating if you did not hire him. To avoid confusion, be sure that the essential job functions are clear in the job description.

The other concept is *business necessity.* Technically, that's the standard an employer must establish to enforce a company rule or policy that may adversely affect protected employees. An employer must prove that rules or requirements are job-related and necessary to the business. For example, a classic court case involved an employer in the South that was requiring all applicants for janitorial jobs to have a high school diploma. Eventually, the case was heard by the U.S. Supreme Court, which expressed concern that the rule was a pretext designed to eliminate African-Americans from the hiring process. The Court held that the employer had failed to demonstrate that it was a business necessity that janitorial applicants be high school graduates.

To protect yourself, make sure that the requirements you make of applicants have a solid business rationale. If it's possible that the requirement adversely affects a protected class, be prepared to demonstrate how it's necessary to the business.

Do at Least the Minimum

- *There are no shortcuts here; you really have to do this.*

Manage Up

Review job descriptions with your boss. Make sure that he or she doesn't have expectations that aren't addressed. Have the description reviewed by HR or legal counsel first, so that your boss knows that the company will have no legal surprises.

Get More Information

Results-Oriented Job Descriptions: More Than 225 Models to Use or Adap—with Guidelines to Create Your Own, Roger J. Plachy and Sandra J. Plachy, AMACOM, 1993.

FLSA Status: A Primer

How employees are classified according to the *Fair Labor Standards Act* (FLSA) is crucial because if you don't pay overtime to employees who are entitled to it, the penalties imposed by the government are severe. Understand the rules and designate people accordingly:

Exempt Employers do not have to pay overtime for work performed by an exempt employee. The most common exemptions are the supervisorial/managerial exemption, the administrative exemption, the professional exemption, and the outside salesperson exemption.

Under Federal law, an employee is exempt as a supervisor if she supervises two or more full-time employees (or the equivalent), has as her primary duty managing a business or a recognizable portion of a business, regularly uses independent judgment and discretion in the course of her employment, and is paid (on a salary basis) at least $250 per week. (Technically, an employee could be exempt under Federal law if he is paid at least $155 per week on a salary basis, but that requires a much more difficult test.)

continued

The requirements for an administrative employee are very similar, except that the primary duty of an administrative employee consists of office or non-manual work that is related directly to the employee's policies or general business operations. Examples of employees in administrative categories who may be exempt include a human resources specialist, a buyer for a large department store, or the person in charge of marketing.

The professional exemption requires that an individual's primary duties consist of work that requires advanced knowledge in a field of science or learning, involves the exercise of creative talent, or entails teaching in a school or college.

To be exempt as an outside salesperson, the employee must customarily and regularly be engaged in selling goods or services at locations away from the employee's place of business. This Federal exemption has no minimum compensation requirement, but the employee may not devote more than 20 percent of a customary workweek to activities unrelated to the employee's own sales.

Other exemptions (and partial exemptions) are more esoteric, such as agricultural exemptions, computer programmer exemptions, used car salesperson exemptions, truck driver exemptions, seaman exemptions, radio announcer exemptions, processors of maple syrup into sap exemptions, and others. Exemptions may vary under state law.

This point is of critical importance: To be exempt, an employee must be free from the obligation to be paid overtime under all three of the potential sources of overtime liability: Federal law, state law, and employer promises (contract law). To compound the complexity, these three sources of the overtime obligation are often inconsistent, and each exemption under each of the three sources typically has many intricate sub-requirements that must be met. Finally, it is typically the *employer's* burden to establish proof of exempt status.

continued

> **Non-exempt**   A non-exempt employee is one that the employer cannot prove is exempt and for whom the employer must pay overtime when the employee works beyond a number of hours specified by law. (Federal law requires paying overtime after an employee works 40 hours in a workweek; California law requires paying overtime when an employee works more than eight hours in a day and when an employee works more than 40 hours in a workweek.) The Federal "overtime penalty" for hours worked over the maximum permitted is 1.5 times the employee's regular rate. Some states (including California) require double-time pay under certain circumstances (for example, when the employee works more than 12 hours in a workday or more than eight hours on the seventh consecutively worked day in a workweek).

BEHAVIORAL EXPECTATIONS: HOW TO DIRECT THE *HOW* OF THE JOB

Know the Issue

We've all faced enough cold soup and rude service to know that simply getting food to the table isn't enough. That's why it's important to include behavioral expectations in a job description. Although the job description explains the *what* of the job, be sure to clarify the *how*.

In setting expectations, clarify the *how* from two perspectives: how to do the job, and how to interact with you. Both are important.

Take Action

- *Tell your employees what the job demands.* Given enough time, most employees will figure out what's expected by watching what happens around them. It's more efficient—and kinder—to simply spell it out. Don't make assumptions. Don't even assume that food servers know how often they should check with diners or that accurate orders are critical. Be prepared to discuss the following:

- Will the employee be required to travel? How often? For how long? To where?
- Will employees routinely be required to work extra hours? Are those extra hours scheduled predictably or unpredictably? How much notice will employees have?
- How flexible are employees' work schedules?
- Are employees permitted to telecommute? Under what circumstances?
- How is vacation time scheduled? How far in advance should employees plan? How often are requests approved?
- Are employees expected to check voice mail or e-mail on weekends or after hours?
- How do employees get assignments? Formally? Informally?
- How often are performance reviews conducted? Are they done on time?
- What is the culture of the organization? (For more information on this topic, please see pages 24-28)
- Make it clear that duties and requirements are subject to change.
- *Tell employees how to win.* Employees are not mind readers. Most will willingly adjust to your preferences if they know what they are. Consider what's really important to you. Think about the following:

- *Personal space*: Do you object to employees leaving things on your desk? Taking things from your desk? Rearranging things on your desk?

- *Time*: Do you value uninterrupted stretches of time? Prefer quiet mornings when you first arrive? Prefer quiet evenings just before you leave?

- *Communication*: Do you prefer structured meetings or impromptu conversations in the hall? Prefer voice mail, e-mail, or notes on your chair? Expect employees to check in while they are on the road, or to save information until they are back in the office? Interrupt you if your family calls?

- *Status reports*: How often do you want to hear from people? Do you only want to hear when the project is complete, or do you want progress reports? Do you only want progress reports if a problem occurs? Is "fine" an acceptable answer when you ask how things are going, or do you want specifics?

  These questions have no right or wrong answers. The point simply is to set employees' expectations.

- *Show that you respect employees by asking what's important to them.* You can't accommodate every foible, but you can accommodate many, and why keep doing something that you know drives someone crazy?

Stay Out of Jail

- *If certain behavioral expectations are so critical that failure to meet those expectations puts an employee's job at risk, be sure they are included in the job description.*

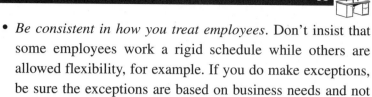
- *Be consistent in how you treat employees.* Don't insist that some employees work a rigid schedule while others are allowed flexibility, for example. If you do make exceptions, be sure the exceptions are based on business needs and not favoritism.

Real World Example

An executive once told this story about one of his employees. From the day he was hired, the employee made it a habit of meeting with his boss first thing in the morning. Dependably, he would spot the boss coming through the front door and then follow him to his office. Then, while the boss took off his coat and turned on the computer, the employee would start asking questions, updating the boss on progress, and so on. The employee was smart, reliable, and productive—the sort of employee we all hope to have, but he was driving his boss crazy.

The boss had always cherished the first hours of his morning. When he arrived at work, he used that time to enjoy his coffee and plan the day. He saw the time as valuable thinking time, and the employee had ruined it. Eventually, the boss began to dread the morning and resent the employee.

When he couldn't take it any more, the executive shared his frustration. The employee, of course, was surprised and wondered why nothing had been said before. Together, they devised a new rule: The boss was to be left undisturbed each morning until 9:00. After that, the employee, who valued face time with the boss, was in the boss's office each day precisely at 9:00. Still, it was a solution they could both live with.

Do at Least the Minimum

- *Be sure employees' expectations are clear about the issues most likely to impinge on their personal time: overtime, vacations, and business travel.*

Manage Up

Find out what behavior your boss expects from you, and do your best to meet those expectations.

4

Sourcing Candidates

"I liked the old days," the manager says. "If somebody wasn't pulling his weight or you didn't like him, you fired him. Then you went out to the line in front of the building and hired a guy to replace him. It was easy."

Those days were "easy" if you didn't care anything about the quality of your workforce. If many people are looking for work, and anyone will do, then filling jobs *is* easy. However, today many people are not looking for work, and they won't be anytime soon. And even if people were looking, times have changed. There are almost no jobs anymore where just anyone will do. Still, many managers continue to believe that if they hire people they've done their job. Trust us: hiring the wrong person is worse than hiring no person.

Don't think of yourself as a fisher, casting a wide net and hoping for the best. Think of yourself as a chef, a jeweler, or a director. In any of these jobs, you'd be utterly reliant on the right resources.

In the end, all the talent and skill in the world won't matter if all you have to work with is bad meat, bad stones, or bad actors. All of your managerial skills won't matter either, if all you have to work with are employees who were compromise hires.

For all those reasons, sourcing candidates is a crucial part of the hiring process. Once you've written a job description and set expectations, you need to find people who can meet those expectations. This means you must promote your job aggressively. Think like a marketer, and then be diligent about making the most of all the sourcing options you have.

CLASSIFIEDS: HOW TO RUN ADS THAT WORK

Know the Issue

Here are some classified job ads that were found in major newspapers and were intended to attract top prospects:

> Secty: 2-3 yrs exp. Lite typing, phones & assisting gen'l mgr. Call . . .
>
> Executive Asst for Int'l co. Fax res to: . . .
>
> Maint. Power washing exp. Req'd. night hrs. good driving rec. call . . .
>
> Cocktail servers. Exp'd. wknd even only. Call Giggles . . .

Excited yet? Can you picture the rewards and fulfillment that lie ahead? Are you ready to spend time polishing your resume, going through the hassle of an interview, and leaving your current job for these thrilling opportunities? We bet that even the prospect of a boss named Giggles isn't enough to get you moving.

At one time, newspaper classifieds were the be-all to fill jobs. Today, they're still black and white, but no longer read all over. Classifieds draw fewer responses than ever for many reasons: the labor market is tight, and fewer people are looking for jobs; newspaper circulation is down; illiteracy is rising; and then there's something called the Internet.

But it's too early to write an obit for the classifieds. They're still a great option for filling many jobs, particularly those that don't require highly specialized skills. For classified ads to work, however, they need to be *advertising*—that is, creative, punchy, and enticing.

Take Action

- *Know your audience.* Newspapers are a mass-market medium. Consider this example: In Anytown, USA, there are two nuclear physicists and 10,000 secretaries. Both physicists read the paper daily, as do half the secretaries. This means that secretaries are 2,500 times more likely to answer a classified ad than the physicist. Yet many labs would run the ad for a physicist anyway. Wrong! It would be infinitely more efficient to simply call both physicists. Classifieds work best when filling the sorts of jobs that are sought by many people: food servers, salespeople, and so forth. If you really must run a classified for a specialized job, run it in a targeted trade magazine or scientific journal, *not* the newspaper.

- *Figure the odds.* Unless someone is trapped in an auto repair shop waiting room and desperate to read *anything*, the only people reading classifieds are active job seekers. These are people either not currently working or unhappy in their current job and ready to make a change. Your ad will be missed entirely by passive job seekers—those who are working but might consider another opportunity if it were presented to them. (Remember, if passive job seekers read want ads, then headhunters would be extinct.) Think about the unemployment rate in your area for the type of job you're filling. If competing hotels in your area are bringing in staff from the Caribbean, running a classified ad to hire housekeepers probably won't work.

- *Sell the job.* Would you plunk down eight bucks at the multiplex to see something known only as *Action Flick*? Of course, you wouldn't. You want to know something about the story, who stars in it, and whether it's supposed to funny or scary. If people won't invest two hours and seven dollars in an unknown, why would they bet their career on a mystery job? Sell what the job has to offer—opportunity, creativity, flexibility, great pay, a cool office, terrific benefits, working for the world's most perfect boss, and so on. Don't scribble a list on an envelope just before the deadline. Write an ad that gets people excited.

- *Don't pinch pennies.* Most classified ad space is sold by the word or line. For some reason, otherwise rational people hear that and become irrational. To save money, they start abbreviating and slashing until the ad reads like Fortran code. Impress people with the job, not with how cheap you are.

- *Don't be coy.* True, you want to cast a wide net and get as much response as possible, but don't get coy to do it. It's a waste of everyone's time to be misleading about salary, job duties, and so forth in an ad. Just as people reading real estate ads resent the euphemism "fixer-upper" to describe a dump, job candidates resent "high-potential restaurant career opportunity" to describe a waiter position.

- *Don't run blind ads.* Some employers run blind ads, in which the job is advertised, but the company name is left out. It's done to spare the company phone calls, or because the company doesn't want employees to know a job is open (or about to be because someone will be fired). Don't do it. Blind ads establish an atmosphere of second-guessing and distrust from the outset. Also, many top candidates won't respond to blind ads, reasoning that if they are sending personal information to someone, they want to know where they're sending it.

- *If you're an equal opportunity employer (and you should be), say so.*

- *Decide how you want candidates to respond.* Do you want candidates to respond through the mail only, or can they fax a resume? Can they send a resume by e-mail? Will you answer telephone inquiries? There is no "right" answer, though generally the more options you offer, the greater the response you'll get. Whatever you decide, include the information in the ad.

- *Develop a plan to respond.* Once the ad runs, you need to be ready to respond. Develop a plan. Who will open the mail? Who will check e-mail? How often? Where will the resumes go? How soon will you respond to candidates? Who will respond to phone calls? (Hint: Choose someone who can actually answer most questions, not merely take messages.) Once you have the plan, communicate it to anyone involved and then stick to it.

- *Acknowledge all responses.* It's good form to acknowledge every application, even if you use a form letter. Anything less than that is disrespectful. And some candidates are receiving unemployment and need to prove that they are making a legitimate effort to find work.

Real Life Example

His long-time secretary had just resigned. She was hard-working, smart, dedicated, funny, and thoroughly professional. They had worked together for years, and trusted each other completely. He wanted to drink a margarita or two and go watch a mindless movie. Instead, he sat down and wrote a classified ad for her replacement. The ad began

> CAN YOU REPLACE MARY POPPINS?
> Our executive secretary has been practically perfect in every way, but now she's moving on. If you can juggle e-mail, voice mail, and notes left on your chair; if you aren't afraid to point out when the boss is being stupid; if you like to make decisions for yourself (and sometimes for other people); and if you keep a magic carpet bag hidden somewhere in your desk, we've got a job for you!

In the next few days, the executive was swamped with resumes, faxes, phone calls, and e-mail. Almost every letter and call made some mention of Mary Poppins. But what really struck him was that almost every call and letter also said something like this: "Wow! I can tell you really respect your secretary . . . " or "I can see that your secretary is really part of the team . . . " or "It's clear that you don't take your secretary for granted . . . " The candidates were excited about the job before they even had an interview.

Stay Out of Jail

- *Don't discriminate in your ad copy.* Don't even think about an ad that reads, "Seeking young women . . . ," "No Latinos," "No one over 40 need apply . . . ," or any other phrase that discriminates against a protected group or groups.

AGENCIES: HOW TO GET RESULTS USING EMPLOYMENT FIRMS

Know the Issue

There it is on your calendar: dinner with a client, a deadline that will demand overtime, or even an out-of-town meeting. Your spouse is unavailable, and your two-year-old will not be welcome. What do you do? Call a babysitter. Those woefully underpaid helpmates can do a lot—everything from making sure that teeth are brushed to keeping the kids alive all weekend. But no one—not even live-in help—can raise the kids for you.

The same applies when dealing with employment agencies. Depending on which you hire and the instructions you give, they can do a lot to make your life easier. But they can't and shouldn't do the hiring for you.

Take Action

- *Figure out what kind of help you need.* Plot out the total hiring process for your open job. Where are you most likely to get bogged down? If you're trying to fill a job that demands highly specialized skills, finding candidates may be the toughest hurdle. On the other hand, if you're recruiting for a job with a broader skill set, just finding time to interview people may be a bigger challenge.

- *Decide what kind of agency would be best to work with.* All agencies are not the same. Four primary types of agencies are available (see "The ABC's of Agencies," page 67), and the services, results, and fees vary. Choose the type that's best for the assignment.

- *Find out whether others in your organization are already working with an agency.* If you work in a company with an HR function, some agencies may already have been chosen. If so, use them. Doing so will probably save money (agencies may offer lower rates on a contract basis) and time (existing vendors probably already know something about your corporate culture). Even if the company has no HR function, other employees in your firm may have experience with specific agencies. Find out.

- *If it is necessary, choose an agency.* If you're a pioneer in using an agency, choose carefully. Interview an agency as if you were interviewing a candidate because, in effect, you are. Find out
  - How long the firm has been in business
  - How large it is
  - How many people it places
  - How long it takes to fill the average assignment
  - What the turnover rate is on jobs they've filled
  - What sort of screening, testing, and background checks they conduct

- Whether they offer a guarantee
- What all the charges are
- Whether they have references you can call

If possible, ask to meet or at least speak to the people you would be working with. What experience does the person or team have? Also consider what the agency asks about you. The more questions, the better. After all, if they don't ask, what reassurance do you have that they'll effectively screen candidates?

- *Tell the agency what you want.* Remember, you're the boss. That means you can have things your way ("Don't call me Monday mornings during my regular staff meeting"), but it also means you're responsible for making sure the agency understands the assignment. Don't be stingy with information; the more the agency knows, the better. Be sure to share

  - The job's title
  - Key responsibilities
  - Necessary experience/skills
  - Salary
  - Benefit plan

- *Share, share, share.* Beyond the basics, be sure your contact at the agency understands the job, the company culture, and you. Talk about what the job entails, and what the job is like day to day. Describe the culture, too. How are decisions made? Is risk rewarded? Is overtime routine? 'Fess up to what it's like to work for you. In short, give the recruiter all the information you would give to a candidate. Yes, the process will be time-consuming, but what you invest now will pay off later—remember, you're telling only one recruiter, not a dozen candidates. Good recruiters will use the information only to better screen candidates, not to prep people for interviews.

- *Clarify expectations.* Be sure that you and the agency are on the same page about how the process will work. Don't assume anything. Think about these issues:

  - How long do you think the process should take? What does the agency think? Be sure you agree. If not, negotiate.
  - How often do you want to be called? When?
  - Is it OK for the agency to work through your secretary or another person, or should your contact only speak to you?
  - How much notice do you need in order to set up an interview?
  - What do you want to see when a candidate comes for an interview? If you need work samples, say so.
  - What sort of out do you have if you're unhappy?

- *Monitor your progress.* Once the process is underway, think about how it's going. Are you seeing the sort of candidate you expected to see? Is the agency responsive? Are you feeling supported or pressured? Do candidates seem too well-prepared? If you have concerns, say so.

- *Don't hijack the process.* You hired the agency to do a job. If they aren't meeting your expectations, try to fix things. If you can't, cut your losses and move on. If you're happy, stay out of their way. In any case, don't get in the middle of the process. Even once you've chosen a candidate, let the agency

The ABCs of Agencies

Temporary help agencies are best known for providing staff to fill in for vacationing employees or to add capacity during busy periods, but many also place people in regular positions after a "try out" period. (This is often described as "temp to perm," but avoid using that language because it may imply a promise of permanent employment.) The firm earns a fee if you hire someone; fees you've paid for an employee's work as a temp may sometimes be applied toward the total fee.

Pros:

It gives you a chance to work with a candidate before extending an offer.

Work can get done during the search process.

Cons:

It works best for the sort of jobs routinely filled by temporary employees.

Employment placement agencies generally help fill lower-level jobs that don't require specialized skills. These firms usually maintain databases of job seekers, and then search those databases when they get an assignment. They earn a fee from the employer (usually a percentage of the job's annual salary, although sometimes a set fee) when the job is filled.

Pros:

It can often produce many candidates quickly.

It can save you time and effort.

Applicants are screened before you meet them.

It costs you nothing if you don't hire someone.

Cons:

The quantity of applicants may exceed quality.

The quality of screening is variable.

continued

It primarily reaches active job seekers.

Prepare to be called and called and called and called.

Contingency search firms can be hired to fill any type of job, though they're most often used for mid-level jobs. They may maintain a database of job seekers, but they also will actively recruit on your behalf. They earn a fee when the job is filled, but the fee is higher than that charged by placement agencies; prepare to pay as much as 30 percent of the job's salary.

Pros:

It can do a lot of work on your behalf.

It may reach passive job seekers.

Cons:

The process may take as long as if you did it yourself.

Firms tend to accept only jobs that they believe can be filled easily because they only get paid when jobs are filled.

Retained search firms are hired most often to help fill high-level and hard-to-fill jobs. They use research, networking, and other techniques to identify top candidates. They earn a fee (often 30 percent of the job's annual salary) whether the job is filled or not, and they usually charge separately for expenses.

Pros:

It's the best option for key jobs.

Firms usually make the greatest investment in understanding the job and your organization.

Cons:

It's usually the most expensive option.

make the offer on your behalf unless you've negotiated otherwise up front.

- *Follow up after the job is filled.* Give the agency feedback about the process, pro and con. What would you like to be handled differently if you work with the agency again? Keep the agency apprised about how the candidate is performing —particularly if the placement is guaranteed.

- *Read the contract.* Don't assume the agency understood all of your requests, or that the account executive translated your understanding to writing. Review the written agreement (that is, the contract) with the agency very carefully to make certain that your company's responsibilities and the agency's obligations are clear and accurate.

Stay Out of Jail

- *Remember, you are still the employer.* An agency can act on your behalf during the process, but you are still responsible. Be sure that background checks, tests, and so on are complete and done within the confines of the law. Ask to see copies of any material, and keep copies of the material in the employee file after the employee starts.

- *Be sure the employee understands the offer.* Review any formal offer *before* the agency makes it. (Insist on that when you hire the agency.) Be sure the agency is not promising something you can't deliver.

- *Be sure the employee understands the offer, including such things as when health insurance coverage becomes effective and how long new-employee probation lasts. Do not assume the agency will take care of it.*

- *Be sure that employees hired through an agency have been subjected to the same tests, assessments, background checks, and so forth as employees hired from other sources.*
- *Be sure that the agency does not discriminate in its hiring practices. Are you seeing candidates of various ages, races, and so forth?*

CREATIVE RECRUITING: HOW THINKING OUTSIDE THE BOX PAYS OFF

Know the Issue

When Chrysler was creating its new auto/minivan hybrid, it would have been easy to play follow the leader and design it to look very much like all the other family-size vehicles out there. Instead, Chrysler took the space and versatility that customers wanted and put it in a retro-styled package that looked like nothing else around. The result, the PT Cruiser, was the hottest American car in years. Chrysler couldn't make them fast enough, dealers were selling them for more than sticker price, and buyers found themselves greeted by *oohs* and *ahhs* and requests for pictures. Sometimes, different is better.

This holds for recruitment, too. Most of the time, the traditional sources work just fine. But sometimes, they don't and then it's time to get creative. As long as you stay within the boundaries of the law and good taste (no providing college kids with free beer, please), there is no limit to what you can do. These ideas aren't by any means exhaustive; they're just intended to get your mind racing. Go ahead —have fun.

Take Action

- *Practice 24/7 recruiting.* Legend has it that teenaged Lana Turner was having a soda at Schwab's drugstore when a studio talent scout spotted her. A screen test followed, and a movie queen was born. Turner herself insisted that the story isn't true, but it has a kernel of truth: casting scouts were on the lookout for talent and did routinely sign performers—just as baseball scouts do today.

  There's no reason that such a proven technique does not necessarily have to be used in the so-called glamour professions. Does it really make sense to assume that the perfect person will appear at the precise moment we need her? Why not improve the odds by acting as a scout and recruiting 24 hours a day/seven days a week? Train yourself to notice potential and be willing to make your pitch when you do. To improve your odds

  - Think about the qualities you need.
  - Think about where the best candidates are likely to be.
  - Talk to your top prospects.
  - Make candidates a top priority if they respond to your interest.

- *Ask employees for referrals.* If Hillary Rodham Clinton were a corporate executive instead of a United States Senator, she might have said, "It takes a lunchroom." That's because Hillary's basic idea—shared responsibility—turns out to be as true in business as in raising children, and shared responsibility at work can be especially valuable when it comes to hiring.

The idea is simple. Employees, who know your business better than anyone, refer people (friends, relatives, neighbors) who they feel would make good employees. Then employees are rewarded if one of their referrals is hired. Study after study has shown that employees hired through referral programs perform better and stay longer than employees hired through any other source.

Of course, for a referral program to work, you can't just send an e-mail to your staff and hope for the best. Instead

- Decide which jobs you'll accept referrals for and who is eligible to participate (Hint: The broader the program, the better), how the referrals will be made (asking employees to complete a form works better than sorting through random voice mails or notes on your desk), and how long the program will last.

- Decide how to reward employees. (You can give a small prize, such as movie tickets, to every employee who makes a referral, but most programs offer more substantial rewards when hires are actually made.)

- Explain in advance that the hiring decisions will be business decisions, not personal ones. Have a plan for contacting the referrals.

- Promote the program.

- Monitor participation. If interest in the program starts to flag, rejuvenate it with new prizes or fresh promotion. If enthusiasm wanes because referrals aren't being hired, think about why. Do people need more explicit information about the kind of people you're looking for?

- *Use your network.* A theory of sociology, popularized by John Guare's hit play *Six Degrees of Separation*, claims that no more than six people separate you from anyone else in the world. Think of it as a chain: you know someone, who knows someone, who knows someone else. Based on how many people we each know, there are no more than six people between you and Queen Elizabeth, or you and the Pope or, yes, you and the perfect hire. The trick, of course, is finding the right six people. There's no sure way to do it, or we'd all be lunching with our favorite TV stars, but networking substantially improves the odds that you'll connect with someone you otherwise would have missed.

Networking is a methodical approach to identifying top candidates:

- Cultivate your network. Remember former employees who left on good terms, former co-workers, contacts at your key vendors, people who write for professional journals or magazines serving your industry, college instructors or professional trainers who work in the field, or consultants to your industry.

- A network is like Madonna's career; without constant attention it will wither and die. Take just a little time each week to attend local meetings of industry or professional associations; call people in the network to swap information.

- If you use your network when hiring, make the calls yourself; don't delegate them. When you call, don't simply ask people whether they know someone who might be interested. Take a few minutes to qualify prospective candidates.

- Handle calls professionally.
- Once you've called a referral, be responsive.
- Don't ask the same person too often.
- Say thank you.

- *Use the Internet.* "The Internet is the greatest invention since the printing press, and maybe the greatest invention ever. It has revolutionized recruiting. In fact, Internet recruiting is the only way to go." Blah, blah, blah. The hype, mostly generated by marketing kingpins at dotcom start-ups, argues that all the above is true. It's not. Yes, the Internet can be a valuable recruiting tool, but it isn't a panacea. (See "The Pros and Cons of Internet Recruiting," page 77). Be smart about when and how to go online to fill jobs:

  - Think about the people most likely to apply for your job. Do *they* have access to the Internet? Which recruiting sites are they visiting? The top sites can give you information about their audience. Find a good match.

  - Find out whether your organization has a preferred site or sites. If you work in a large company, HR may have already contracted with one or more recruiting sites. If so, follow their lead. If the company has no formal policy or agreement, network with other managers to see if they've had good luck with a site.

  - Get information from several sites that match your needs. Find out job posting options, pricing, audience demographics, traffic, currency of resumes, and site reliability. Get references.

  - Post your job and track the responses. Track how many responses you get, how quickly you receive responses, how

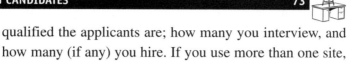

qualified the applicants are; how many you interview, and how many (if any) you hire. If you use more than one site, compare how each performs.

- *Hang out where your candidates hang out.* Be the employer that candidates see when they do whatever it is they normally do. You want them to think of your firm when they think about job opportunities. For example, where do disenfranchised software programmers hang out? The Dilbert Web page! So that's exactly where Cisco Systems placed job ads. The ads linked directly to Cisco's job page. Because research showed that most people were visiting the site between 10 a.m. and 2 p.m. (when they were supposed to be working), Cisco made it possible for candidates to profile themselves in just 10 minutes. And, in case they were caught in the act, a single keystroke brings up a disguise page that reads "Seven Successful Habits of Great Employees." Meanwhile, the approach at Olds Products, a mustard manufacturer, is about 180 degrees less irreverent. Representatives for Olds went looking for people at churches, synagogues, and mosques—trading $100 donations for job candidate leads.

- *Hire for attitude, train for skill.* If you were looking for an information analyst, you'd go to the Juilliard School and hire a violinist, right? That's just what Electronic Data Systems (EDS) did after realizing that they were duking it out with their competitors for the same small pool of high-tech grads. It makes sense if you think about it: any violinist who gets to Juilliard is driven and detail-oriented. He can learn information analysis.

- *Take college recruitment a step further.* Going to college career fairs is swell, but to really stand out on campus, think big. EDS became the primary sponsor of the U.S. Sunrayce, an intercollegiate competition to build and race solar-powered cars. The company provided scoring and timing devices, location tracking systems, and even technical engineers. While students were winning races, EDS was shaking hands with several bright engineering graduates who eventually accepted job offers. But the race only happens once a year. What else could EDS do? Race down the ski slopes with flyers and t-shirts to recruit students on their winter break.

Stay Out of Jail

- *Don't make promises.* Remember, you're expanding your options—not promising to hire anyone.
- *Keep hiring information confidential.*
- *Don't rely too much on any program if the result is that all applicants start "looking alike."* You could find yourself accused of discrimination if it effectively excludes applicants from protected classes.
- *Find out whether candidates have an employment contract or have signed a "do not compete" clause that prohibits them from working for a competitor in the same industry.* If they have, it could result in legal problems you don't need.
- *Be politic.* When networking, don't say anything about anyone else that you wouldn't want repeated.
- *Don't use the Internet exclusively.* Not everyone has access to the Internet. In fact, fewer than half of Americans have ever been online. Those who are online are disproportionately white and middle or upper class. Because of that, there's some

concern that posting a job online only (as opposed to online and in traditional media) puts minority candidates at a disadvantage in getting those jobs. Our opinion is that a lawsuit is waiting to happen. Be prudent, and use several options available to you.

- *Don't even think about using discriminatory language (for example, "no one over 40 need apply") in any job posting.*
- *Protect the privacy of applicants.* Do not sell resumes you receive over the Internet or forward them to other prospective employers without the candidate's permission.

Real Life Examples

At DoubleClick, a growing Internet advertising firm, 30 percent of all 1999 hires started with an employee referral; for the first quarter of 2000, that jumped to 43 percent. The company makes it easy: Employees can make referrals online. The resume gets captured, and then it is sent to an administrator who looks at it and distributes it to recruiters. The system also records the employee's name because whoever has the most referrals hired wins a prize. This system has East Coast, West Coast, and international quarterly winners. An annual winner receives a Harley-Davidson motorcycle. Two Harleys sit in reception areas, with signs reading, "Wanted: internal referrals—win prizes."

Charles Schwab & Co., Inc. also boasts a 30 percent employee referral rate. One event the company promotes is a "Suitcase Social." Employees bring friends, introduce them to recruiters, and toss their names into the Suitcase Social raffle; the prize is a trip. Not only does the event net Schwab new employees, it's a great marketing tool to promote the referral program throughout Schwab.

Manage Up

- *If you try something creative and it works, be sure your boss knows about it. Who wouldn't be happy with an employee who can solve problems creatively?*
- *Don't forget to include your boss in your network.*

Get More Information

www.careerbuilder.com

www.careermag.com

www.careerpath.com

www.cruelworld.com

www.dice.com (specializes in high-tech jobs)

www.flipdog.com

www.freeagent.com (specializes in independent contractors)

www.HeadHunter.net

www.hotjobs.com

www.iminorities.com (specializes in minority candidates)

www.jobfind.com

www.joboptions.com

www.jobs.com

www.monster.com

www.webhire.com

The Pros and Cons of Internet Recruiting

Pros

- *Internet recruiting saves time.* One hospital cut 18 days from the average time to fill jobs and some recruiters were able to connect with candidates within 10 minutes of their entry into the hospital's computer system.

- *It saves money.* The average cost per hire using the Internet is $377 versus $3,295 using traditional media.

- *It extends the scope of your search.* You're no longer limited to reaching readers of the local newspaper.

- *It offers greater control.* Free yourself from the tyranny of newspaper deadlines. Enter the data yourself and avoid finding typos in your phone number. It doesn't limit your recruiting efforts to regular business hours.

- *It allows better searches of your applicant pool.* Electronic records are much easier to sort than stacks of paper.

- *It helps candidates know more.* Ideally, candidates can use the Internet to learn about your organization, business results, corporate culture, and more. Theoretically, the candidates who apply at that point are pre-sold on the company.

- *It makes the hiring process virtually paperless.*

Cons

- *Internet recruiting shortens hiring time.* Applicants using the Internet expect an almost immediate response to their application and they won't tolerate a protracted interview process. You'll have to move quickly to get the best candidates.

- *It extends the scope of your search.* Currently, more than 100,000 Internet sites have job listings, and more than 2.5 million resumes are posted publicly. In addition, more than 600,000 jobs are available online. This means that you should

continued

be prepared to get resumes from all over the world whether or not you're in a position to hire from abroad. It also means that it'll be tough to call attention to your open job.

- *It increases the volume of responses to an opening.* Without a computerized tracking system, keeping up with the volume can be overwhelming.

- *It isn't always current.* Many of the resumes online are dated. Some sites have begun purging and cleaning to correct this, but you should still pay attention to how long resumes have been posted.

- *It is not an effective way to reach passive job seekers.* It is even less likely than the newspaper to be browsed casually.

- *It is not an effective way to recruit for entry-level jobs or jobs requiring minimal experience or skills.*

- *It may increase the number of vendors you're managing.* Each site has its own rules, pricing, processes, and so forth. How many do you want to learn?

- *It overemphasizes skills.* Most people succeed or fail in jobs based on their interpersonal competencies, not on job skills. Yet Internet recruiting usually hinges on key words and other data bytes, which make it tough to assess for anything *except* skills.

5

Assessing Candidates

Consider the typical process for buying a car. First, we eye every car on the road, picturing ourselves behind the wheel: Too Mid-Life Crisis? Too Soccer Mom? Enough "I Made It?" Then, in our minds, we customize with a sun roof and tasteful pin striping.

The process consumes us. Car ads become more interesting than the articles in our favorite magazine. We postpone the microwave popcorn ritual to actually watch the car commercials. We talk to everyone we know about their cars, until we become more obnoxious than the salespeople calling about our long-distance calling habits.

Finally, we're ready to go hands-on. We peer in windows, open doors and trunks, and sit in drivers' seats. When we can no longer resist the charms of the hot shot salesperson, we agree to a test drive. Then we dicker over options and price and terms and credit and an extended warranty. Only then do we drive off the lot in our dream car.

If only a fraction as much time were spent in assessing the average job candidate, but it isn't. Too often someone is hired on little more than a cursory interview and a gut feeling. To be fair, assessing candidates is difficult. It requires us to turn off (almost) all our emotional responses to people to focus on objective data. It demands that we use listening skills usually reserved for talks with doctors, divorce attorneys, and traffic cops. The process is also constrained by legal straitjackets, large and small.

Don't despair. Great assessment skills can be learned. And with patience—and dogged determination to follow a fair, thorough assessment process —you'll improve your odds of success far beyond any you'll find in Vegas.

APPLICATIONS: HOW TO GET THE BASIC INFORMATION YOU NEED

Know the Issue

You're at the hospital. All you really want is for your test or procedure or surgery to be over with so that you can go home. But before they ever get started, there's . . . paperwork. Lots of it. It's exasperating, but the forms make it possible for every doctor and nurse you encounter to get key information about you. Odds are that the form includes a release granting the hospital the right to treat you. Yes, there's a lot riding on those forms.

There's a lot riding on employment application forms, too, but most companies pay about as much attention to them as they do to the reading material in the lobby. In many cases, applicants who have resumes aren't even asked to complete an application. But applications can do much more than express a candidate's interest in working for you. They also standardize the information you collect (lawyers love that), and they provide a great place to give candidates important legal information (such as your at-will and non-discriminatory hiring practices). The few minutes it takes a candidate to complete an application can be invaluable to you.

Take Action

- *Find out whether your firm has an application form.* If you work in a large or well-established firm, there's probably an existing form to use. Track one down. You should be able to get one from HR or from other managers.

- *If there is no form, create one.* If your company doesn't already have a form, you need one. Forms are commercially available. Or create a form yourself. If you do that, limit the information you collect to what's relevant to the job. Good forms ask for

  - Name, address, and telephone number
  - Date of application
  - Social Security number
  - Position applied for
  - Previous applications to or employment with the company
  - Employment history (including employers' names and addresses, job titles, salaries, and dates of employment)
  - Special skills
  - Education, including school names and addresses, dates attended (except for dates of grammar school and high school), courses of study, degrees earned, and honors awarded

Good forms also ask questions to help employers comply with the law. For example:

- "If you are under 18 years of age, can you provide required proof of your eligibility to work?"
- "Are you legally eligible for employment in the United States?"
- "Have you been convicted of a felony (or a misdemeanor involving violent or fraudulent conduct)? If yes, please state the location, the date, and the crime(s) for which you were convicted." (*Note: The form should include an advisory that a conviction will not necessarily disqualify an applicant from employment.*)

  "Have you ever been arrested for any criminal violation for which you are currently out on bail, out on your own recognizance, or otherwise on release pending trial? If yes, explain." (*Note: Different states have different laws relative to questions about convictions; check with a labor attorney before you put this question on an application.*)

Applications may also ask for practical data, such as when an applicant will be available to begin work and whether the applicant is available to travel, should the position require it.

Applications often advise candidates of employment requirements (such as passing a drug test or background check). When permission is required (as when doing a background check), the form may ask candidates to grant permission and sign it.

Finally, a good application clearly states employment policies, such as at-will employment, the necessity that the application be honest, the fact that the employer resolves disputes by arbitration, the employer's position on drug testing and background checks and the following with respect to non-discrimination:

"We consider applicants for all positions without regard to race, color, religion, creed, sex, marital status, age, national origin, ancestry, physical or mental disability, medical condition, sexual orientation, or any other consideration made unlawful by Federal, state, or local laws. We are an equal opportunity employer and we offer employment on the basis of ability, experience, training, and character."

- *Have every applicant complete the form* —even if they have supplied a resume that includes most of the information.
- *Keep the completed applications in confidential files.*

Stay Out of Jail

- *If you create an application form, have an attorney review it before you use it.*
- *Verify the information provided, such as employment history and Social Security number.*

Do at Least the Minimum

- *Have every applicant complete a form before he or she is hired.*

RESUMES: HOW TO SPOT THE HYPE AND FIND THE TRUTH

Know the Issue

When Lily Tomlin observed, "No matter how cynical you become, it's never enough to keep up," she probably didn't have resumes in mind. But you should, because too many people out there are, well, creative. Some submit resumes far funnier than anything you'll see on TV tonight. If you doubt it, Robert Half, a veteran of the temporary staffing industry and an expert recruiter, collects what he calls "resumania." A few samples:

"Education: Married junior year at University of Florida, twins 10 months later."

"I have incredibly entertaining hair."

"I have mobile living equipment and can live on-site if needed."

Granted, few resumes are that entertaining, but they may not be very helpful either. Remember that what you see as basic information, the candidate sees as unabashed marketing; and marketing, as we know, isn't rich with truth. Robert Half reports that surveys done by his company, Robert Half International, show that 30 percent of job seekers lie on their resumes. Many of the rest exaggerate.

None of this gives you license to throw a stack of resumes down a flight of stairs and hire the people whose resumes get to the bottom. For one thing, enough resumes are totally legit to keep things interesting. For another, jurors are more kindly disposed to managers who hire using some sort of uniform rationale. Resumes are the best place to start.

Take Action

- *Give resumes a careful reading.* Here's how.

  - *Presentation counts:* Give priority to resumes accompanied by a cover letter. Look for resumes that are typeset or created in a word processing program (as opposed to hand written carelessly), and printed on something other than an old napkin or the reverse side of a grocery list. Deduct points for changes made by hand or cute symbols like smiley faces.

  - *Beware of hyperbole:* Suppose, for example, a resume states, "Set new sales record." It sounds impressive, but guessing all the things it might mean while still being 100 percent accurate could keep a frat house busy all weekend. "Set new record for lowest sales" and "Set a record for new sales while losing all existing clients" are two that come to mind.

  - *Beware of name droppers:* If a candidate cites experience at a brand name employer, make sure their experience is relevant. Flipping burgers or dressing as a giant mouse may not prepare them for the work you need done.

  - *Beware of job hoppers:* You want employees with ambition, but if a candidate has a history of changing jobs every 18 months, beware. Odds are that the employee wouldn't stay with you any longer, which means you'll never see a return on your investment in hiring and training. There may be instances when frequent job changes genuinely were beyond the candidate's control. If a candidate is otherwise top notch, inquire about job changes in the interview.

- *Look for gaps:* Candidates who drop out of the workforce temporarily for legitimate reasons (a job search or protected leave) usually say so. If they don't, something has been omitted for a reason. Did the candidate spend time in prison as a convicted felon, or get fired for embezzling or sexual harassment, or spend a long time collecting unemployment because other people were smart enough not to hire him?

- *Beware of career students:* Recent college graduates have reason to emphasize their education. Candidates who have earned a degree while working full time are justified for tooting their own horns. For everyone else, education should be given less emphasis than work experience. There's a reason they call life off campus the "real world."

- *Beware of extraneous data:* Sure, you want a well-rounded candidate, but that doesn't mean you need to know about their pets, voting history, or must-see TV shows. It's helpful to know that she's joined professional associations to network or to hone her skills. It's less helpful for you to know about her membership in the Book of the Month Club or frequent-flier program.

- *Logic counts:* Look for job history in chronological order. Organization by function or other order that makes you work to figure out job tenure and history has probably been packaged to conceal something.

- *Spot the top candidates* by looking for the following:

  - *Specific accomplishments:* Are there concrete examples of what the candidate has accomplished, or glittering generalities about their responsibilities? In sales, for example, look for dollar volume, market share, or increased percentage in sales. Market data and timelines are an added bonus: "As sales rep for one of five national territories, moved sales from lowest market share against four competitors to highest market share in 18 months."

- *Training:* Does the candidate indicate any special training he has had? Depending on your business, anything from university extension courses to conference seminars could be helpful.
- *Customization:* Has the resume been drafted for your job—or at least a similar job—or is it a generic one-size-fits-all resume?
- *Career progress*: Has the candidate made job changes leading to progressively more responsibility and higher pay, or simply seem stuck? Does the candidate seem to have a career plan?
- *Does the candidate focus on the bottom line*? Does he mention cutting costs or making money?

Stay Out of Jail

- *If candidates include personal information in their resumes, ignore it when evaluating their qualifications.*
- *Keep all the resumes submitted in application for the job.*
- *Be careful if you are fully reliant on resumes that have been scanned into databases.* There have been legal challenges to resume scanning on the grounds the key words used adversely affect protected minorities.

Get More Information

Finding, Hiring, and Keeping the Best Employees, Robert Half (John Wiley and Sons, Inc., New York, 1993)

Hiring Smart!, Dr. Pierre Mornell (Ten Speed Press, Berkeley, CA 1998)

Smart Staffing, Wayne Outlaw (Upstart Publishing Co., Chicago, 1998)

VALUES TESTING: HOW TO BE SURE CANDIDATES WILL FIT IN

Know the Issue

Remember the Man in the Gray Flannel Suit—that '50s archetype of the corporation man? Today, he's as extinct as the T-Rex. His habitat is now home to a variety of new species: Bernie Brainstorm, Natalie Numbers, Monica Meetings, Donna Deadlines, and Peter Policy among them. But evolution is a tricky thing. Although the Man in the Gray Flannel Suit is unlikely to survive as the fittest almost anywhere today, choosing the fittest of today's employees is a tough call. That's because today's leading organizations have distinct cultures; and in the best of them, the culture assumes cult-like dimensions. So Bernie Brainstorm may set runways ablaze at Southwest Airlines, for example, while Peter Policy almost certainly won't. That's both good and bad, but when hiring, it means that choosing a candidate who won't fit into the culture is a waste of time.

Furthermore, within each culture people are working together more closely than ever. As a manager, that can be challenging.

Monica Meetings and Donna Deadlines may complement each other —may even need each other—but keeping them from killing each other is an art.

All of which, believe it or not, leads us to testing. Ultimately, you can't change someone's personality, but you can identify it, and work hard to put the right person into the right job and the right culture.

The tests in question are most commonly called psychological tests or personality tests, but both are misnomers. These tests don't really measure personality; they measure values, thinking style, and behavioral preferences, among other things. By whatever name, they can help you figure out whether a candidate is likely a good fit with the open job and with your organization—or not.

Take Action

- *Review your diagram of the culture* (page 27). What are the norms? What attributes are imperative for success? What behavior will really stand out?

- *Review the job description.* Pay close attention to the behavioral expectations. What sort of person are you looking for? An idea person? A doer? An enforcer?

- *Review your organization's testing policy.* If there is a policy, follow it. If there is no policy, draft one for your department. Have it approved by HR. If there is no HR department, have it reviewed by the legal department or an attorney.

- *Review testing options.* American consumers can choose from 23 different kinds of catsup, so you can imagine how many choices you have to assess values and behavior. The task of sorting through them might be scary enough to permanently alter your own behavior, so let's state up front that there is no single right answer. Any number of professional tests are just fine. What's important is to find one that works for you. (See "Values Testing: A Primer" on page 94 for a look at some of the best-known assessment tools.) Although each approach is somewhat different, there's remarkable consistency in the results they produce.

- *Test the test.* Once you've identified an approach that seems right to you, take the test yourself. Do the results seem to describe you accurately? Do your boss, spouse, partner, or co-workers agree? If so, the test is probably a good choice for you. If not, you may wish to try another option.

- *Consider the practicalities.* How expensive is the test? How long does it take to administer? Can the test be taken anywhere? How is it interpreted? Can you determine the results or must an expert do it? Choose a test you can live with long-term.

- *Use the test.* Depending on which test you use, you can administer it either before any interview, between the first and second interview, or after all interviews. It's best to administer between the first and second interviews.

- *Tell the candidate how the test will be used.* Explain the test's role in your hiring process. Identify who will see the results. (It may be only you; if you're using team interviews, however, there may be occasion to show the results to other interviewers.)

- *See how the candidate reacts to the results.* Share the results with your top candidates during a follow-up interview. How does she react? We all have personality quirks; some people manage theirs while others indulge them. Is she most interested in learning about herself or in arguing with you about the results? Does she explain how she manages her quirks? Offer examples of how they surface on the job? You're not looking for a perfect person, but ideally you'll find someone self-aware and honest about who they are.

- *Discuss the results.* Use the results to help frame discussion. For example, suppose a test shows that a candidate craves variety, and you know the job won't offer much variety. Be honest and see how the candidate reacts. Can she see trade-offs (such as the chance to learn in exchange for limited tasks)? Does she really hear you?

Stay Out of Jail

- *Don't rely too heavily on tests.* Look at test results alongside credentials, the interview, and other data; don't make the hiring decision on tests alone. Most tests measure preferences, not skill. For example, just because someone likes to work on several projects at once it doesn't mean they are adept at it.

- *Have an attorney review the test you use.* Some candidates have objected to the questions asked on some tests, claiming they invade privacy. Some also claim that the questions are unrelated to job performance. In several instances, the courts have agreed. In one case, candidates complained about an assessment in which they were asked to decide how applicable certain statements were to themselves. The judge ruled in favor of the candidates. In his opinion, he cited these statements—among others—as objectionable:

I shouldn't do many of the things I do.
I often lose my temper.

In school, I was frequently rebellious.

I hate opera singing.

To further add to the confusion, what's acceptable in one state may not be in another. Bottom line: Run the test by an attorney.

- *Be sure the test you use is validated.* (For more on validation, please see page 95.)
- *Get proof of the test's validity and proof that it does not adversely affect a protected group.* Keep the proof on file.
- *Keep the results of all the tests you administer in confidential applicant files.*
- *Be consistent.* Once you've chosen a test, use it on all applicants; don't pick and choose. (If you test for one job, you needn't test for all. But if one candidate for a job is tested, then all the candidates for that same job must take the test.) Keep the environment and other circumstances as consistent as possible when the test is administered.

Do at Least the Minimum

- *Use behavior or values tests when filling the key jobs in your department.* A lot is at stake in those cases.

Get More Information

Books

Hiring Smart!, Dr. Pierre Mornell, Ten Speed Press, Berkeley, CA

Tests

The BarOn EQi™

Multi-Health Systems Inc.

3770 Victoria Park Ave.

Toronto, ON Canada

M2H 3M6

800/268-6011

www.mhs.com

Personal Preference Inventory (PPI) and Job Preference Inventory (JPI)

Compass Learning Systems

PO Box 2144

Lake Arrowhead, CA 92352

909/337-9854

Kolbe A Index™

Kolbe

3421 N. 44th St.

Phoenix, AZ 85018

602/840-9770

www.kolbe.com

Herrmann Brain Dominance Instrument

Herrmann International

794 Buffalo Creek Rd.

Lake Lure, NC 28746

828/625-9153

www.hbdi.com

The Myers-Briggs Type Inventory (MBTI) is administered by many organizations and professionals.

Values Testing: A Primer

The Myers-Briggs Type Inventory (MBTI) is the most widely used assessment in the world. It identifies people as one of 16 broad personality types, on the supposition that personality drives behavior. The 16 types are derived by measuring four traits (extroversion/introversion, sensing/intuition, thinking/feeling, judging/perceiving), each of which is assigned a scale. (For example, someone might be either an extreme introvert or extrovert, or be placed somewhere toward the center of the scale and have characteristics of both.) The 16 types reflect the dominant tendency in each trait. An INTJ, therefore, is an introvert, intuits, thinks, and judges. These personality types can help predict behavior in the individual alone and in relation to other personality types.

In contrast, *The Personal Preference Inventory* (PPI) makes no claim to assess motivation or personality type. Instead, the instrument gauges the behavior people prefer to exhibit at work. Tom Dortch, co-developer of the PPI, says that everyone seeks to meet their behavioral preferences in a job. He argues that the impulse is so strong that people work to change the job (or quit) if their preferences aren't being met. The PPI measures several preferences, including autonomy (how much freedom do people want on the job?), task involvement (does someone prefer to focus on just one activity, or to do many different things?), and performance feedback (does a person rely on objective data such as a balance sheet, or on subjective feedback such as a "Way to go!"?). The tool places people on a scale for each measurement. (Therefore, Brian may be "high" on subjective feedback while MaryLou is "low.") The PPI can be used alone or in conjunction with a *Job Preference Inventory* (JPI). Dortch says that every job demands certain behavior—rocket scientists must process a lot of objective data, for example, while hairdressers do not. The JPI measures the behavior required in each job (determined by a manager, the person in the job, both, or a team of people). If the instruments are used together,

continued

an individual profile can be matched against the job demands to identify potential stressors and challenges.

Although the PPI measures overt or known behavior preferences, the *Kolbe A Index* measures instinctive behavior—how we actually behave, particularly under stress. The tool identifies cognitive strengths in four zones (Fact Finder, Follow Thru, Quick Start, and Implementor). The results show how we solve problems, and what we will or won't do on the job. The results also offer advice that may not be 100 percent flattering, but is realistic ("turn to others to institute procedures, and cut a deal to avoid most of them").

The *Herrmann Brain Dominance Instrument* doesn't measure behavior at all; instead it measures thinking style. The HBDI looks at the brain in four quadrants (quadrant A is logical, for example, while quadrant D is artistic). The tool acknowledges that we all use all four quadrants, but identifies which quadrant is our dominant thinking style and how the quadrants influence one another. (More than 30 different profile types are identified using the HBDI.) The HBDI can be used to help identify thinking styles best suited to particular professions or organizational cultures. For example, someone whose thinking style uses very little of the artistic quadrant may not be suited to an advertising career.

The *BarOn EQi* is the first scientifically developed, validated measurement of emotional intelligence. (For more on emotional intelligence, see pages 191–199.) The assessment takes about 30 minutes to complete and measures competencies and skills in 15 scales (such as flexibility, empathy, and problem solving). The result is a score (100 is average) similar to the IQ that measures cognitive intelligence.

Validation: A Primer

If you're doing virtually any kind of pre-employment testing, validation is a concept you should be familiar with—and no, we're not talking about a group hug. Validation is the process of proving that a test is relevant to a job, that it tests only what it claims to test, and it doesn't discriminate against any protected groups or individuals applying for the job.

To understand validation, you must first know about the Uniform Guidelines on Employee Selection Procedures. The Guidelines were created jointly in 1978 by several Federal agencies, among them the EEOC, the Department of Labor, and the Department of Justice. The Guidelines were written to help employers hire without discriminating. What does that mean for testing? It means that if you use a test to make hiring decisions, you must look at the people who have been hired after taking the test. Look first at the people who were hired most often—say people with blue hair. To make the math easy, say that 100 people with blue hair were hired. If fewer than 80 of any other group (say people with red thumbs) were hired using the test as a basis, then the selection rate is considered substantially different and therefore unacceptable. Of course, we don't live in a world where people naturally have blue hair or red thumbs, so the government looks instead at race, sex, religion, and national origin.

Validation is proof of any test or procedure's nondiscriminatory job-relatedness. Generally, the process begins with an analysis to identify the job requirements. The next step is to identify selection tools and standards that will isolate the applicants that meet those requirements. (Testing current employees and applicants without using the results to make hiring decisions can help measure the test's effectiveness.) Validating a test takes place over a long period of time and is applied to a large sample population. The final stage is to draft a report that outlines the steps taken and the results. Industrial and personnel psychologists with specific expertise in such research usually validate tests.

continued

Three methods can demonstrate validity:

- *Criterion-related validity* is a statistical correlation between test scores and the job performance of a sample of employees.
- *Content validity* demonstrates that the content of a test represents important aspects of job performance.
- *Construct validity* shows that a test measures something believed to be a basic human trait (such as honesty) and this trait is important for succeeding in a job.

Of these, content validity is used most often.

As with flamethrowing and stunt skateboarding, validating a test is probably something you shouldn't try at home. Buying a validated test is easiest. If you decide to develop a test yourself, have it reviewed by an attorney; you may ultimately need to have it validated. After all, the Uniform Guidelines apply to all private employers with 15 or more employees, state and local governments, labor organizations, and contractors and subcontractors to the Federal government.

DRUG TESTING: HOW TO USE THE FIRST LINE OF DEFENSE IN EMPLOYEE SAFETY

Know the Issue

Pop quiz. Decide whether each of the following statements is true or false:

1. The National Institute on Drug Abuse estimates that on any given day, 12 to 25 percent of employees age 18 to 40 would test positive for illegal drug use.

2. The Research Triangle Institute estimates that the United States loses $26 billion annually because of drug abuse.

3. According to the American Management Association, approximately 76 percent of employers require pre-employment drug testing.

4. In order to protect the safety of employees, customers, and the public, you have a legal obligation to require pre-employment drug testing for at least some positions.

5. Pre-employment drug tests will deter users of illegal drugs from applying for jobs at the organizations that require them.

6. Pre-employment drug testing may undermine morale.

7. Pre-employment drug testing does not guarantee that your workplace will be drug-free.

OK, we admit we rigged the test—all the statements are true.

Even in today's highly complex workplace, few issues are as complex as drug testing. That's because illegal drugs are a little bit like the elephant being described by the blind men. Some see drug use as a health issue, and others as a legal problem. Some see illegal drug use as a moral failing, while others see it as recreational activity. For some, drug use is a major public policy challenge, and for others, it's the flashpoint of discussions about personal privacy. For all those reasons, drug use is also an employment issue.

Much of the debate centers on illegal drug use of employees (not applicants) and we address those issues in "Drug and Alcohol Abuse" (see pages 399–405). For now, our concern is on pre-employment testing.

The goal of pre-employment testing is pretty straightforward: To discourage users of illegal drugs from applying to your organization, and to identify those who do apply before they're hired.

Almost nothing else about drug testing is so straightforward. Although the tests can identify illegal drug users, they also can be insulting to people who have never used illegal drugs. People who use drugs may go undetected (many users have become skilled at foiling the tests), while non-users may be stigmatized by false positive results. Most tests detect only the presence of drugs in someone's system; they do not measure whether the person's performance is impaired. Finally, relatively few employers test for alcohol abuse, though alcoholism is much more prevalent than illegal drug use.

In short, drug testing is imperfect. If your organization already has a testing policy, follow it. If not, weigh the potential benefits against the downsides and decide what seems best.

Our advice is to require testing when impairment because of illegal drug use puts the employee, co-workers, customers, or members of the public at risk. Consider these risk factors:

- Is the employee directly responsible for public safety (such as health- and dental-care personnel, airline personnel, bus drivers, emergency response workers, and security personnel)?
- Does the employee work with children?
- Is the employee indirectly responsible for public safety (such as truck drivers and public utility workers)?
- Does the employee work with heavy equipment, chemicals, live electrical wiring, or other dangerous or hazardous equipment or materials?
- Is the employee required to climb or work at a potentially risky height (such as washing windows)?
- Is the employee responsible for valuable or breakable merchandise?

Keep in mind that your organization may run the risk of a claim of negligence if you *don't* test applicants for such positions.

If you test for illegal drug use, drug tests can be required in three points of the hiring process:

- Before an offer of employment is made
- After a conditional offer is made, but before a candidate is formally hired
- Soon after the employee begins working, with the understanding that employment is still conditional on passing the test

Generally, requiring a test after extending a conditional offer of employment is best.

When requiring a drug test, keep in mind that there is no single test. Several options exist; see the accompanying chart for specifics.

Take Action

- *Know your organization's policy.* Review your employee handbook. Most organizations have a stated policy about drug testing and illegal drug use. Whatever the policy, follow it. Don't be the only manager to require pre-employment drug tests *unless,* for example, you manage the only department in which employees directly affect public safety.
- *Don't keep the policy a secret.* If you require employees to pass a drug test as a condition of employment, make that clear up front. Include a statement to that effect on the application form, and advise candidates of the policy during the interview. (At one auto repair chain in the Midwest, a high percentage of applicants failed the drug test. When the firm began advising candidates of the testing policy in advance, 40 percent of applicants were no-shows for the interview, which saved the company the time interviewing and the cost of testing).

- *If there is no company policy, develop a policy for your department.* Don't ask for drug tests using the whim system. Determine for which positions you'll require a pre-employment drug test and which you won't. Make sure the legal department or an attorney approves it.

- *If you require a drug test, use a vendor recommended by your HR department.* If there is no HR function in your organization, or the HR function has not recommended a vendor, find a reputable firm. How do you know if a firm is reputable? Ask the following questions:

  - How long has the firm been in business?
  - What sort of tests does the lab do? (Please see accompanying chart for the options.)
  - How does the lab maintain confidentiality?
  - What is the lab's chain of custody procedure for the sample?
  - Is testing done under the direction of a board-certified toxicologist?
  - Is the lab Federally certified?
  - Has the lab been checked?
  - Is the lab insured?
  - Will the lab guarantee its work?

Then, ask for references—and call them.

Stay Out of Jail

- *Be certain about the law in your state.* If you have any question, contact an attorney.

- *Be consistent.* If one candidate for a job is asked to have a pre-employment drug test, *all* the candidates for the job should be required to have a drug test.

- *Keep the results of any drug test confidential.*

- *Where practical, use the same lab to assure uniformity of testing.*

- *If you are in the transportation industry, be well versed with the Department of Transportation regulations regarding drug testing.*

- *The* Americans with Disabilities Act *(ADA) provides that a medical examination can be required only* after *a conditional offer of employment and before an applicant is formally hired.* The ADA allows employers to require a drug test even before making a conditional offer of employment *provided that*

  - The test must be designed to accurately identify only the illegal use of drugs

  - The test should not be performed in conjunction with a pre-employment physical

  - The test should not require an applicant to reveal information about prescription drug use, unless a positive test result may be explained by use of a prescription drug

  - *The ADA also stipulates that pre-employment alcohol testing* is *considered a medical examination and therefore may only be required*

  - After a conditional offer of employment has been made

  - In accordance with ADA regulations of pre-employment physicals. (see Chapter 8, pages 230–233)

- *Ask for applicant consent.* If your firm has a form in which candidates or employees consent to a drug test, use it. If not, have an attorney draft a consent form and then ask candidates to sign it.

- *Candidates who test positive for illegal drugs may claim that they are not users.* In such cases, they may ask for another test to confirm the results. (Normal protocols for testing stipulate that labs test only one-third of the sample provided. That means that they can conduct another test without getting another sample.) You are not obligated to pay for the second test. However, false positives are possible. Many employers choose to pay for the second test as a matter both of fairness and precaution. Applicants who are rejected on the basis of a drug test may sue for invasion of privacy, wrongful failure to hire, defamation, and negligence, among other things. It pays to be certain of the facts.

Real World Examples

Two sides of the drug-testing coin occur:

- A candidate for a management position was asked to take a drug test. At the lab, he was asked to pass through a crowded waiting room carrying a specimen cup. A lab technician then watched while he urinated, ostensibly to ensure that the sample wasn't tampered with. Then the candidate had to pass through the crowded waiting room again, this time carrying the full specimen cup. The experience didn't do much to preserve the candidate's dignity, or to give him a favorable impression of his prospective employer.

- During his initial interview, a candidate for a sales management position seemed distracted and edgy. He had a hard time sitting still. He drank a lot of water and sweated profusely. He apologized for all of the behavior and chalked it up to nerves. Still, the executive filling the position suspected a problem and scheduled a second interview in the evening, over dinner. At that interview, the candidate seemed relaxed and comfortable. The candidate seemed well qualified, and he was hired. Less than six months later, he was terminated for poor performance. Afterward, one of the salespeople who had reported to the sales manager stepped forward. He said that during an out-of-town sales trip, the manager had admitted to spending much of the night in a city park looking for drugs and had shown up for their first sales call strung out and acting bizarrely. In addition, the salesperson reported that sales calls often were compromised by the same behavior that the executive had seen during the initial interview. A drug test could have spared the company—and its sales staff—some embarrassment and an expensive lesson.

Get More Information

Center for Substance Abuse Prevention Hotline, 800/843-4971

The AMA Handbook for Employee Recruitment and Retention, Mary Cook, editor, The American Management Association, New York, 1992.

Types of Drug Tests

Urine tests. The most widely used urine test is the *Enzyme Multiplied Immunoassay Technique* (EMIT). This inexpensive test can detect the presence of enzymes into which drugs metabolize. It's highly accurate, but also has a high false-positive rate.

Gas chromatography and mass spectrometry. This is the superior test. It's highly specific and very accurate. Naturally, it's also the most expensive.

Blood tests. Blood tests detect the presence of drugs or alcohol in the bloodstream, but are of little value just a few hours after the drugs are taken. Such tests therefore are best used when an employee's on-the-job behavior suggests his performance may be impaired by illegal drug use.

Saliva tests. These tests are extremely nonspecific and their accuracy is questionable.

Hair tests. Radioimmunoassay analysis of metabolites imbedded in a single strand of hair offer rough estimates of the quantity of illegal drugs consumed and approximately when they were taken. This test is more expensive than the EMIT, and its accuracy is unproven.

Nonmedical tests. Another option is to test for impairment, rather than for the chemical presence of illegal drugs. Such tests include *balance and reflex performance checks* and *critical tracking tests,* which measure hand-eye coordination and quick reaction time. Beware, however, that these tests could discriminate against people with certain disabilities or impairments.

Source: *The AMA Handbook for Employee Recruitment and Retention,* American Management Association, New York. 1992.

PHYSICALS: HOW TO BE SURE THE CANDIDATE WILL BE ABLE TO DO THE JOB

Know the Issue

Around the turn of the last century, a young Scottish man chose his bride by considering which of the eligible young women was healthiest. He planned to emigrate to the United States and he wanted a companion who would survive the trip and be strong enough to work hard after they arrived. Not exactly the romantic fantasy of a Julia Roberts movie, it's nonetheless an honest reflection of the economic realities the young couple faced.

Although no employer today would openly seek the healthiest girl in the village, many do require physical exams. Sometimes they should. None of us wants to board an airliner wondering whether the pilot is at high risk of suffering a heart attack.

But it would take an unabashed fan of managed care to really love pre-employment physicals. The laws are complex, confidentiality is paramount, and the emotional stakes can be high.

If you decide a physical is warranted, focus on what's relevant to the job. Remember, the purpose of a pre-employment physical is not to get the complete medical history of the candidate. You have three responsibilities:

1. To protect employees from on-the-job injuries
2. To protect co-workers and customers from injury
3. To protect the company against false claims that it is responsible for an employee's disability or medical condition by having a "baseline" test on file

Take Action

- *Revisit the physical requirements for the job noted in the job description.* Most white-collar jobs don't require much physical activity, so there's little reason to require a physical. The cost probably outweighs any value to the company. If, however, the job requires something more, a physical might be appropriate. Consider whether the job requires
  - Heavy lifting (Here's the test: Can the employee, without difficulty or with a reasonable accommodation, perform the essential job functions without endangering his or her health or safety, or the health and safety of others.)
  - Exertion (such as climbing stairs or walking long distances)
  - Working at elevated heights (for example, on ladders or a multi-story construction site)
  - The ability to respond to safety warnings (such as flashing lights, alarms, or other devices)
  - Licensing that requires specific physical abilities
  - Normal vision (employees who work with color-coded electrical wire, for example, could be in danger if they are color blind)

  or anything else beyond the norm.

Stay Out of Jail

- *Asking a job candidate to have a complete physical is legal.* However, the ADA prohibits requiring a medical exam *before* an offer of employment is made. Extend a job offer based on the candidate's experience and skills, but conditional on passing the job-related physical. As far as the law is concerned, a physical may be far less than an exam by a doctor. None of the following is permitted before a job offer is made:

- Any procedure administered and/or interpreted by a health care professional

- Any procedure intended to reveal the existence, nature, or severity of an impairment

- Any invasive procedure (such as requiring the drawing of blood or urine)

- Any test that measures physiological or psychological responses

- Any procedure that employs medical equipment or devices

- *Limit the tests to job-related functions.* This is one case in which less is more. If, through whatever means, you know that a candidate is pregnant, suffers from migraines, or is a cancer survivor, you may be accused of discrimination if you do not hire that person. Even if the charges are unfounded, defending yourself will be time-consuming and expensive. Stick to what's relevant to the job.

- *Physicals must be required of* all *applicants for a job; you can't pick and choose who gets one.*

- *Information obtained must be maintained and collected on separate forms and in confidential medical files separate from an employee or candidate's primary personnel file.*

- *Medical information may not be disclosed.* Your organization may require that physicals be administered through HR or an employee health department. If so, do not expect to see the results yourself. Legally, you have no right or reason to know the particulars of an employee's medical condition. Therefore, you're likely simply to get a report stating whether the candidate can perform the essential job functions. If somehow you do see other information (such as a diagnosis), tell HR there has been a breach that must be corrected, and *keep the information to yourself*.

- *There is one exception to the confidentiality: Candidates may ask to see the results of their own physicals.*

- *If the physical discloses a disability, and you decide not to hire a candidate because of that disability, you must show that the disability cannot reasonably be accommodated and that the job tasks you require that cannot be performed are core functions of the job.* It is a very difficult standard.

- *You may require a candidate to see a specific doctor.* In theory, this prevents the employee from unduly influencing the results. If you exercise this option, however, do it consistently. And remember that doing so sends a signal that you don't trust people.

- *If the applicant refutes the results of a physical, he or she may opt to have another doctor do a physical.* If those results are different, you aren't obligated to accept them. However, if the applicant is otherwise a good choice for the position, or simply to show good faith, you may wish to get a second opinion. Make it clear that doing so is at your discretion, and isn't a precedent for the future. (Note: In a few selected cases—such as truck drivers—a neutral third doctor may be required to settle the dispute.)

Do at Least the Minimum

- *Require physicals for jobs in which employee health and safety (or the health and safety of others) may be at risk.*
- *Limit tests to job-related abilities.*
- *Keep any medical information you have confidential.*

REFERENCE CHECKS: HOW TO GET THE WHOLE STORY

Know the Issue

There's a body on the floor of the parlor: The owner of the manor has been murdered and his priceless heirloom painting is gone. The security log shows that other than the victim, no one was in the house that night except the maid; and she denies she did it.

Would Hercule Poirot or any other self-respecting detective simply accept her statement? Of course not! He would talk to witnesses to get their version of events, comparing each person's story to the others in an effort to find the greater truth.

Most job candidates aren't hiding smoking guns, buried ransom, or forged wills. But they are working hard to present themselves at their very best; and you owe it to yourself to be sure you've heard the whole story. Sure, Ms. Perfect might have been the most accurate checker at the supermarket. But was she also the slowest? References can help answer questions.

A warning: It won't be easy. Because of some successful lawsuits filed by candidates who felt they were defamed by previous employers, many companies have limited references only to confirming dates of employment and job title. That makes it tough even to get *positive* references, let alone cautionary ones. Just working through voicemail to find the right person can be overwhelming. If Sam Spade had so many obstacles to overcome, we *still* might not know who stole the Maltese Falcon.

Stick with it. If you persevere, checking references can be very worthwhile.

Take Action

- *Figure out what you want to know.* Calling references to ask generic questions ("How long have you known Nancy?") isn't likely to yield much that's worthwhile. Review your interview notes. Has the candidate talked about an accomplishment you'd like to confirm? Would you like to know more about the environment she worked in? Are there pieces of the puzzle that don't fit? References can help answer whatever questions you still have.

- *Ask the candidate for references.* Some candidates list references on their resume. Others provide them in a cover letter. However you get them, ignore them if the candidate volunteered them. Applicants choose people ready to tell you how wonderful they are, but those may not be the people who can answer your questions. Tell the candidate the areas you'd like to explore ("I'm interested in finding out more about the events you organized") and ask her who you should call. That way, she knows who you'll be calling; and you won't waste time calling people who can't help you anyway. Just don't give away too much about what you'd like to ask; you don't want the candidate to prep the reference.

- *Tell the candidate whom you're calling and when.* Too many bosses have found out that their employees were job hunting when a potential boss called for a reference. Don't put a candidate in that situation.

- *Don't limit yourself to the candidate's boss.* Yes, the candidate's current or previous boss can answer questions, but don't stop there. Is the candidate a member of a professional association? Call another member to find out how the candidate participates. Has the applicant published in professional journals? Call the editor and ask how it was to work with the candidate. Be creative in your thinking. Just be sure to limit questions to job-related topics. Develop some specific questions related to these issues:
  - Technical competence
  - People skills, where relevant
  - Motivation

- *Use voicemail.* If you're pressed for time, Dr. Pierre Mornell has a great suggestion. Call references during their lunch hour and leave a message. Tell them that Joe is a candidate for a job in your firm, and ask them to call back if Joe is outstanding. What happens next is telling. If Joe is great, most people will happily call back. If no one does, you've learned something without anyone saying something negative.

- *Be persistent.* If references agree only to confirm employment, at least do that. Then keep calling. Eventually, someone will talk. People are more likely to answer specific questions ("What percentage of Jane's students were promoted to the next grade last year?") than generic ones ("Did Jane's students like her?").

- *Meet in person.* It's often not possible, but, if you can, meet key references face to face. Buy them lunch or a morning latte and have a conversation. You're more likely to get anecdotes and better examples of the candidate's work in a relaxed environment without distractions.

- *Take the focus off the candidate.* If a reference can't—or won't —tell you more than the basics, try another approach. Ask about the qualities she was looking for in the person hired to replace your candidate. Are the qualities she mentions consistent with what you've seen in interviews with the candidate? Or is she describing someone who sounds like the opposite of the person you've been talking with?

- *Talk to your own staff.* Don't ignore your own *internal* references. If someone else scheduled the interview, talk to that person. Talk to the receptionist, the parking garage attendant, and anyone else the candidate interacted with. Did they seem the same qualities you did? Or did they meet someone rude or telling inappropriate jokes?

Stay Out of Jail

- *Should there ever be a problem after a candidate is hired (such as violence or sexual harassment), the better your due diligence was up front, the better off you'll be.*
- *Keep your questions focused on the job—don't get personal.*
- *Keep whatever you hear from a reference confidential.*
- *Keep a record of which references you spoke with and when.* Take notes during the conversation.
- *Don't tape record your conversations.*
- *Never claim to be someone else, or misrepresent the call.* Be up front about who you are and why you're calling.

Real World Example

One executive has a strategy for hiring sales talent. He asks job candidates to identify their toughest sale, and then he calls that client. The information can be invaluable. How long did it take to close the sale? How did the candidate keep the conversation open? What information did he give the client? How did his performance compare to his competitor's sales pitch? After the sale, did the candidate offer good service or disappear?

Do at Least the Minimum

- *Verify employment dates, titles, and salary.*

BACKGROUND CHECKS: HOW TO FIND OUT WHAT CANDIDATES DON'T WANT YOU TO KNOW

Know the Issue

You've found your dream house, and you can't wait to move in. But during escrow the extras begin: title searches, termite inspections, radon gas tests, and on and on. It can be irritating and expensive, but it can also save you from making a $200,000 mistake.

Odds are, a background check won't uncover wood rot in your top candidate. But it might uncover something else that you really need to know before you make a job offer. Protect your employer—and your reputation. Do a thorough check to verify the facts.

Take Action

- *Find your employer's policy and follow it.* If you work in a large firm, there's probably a policy on background checks. If so, follow it. The firm may also require that the HR department conduct or monitor any background checks. If there is no policy or HR function to help, then follow these guidelines.

- *Make sure the candidate is who he says he is.* Verify his name, address, and Social Security number.

- *Determine the credentials the job demands.* Review the job description to see whether a high school diploma or a college or post-graduate degree is required. Then consider other requirements. Many positions—from attorneys to cosmetologists—require licenses. Others (accountants, for example) require certification of their skills. Still others (such as teachers) require periodic training to keep current. Make a list of everything necessary.

- *Verify his credentials.* Did the candidate really earn the college degree he claims to have? You may want to know simply to test the candidate's honesty. In other situations, the data may be more critical. If you require a degree for a particular job, it's best to get proof of the degree. (Universities generally verify enrollment dates and degrees earned.)

If the job demands other credentials, verify those, too:

- Licenses (including a drivers' license *if* the job requires driving)

- Certification (a prominent hospital was embarrassed when a physician on its staff turned out not to have the board certification he claimed, which imperiled his license to practice)

- Training hours, if required

- *Identify work-related risks.* An employer assumes some risk every time an employee is hired. But some positions carry specific risks that should not be ignored. For example, if the job requires management of money (cash or credit), it's prudent to check a candidate's credit history. A credit check, however, isn't really relevant if hiring an appliance repair technician. On the other hand, recent felony convictions may be relevant if a position requires that an employee directly interacts with customers or other members of the public, either at the workplace or in customers' homes. Stick to the facts (not hearsay or opinion) and make sure inquiries are job-related. But get the information you need.

- *Collect the data.* Much of this information (such as licenses) is a matter of public record. Other information (such as credit history) can be obtained from reporting agencies. But collecting data can be tedious and time-consuming, particularly if you're filling several jobs at once. Therefore, you may want to hire a professional firm to conduct the check for you. If you elect to hire a firm, be sure you hire a reputable one:

  - Ask for a list of clients and call some of them.

  - Find out how the firm gets its information.

  - Does the firm do a national check, or merely a local one?

  - Does the firm guarantee its work?

- Keep the data in a confidential candidate file.
- Comply with the Federal and state legal requirements when you use a third party to get information.

Stay Out of Jail

- *Be consistent.* Verify the same information for every candidate for the same job. Don't conduct a check on some candidates and not others, for example. What you check may vary from job to job, but in each case there should be a business rationale for your decision.
- *Limit what you inquire about.* For example, it may be illegal— or evidence of unlawful discriimination—to explore:
  - Arrest records or misdemeanor convictions
  - Workers' compensation claims
  - Legal activity (including employment-related lawsuits)
  - Marital status
  - Physical or mental disabilities
  - Political activities
  - Bankruptcy
  - Sexual orientation
- *Comply with the* Fair Credit Reporting Act *(FRCA).* The FRCA governs the retrieval and use of consumer information from credit reports, criminal records, and department of motor vehicle reports among others where it is obtained by a consumer credit-reporting agency. The law is complex, and the definition of a credit-credit reporting agency is broad, but you should know about certain provisions:

- You may not use consumer reports unless you notify applicants that such a report may be used and obtain their permission to use it.

- If you use any background check as a reason (either as the whole reason or as a contributing factor) *not* to hire someone, you must provide the candidate with a copy of the report and a summary of his rights. Copies of the rights usually are provided by the reporting agencies.

- Before taking any adverse action based on the report, it's best to allow candidates a reasonable time to explain any information that may not be correct in the report. The law does not specify what's reasonable, but courts have held that five days is acceptable.

- Be prepared to explain how adverse information obtained in a report is job-related and sufficient to render the applicant unsuitable for a particular position.

Real Life Example

She seemed too good to be true. A manager in a small business was searching for a new employee, and the woman across from him had every qualification he had hoped to find. She seemed to have all the answers to his questions before he even asked them and she seemed reliable—she had made very few job changes.

Her resume did include a four-year gap in employment, which she explained by stating that she had chosen to stay home and care for her young children until they started school. Now she was ready to re-enter the work force.

The manager hired her and she was one of the best employees the company ever had. She quickly learned every position in the office. Everyone thought she must have been sent from heaven.

Then one day the perfect employee took a day off. As it happened, the owner's wife was filling in that day and answered the phone. It was a call from the bank, inquiring whether the company was aware that its checking account was overdrawn.

The call led to an investigation, which revealed that the perfect employee had been embezzling for six years. She had stolen more than $400,000. Later, the police told the manager that the perfect employee had not spent four years at home caring for her children; she had spent that time in prison for stealing from a previous employer. For the second offense, the perfect employee was sentenced to six years in the state penitentiary. She lost her home, her husband, and her family, and has been paying the company $50 a month in restitution.

The manager who hired her wonders what her resume looks like today and is glad he wasn't fired for his failure to do a background check on the employee.

Do at Least the Minimum

- *Be sure that the candidate is who he claims to be.*
- *Verify that the candidate has any valid licenses or other certification required by law.*

NEGLIGENT HIRING: HOW TO AVOID THE LEGAL NIGHTMARE OF MAKING A BAD HIRE

Know the Issue

What's the worst thing that can happen if you make a bad hire? You just have to fire the person later, right? Wrong! A truly bad hire—someone who is unstable, or undependable in performing his or her job—can be a financial and public relations disaster for your company. That's because the law says that managers are obligated to protect their organization, its employees, and its customers. Unstable and undependable employees are a potential danger to all three. If a person you hired somehow causes injury to another person, your company—*not* just the employee—can be responsible for the damages.

In other words, your negligence in making a hire will have exposed your company to unnecessary risk. You can imagine how your boss will feel about that.

Take Action

- *Require a completed application form before hiring someone.*
- *Call all references and previous employers to get as much information as possible about the applicant.*
- *Document all answers given by references and prior employers, including refusals to give information.* Keep your notes in the candidate's file.
- *Do a background check that's directly applicable to the job tasks required.* For example, check driving records if you're hiring a truck or school bus driver. (For more information, see "Background Checks," pages 114–118.)

Once the employee is hired, protect yourself from being vulnerable to negligent supervision: Provide adequate training and take corrective action as soon as there's a problem. For more information, see pages 294–297.

Real Life Examples

An employer attended a Rotary Club luncheon and was convinced by the director of a state-licensed residential treatment center that hiring disadvantaged teens is a benefit to society. Afterward, the employer hired a teen who was living at the center and serving probation following a burglary. At the time, the employer made it clear to the staff at the center that he did not want to hire a troublemaker or someone who was violent. Yet within a few months of being hired —and while working at the employer's store—the teen beat a customer in the head and face with his fists and a hammer. The employer then claimed that he had relied on the residential treatment center to do the necessary screening. But the court said that the employer's duty to hire competent, non-violent employees is paramount, and that it was not enough to rely on an outside agency for screening.

Do at Least the Minimum

- *There are no shortcuts when it comes to following the law.* Skipping steps here puts your company at risk. Period. So bite the bullet and do what you need to do.

Manage Up

- *When you've made your hire, make sure your boss knows that you've completed the reference and background checks.* Don't make her ask later.

- *Should there be a problem with the employee (despite your best efforts) don't wait to be asked for the documentation you have.*

6

Interviews

Just be quiet. That's our first and best advice for doing an effective interview.

The whole point of an interview is to find out what and how the candidate thinks, yet most managers barely come up for air once the interview starts. They rattle on about the company, the job, their own work history, or the basketball playoffs. They do it because they're nervous (admit it—it's not just the candidates who find interviews stressful), because they like the candidate and try to sell the job, because they find silence uncomfortable, or just because they like to talk.

Whatever the reason, the impact on the interview is almost entirely negative. Here's what happens. Chatty Hattie is filling a key job in her department. The more she talks, the better she likes the candidate. The conversation is easy. They joke. They laugh and nod. The candidate, when she's allowed to talk, says just the right things.

Hattie likes the candidate because she's had a good time during the interview. In other words, Hattie has decided she likes herself! And the candidate says all the right things because Hattie gave her more lifelines than if she were answering questions on "Who Wants To Be a Millionaire?"

Hattie may be a swell lunch date, but she's a bad, bad interviewer. Remember: An interview and a conversation are *not* the same thing.

An interview has one purpose and one purpose only: To get information to help you determine whether the candidate is qualified to do the job. Getting that information means consistently following a well-structured, objective plan. It may not be as much fun as a three-brewski lunch, but you're much less likely to hire a loser or end up in court.

PREPARING FOR INTERVIEWS: HOW PLANNING SAVES TIME

Know the Issue

Without preparation, any job interview you conduct has all the downsides of a blind date and none of the potential upsides.

Too often, this is how it happens. On interview day you bounce out of bed with a smile on your face and a song in your heart. You whistle through your shower and sing harmony with Barbra Streisand in the car. Why not? There's a neat stack of resumes to review. You pour yourself a hot jolt of java and sit down to prepare for your quality time with eager job prospects.

Then the phone rings. Someone rushes in with a question that must be answered now. Your boss calls an unexpected meeting. Soon, you've lost control of the morning. When the first candidate arrives, you realize you haven't really studied her resume. You have her wait, and sit down to read. The phone rings again. You decide it'll be better to just get on with it. You start the interview, glancing at the resume to prompt questions.

The candidate across the table looks at you warily. She's taken time from another job to be there, and because she's brighter than the average third grader, she's figured out that you haven't read her resume. Two things happen: She decides you're unprepared (and therefore not the boss of her dreams) and she seizes control of the interview. She makes it her mission to be sure you understand what's on the resume and spends most of her time reiterating what you already know or should know. Interviewing is an art, and you're doing a paint-by-the-numbers portrait.

There is a better way.

Take Action

- *Interview fewer people.* Most managers interview too many people and then let disastrous interviews drag on too long. Spend the time up front narrowing the field, and then give your two or three top candidates their full due.

- *Limit interruptions.* Preparing for an interview takes your full concentration. Do what you need to do to get some quiet time. Close your door, let voicemail answer the phone, and focus. If you absolutely can't limit interruptions at work then prepare offsite.

- *Ask the candidate to reconfirm your appointment.* Unless you schedule an interview only a day ahead, ask the candidate to confirm the appointment. Doing so makes it less likely you'll face a no-show; you'll also find out whether the candidate can follow directions.

- *Prepare questions.* You've already carefully read the resume and made notes. Review them now, and write some sample questions. The goal of your questions should be
  - To answer any questions you may have (such as what was happening during the two years that are unaccounted for on the resume)
  - To check the accuracy of any conclusions you may have reached ("It looks as though you were promoted twice during a relatively short period of time at your previous employer. Is that right?")
  - To ask the candidate to relate her experience to the open job
  - To explore behavioral issues (if punctuality is a hot button for you, for example, ask about it)

- *Reserve a room to meet in.* Neutral places are better than your office. Be sure that the room has paper and a pen. If there's something you plan to show the candidate (such as a product sample, sample ledger, or advertising campaign), have it ready. And have water for both of you.

- *Plan your schedule.* If you've done your homework, the interview should be time well spent. Allow about an hour for your meeting. Pace yourself. If you're meeting with several candidates in a single day, allow at least a half-hour between meetings in which to make notes and catch your breath. Also work hard to be prompt. Keeping people waiting is rude and makes it harder to establish rapport.

- *One proviso: These guidelines assume that you're interviewing for a position that requires at least some experience.* If you're hiring counter staff at a fast food store or janitorial help at a hotel, you can limit your prep time, but all candidates deserve the courtesy of a prompt meeting in a comfortable environment.

Do at Least the Minimum

- *Limit the number of people you interview.*
- *Hide in the restroom if that's what it takes, but spend at least a few minutes prepping for every interview.*

Manage Up

- *Let your boss know that you've scheduled interviews.* Give her a sentence or two on the strengths of the candidates. Explain what you hope to find out during the interview.
- *Trust us: There's something your boss will really want to know about your top candidates.* Find out before your interviews what it is.

DIRECTING INTERVIEWS: HOW TO GET THE INFORMATION YOU NEED

Know the Issue

There's a reason Ingrid Bergman doesn't leave town in the opening five minutes of *Casablanca*: Good storytelling takes time. You'll never win an Oscar or earn DVD residuals for doing it, but do everyone a favor and "direct" the interview so that candidates can really shine: Let them tell their story. And when you direct, remember that Ingrid is almost silent in the final scene. That's because great lines ("We'll always have Paris," "Here's looking at you, kid") need a receptive audience. Listen to what candidates have to say.

Take Action

- *Set the stage:*
  - Thank the candidate for coming.
  - Introduce yourself. *Briefly* explain your role in the organization. (Even if you already explained this during the telephone interview, explain it again. Do your parents understand your job? And how often have you explained it to them?)
  - Let the candidate know that you will be making the hiring decision.
  - Tell the candidate how much time you anticipate spending. Keep it short: The first interview should never be longer than 90 minutes. Anything longer may be misinterpreted as a hostage situation.
  - Offer a brief (two or three sentences) overview of the topics that you'll be covering.
- *Begin the interview.* To get the most out of it
  - Don't start with the big questions. Would you break the ice on a first date by asking about child-rearing philosophy? Of course not. Ask simple questions first to help candidates relax. Just don't ask, "What's your sign?"

- Follow a logical train of thought. Begin by asking about a candidate's experience, then his current or most recent job, then the job you have open, and then his long-term career plans. Jumping around confuses everyone, and yes, you can revisit a topic if you forget something or later answers raise questions.

- Vary the questions. Give candidates some variety by asking both close-ended questions ("What was your salary in your last position?") and open-ended ones ("What is there about this job that appeals to you?").

- *Limit your role.* Throughout the interview, keep this rule in mind: The candidate talks 80 percent of the time; you talk 20 percent of the time. (You can open up during subsequent interviews. By then you'll have the data you need, and you'll want to explore what kind of give and take you can have with a candidate. But that's later.) Here's the second rule: Anything you say should be said almost entirely at the beginning of the interview and at the end. Here are a few tricks that make it easier:

  - Tell the candidate up front that you'll answer questions at the end of the interview. Interviews get off track when candidates jump in with questions and interviewers answer them. You want answers that are as genuine as possible, not answers shaped by information you've provided. If candidates ask anyway, gently remind them that you'll be happy to answer their questions later.

  - Dr. Pierre Mornell, author of *Hiring Smart!,* suggests asking all your questions at the outset and then letting candidates answer.

- Tolerate silence. If candidates struggle to answer a question, don't rescue them. Let them think. If you must say something, simply encourage them to take their time.
- Find your own tricks to keep quiet. One interviewer trained himself to take a drink of water every time he wanted to say something. Another leaned on the table and put her hand over her mouth as a reminder. Find a way that works for you.
- Be prepared. Interviews get off track when there's no agenda. Certainly, some questions will occur to you as the candidate talks. Ask them, but have a general plan and follow it.

Stay Out of Jail

- *Take notes.* You won't remember everything and it may be helpful later (should there be a legal dispute) to have a record of the interview. Make notes of what you say in addition to what the candidate says.

Do at Least the Minimum

- Put duct tape over your mouth if need be, but be quiet and listen.

Get More Information

Hiring Smart!, Dr. Pierre Mornell, Ten Speed Press, Berkeley, CA, 1998.

Smart Staffing, Wayne Outlaw, Upstart Publishing Co., Chicago, 1998.

PREDICTING BEHAVIOR: HOW TO FIND OUT WHAT THE CANDIDATE IS *REALLY* LIKE

Know the Issue

Suppose Barbara Walters had asked Monica Lewinsky just one question: "So, Monica, were you in love with the President?" Would we have been satisfied? Of course not! Walters gets paid the big bucks to dig deeper. We wanted all the teary details.

Happily, the interviews that you do are probably less emotional (and much less prurient!), but they should be just as thorough. The more you know about how candidates behaved before, the more you know what to expect should you hire them. And at the risk of sounding too Marin County, you also want to know how they felt about it.

Take Action

- *Ask the candidate to describe a typical day in their current or previous job.* Then listen and probe for specifics: What excited them? What bored them? Who did they interact with? How did they respond to interruptions? What was their greatest frustration?

- *Explore how they like to be managed.* Their potential working relationship with you is paramount. Ask what they like most about their current boss, and what they like least. Ask them to describe their ideal boss. If they want someone who will make decisions for them, while you want an independent thinker, you're headed for trouble.

- *Skip the greatest strength/greatest weakness question.* It's too abstract and most candidates have rehearsed the answers.

Instead, try the following: "If I were to ask your current boss what she values most about you, what would I hear?" and "If I were to ask your boss what about you drives him or crazy, what would I hear?" (One candidate answered the latter question by admitting to sneaking into the boss's office after hours and rearranging everything on her desk because "the way she kept things on her desk didn't make any sense").

- *Ask how they make decisions*: How they establish priorities; when they ask for help, rather than doing it alone; where they go for information; when they make a decision on their own and when not; how they learn from their mistakes.

- *Identify some recent situations in your department that you thought were especially well handled or were not handled well at all.* Give the candidates the background and ask how they would have handled the situations.

Stay Out of Jail

- *Base your questions on work-related situations, not the candidate's personal life.* (See "Don't Get Personal: Toxic Questions and Antidotes," pages 134–138)

Real Life Example

Ann Perle, an experienced HR professional and consultant, stresses the importance of looking behind the info on the resume. She tells the story of two recent college grads. One graduated in four years with a high grade-point average and had several extracurricular activities to his credit. The other candidate took five years to complete her degree. She had a mediocre GPA and no extracurricular activities. On paper, one seemed to be the more ambitious, accomplished choice.

The interviews, however, told a different story. Both were asked to describe their college experiences and to summarize how they felt about them. The first candidate explained that he had had a great time. His father had paid for school, he had managed to find the easiest classes to take, and he hadn't worked hard. In effect, he had been at one long party. The other candidate might never have been to a party during school. She had been responsible for helping her mother keep up the mortgage payments and raise her younger siblings. She had worked two jobs to put herself through college. She had challenged herself throughout and felt proud of what she had been able to learn and do. Guess which candidate got the job?

Perle suggests that one way to get at this perspective is to ask candidates, "What is there about you that made that possible (or made that happen)?" When someone tells you, for example, "I always meet my deadlines," you may find out that the person is well organized and plans ahead, or that she is simply able to persuade others to help.

Do at Least the Minimum

- *Ask candidates to describe their current or most recent job carefully.*
- *Ask what they're looking for in a boss.*

Don't Get Personal: Toxic Questions and Antidotes

OK, wouldn't you think common sense would tell you that drinking drain opener is a really bad idea? But there is still the danger that people will drink it, which is why manufacturers label it carefully and point out that it is toxic. And people still ask pointless, and often illegal, interview questions. So we feel compelled to label them with a skull and crossbones and point out that asking personal questions is hazardous to your legal health. Fortunately, you can ask safe questions instead.

TOXIC QUESTIONS	ANTIDOTES
"How old are you?"	"If hired, can you show proof of your age?"
"When were you born?"	"Are you over 18 years of age?"
"What is your date of birth?"	"If you are under 18, can you, after employment, submit a work permit?"
"When did you graduate from high school?"	A statement that being hired is subject to verification that the candidate meets legal age requirements
"When did you go to elementary school?"	
"Where were you born?"	"Can you, as a condition of employment, submit verification of your legal right to work in the United States?"
"I love your accent. Where are you from?"	
"Is your husband [or wife] from around here?"	
"Are you a U.S. citizen?"	
"May we see your naturalization or alien registration papers?"	

continued

TOXIC QUESTIONS	ANTIDOTES
"What's your maiden name?"	"Have you ever used another name?"
"Is any further information relative to a name change or use of an assumed name or nickname needed for us to verify your education or job history? If yes, please explain."	
"What's your native language?"	"What languages do you speak, read, or write?" (Even then, don't ask unless the answer is relevant to the job.)
"I see from your resume that you're fluent in Spanish. Did you learn that in high school?"	
"Has your family been in this country a long time?"	
"That's an interesting last name. What nationality is it?"	
"Do you have a big family?"	There's no legal way to ask about family status. Just don't go there.
"Are you currently using birth control?"	
"Planning to have kids someday?"	
"How many children do you have?"	
"How old are you kids?"	
"Who takes care of your children while you're at work?"	
"Who lives with you?"	
"Are you gay?"	

continued

TOXIC QUESTIONS	*ANTIDOTES*
"What's your husband's (or wife's) name?"	"If you are under 18, what is the name and address of your parent or guardian?"
"What are your children's names?"	"Do any of your relatives work for this organization? If so, what are their names? What positions do they have?"
"What race are you?"	A statement that, after employment, a photograph may be required for the candidate's personnel file or ID badge
"So, are you 100 percent African-American or mixed race?"	
"Wow! Do you sunburn easily at the beach?"	
"Is that your natural hair color?"	
"Do you have any physical disabilities or handicaps?"	A statement that a job offer may be contingent on the candidate passing a job-related physical
"Are you sick much?"	
"Have you been paid a lot of workers' comp money?"	
"Have you ever had cancer?"	
"Do you have AIDS?"	
"Have you lost a lot of weight lately?"	
"Have you tried dieting?"	
"Do you see a shrink?"	
"Are you religious?"	A statement of regular days, hours, or shifts to be worked

continued

TOXIC QUESTIONS	ANTIDOTES
"Do you got to church? Which one?"	
"Do you pray?"	
"Have you been baptized?"	
"Does your religion prevent you from working weekends or holidays?"	
"Do you observe any religious holidays? Which ones?"	
"Do you belong to any clubs?"	"Are you a member of any job-related organizations, clubs, or professional associations?" (Please exclude the name or character of any organization that indicates the race, color, creed, sex, marital status, religion, national origin, or ancestry of its members.)
"Are you a member of any organization?"	
"When you registered to vote, which political party did you choose?"	

continued

TOXIC QUESTIONS	ANTIDOTES
"Have you ever been arrested?"	A question on the application asking whether the candidate has been convicted of a felony, within the past __years (check state law) along with a notation that a conviction will not necessarily eliminate the possibility of employment. (Note that employers that have a direct responsibility for the supervision, care, or treatment of children, mentally ill or disabled persons, or other vulnerable adults may, depending on the law of the state in which the employment occurs, have greater latitude to inquire into an applicant's arrest and conviction record.)
"Have you ever been in trouble with the law?" "Have you ever been to jail?" "Have you ever been convicted of a crime?" "What is the name and address of a relative for us to contact in case of accident of emergency?"	"What is the name and address of a person for us to contact in case of accident or emergency?"

THE FINISH LINE: HOW TO LEAVE CANDIDATES WITH THE BEST IMPRESSION

Know the Issue

It takes years of sacrifice and hard work to get to the Olympics, but in the end, the difference between a gold medal and no medal is often just hundredths of a second. In other words, how you finish counts.

When hiring, you don't have endorsement contracts, a parade at Disney World, and a broadcasting career on the line, but you may well have the best hire at stake. Your "finish" is the last impression a candidate has of your meeting. Don't squander the opportunity.

Take Action

- *Be quiet.* Once you have asked the candidate all your questions, let her know how much time is left and invite her to ask her own. (Time the interview so that there will be time for the candidate's questions. If the interview is running long and you'll need extra time, ask for it; that shows respect).

- *Answer questions honestly.*

- *Stay focused.* During this initial interview, the primary goal is to determine whether the candidate is a serious contender for the job. If he is, he'll be invited back for another interview and will have the chance to ask many questions then. If he isn't, you don't want to waste either his time or yours answering detailed questions about the job now. However, to be fair to the candidate, be sure he leaves with enough information to decide whether he's interested in pursuing the job further. Be sure to address basic concerns:

- Salary (offer a range, not a specific figure at this stage)
- Overtime or travel requirements
- Appearance standards (including uniforms)
- Work hours (particularly if you are hiring for night, week-end, or other non-standard hours)
- *Offer a five-minute warning.* Let the candidate know when time is almost up. When time is up, bring the interview to a conclusion:
  - Explain the next steps in the process. (For example, if there will be a second or third interview, now is the time to say so.)
  - Offer an estimated timeframe for making your decision.
  - Make yourself available for follow-up questions. Give the candidate your card.
  - Take care of any incidentals (parking validations, for example).
  - Thank the candidate for coming.
- *Review.* After the candidate leaves, allow time to review your notes and make sure they're clear while the interview is still fresh in your mind.

Stay Out of Jail

Be careful not to say anything that might be construed as a promise. If a candidate asks about career development opportunities, for example, offer some examples of career paths other employees have followed. Be clear, however, that if you hire the candidate, her performance will be evaluated individually and that you can't guarantee a promotion. If she asks a question and you do not know the answer (about the benefit plan, for example), say so and offer to get the answer. Don't make something up.

Do at Least the Minimum

- *Be respectful of the candidate's time and thank the candidate for coming.*
- *Don't make promises.*

INTERVIEW FOLLOW-UP: HOW TO KEEP CANDIDATES INTERESTED

Know the Issue

Most airlines and hotels require that reservations be confirmed. Etiquette demands that we send "thank you" notes for gifts. If we subscribe to a magazine, we expect to be hassled by renewal notices for the rest of our lives. So why, in a culture obsessed with follow-up, do so many managers drop the ball during the hiring process? Candidates complete the interview only to face deafening silence. Has the job been filled? Are they still in the running? Has the interviewer fled to Cancun with embezzled funds?

Such "out of sight, out of mind" behavior is always rude. In today's tight labor market, it's also stupid. The times in which you're the only one courting a qualified candidate are about as rare as good airline food. The longer you're silent, the more likely your dream candidate will accept another job. So do yourself a favor and keep the lines of communication open.

Take Action

- *Keep your commitment.* Ideally, you gave the candidate an estimate of when you would hire someone. Stick to that schedule if possible.

- *Let candidates know when the schedule changes.* Times will occur when it isn't possible to stick to your original schedule. When that happens, let the candidate know that there's been a delay, why it's happened, and what your new target is.

- *Respond to candidate inquiries.* If candidates call or send email inquiring about the status of the job, respond or be sure someone responds on your behalf.

- *Enlist the candidate's help.* If a delay is caused by an inability to connect with references, or another situation in which a candidate might help, ask for that help. Remember, candidates have a vested interest in the outcome.

- *If a candidate receives another offer during this stage, take it seriously.* The market is competitive and other offers are likely. Without making promises, give the candidate a realistic sense of his or her chances. Then let the candidate decide whether to remain in consideration for your job. Don't be pressured into making a premature decision, but don't cost someone another opportunity either.

Manage Up

Let your boss know what timeframe you're working within. Keep her informed if things change. You don't want her thinking that nothing is happening, or that you can't make a decision.

7

Making Successful Hires

There's a gentle tug on the end of the line; then a stronger one. You've hooked a fish! It begins to thrash, and as it breaks the surface of the water, you can see it's a beauty—easily the best catch of the day.

What do you do next? Settle back onto your seat and pull a hat over your eyes to nap while the fish swims to the boat and leaps into a waiting bucket? Only if the fish on the line is a Disney creation. Otherwise, you'll use all your fishing expertise, and a lot of hard work, to reel it in.

When you get to the end of the interviews, assignments, tests, and reference checks and you've found the candidate of your dreams, it's easy to just exhale and think your job is done. But this is no time to kick back and assume the candidate will happily flop into your boat and accept an offer.

You'd be far better off developing a Captain Ahab complex and pursuing your top choice with relentless intensity. OK, maybe Captain Ahab is a little scary, but you should work hard to close the deal.

Even after your top candidate says yes, you can take certain steps before she starts, and during her first 90 days, to improve the odds that she'll succeed.

DETERMINING THE OFFER: HOW TO STRUCTURE A WIN-WIN PACKAGE

Know the Issue

Going once . . . going twice . . . sold! The Pez dispenser is yours—for only $3,400. You're elated at first. It's a great addition to your collection, but then you think about it. You've seen others just like it on the market, and they were priced lower. Much lower. In the heat of the auction you've let your emotions get the best of you and you've paid far more than the dispenser is worth.

Even if we don't have a $3,400 Pez dispenser at home, we've all paid too much for something at one time or another. It's almost always because we bought using our hearts instead of our heads. Usually, the most dire consequences are a high credit-card balance and a tongue lashing from our incredulous spouse.

The consequences are much higher, however, if we use our hearts instead of our heads when we determine a job offer. In hiring, we're spending someone else's money and we're paid to spend it wisely. Offering a candidate more than he or she is worth can have several repercussions. It can throw your budget out of whack, raise fairness issues, put pressure on you to raise all salaries, and give you no maneuvering room to give the employee a raise.

No matter how appealing a candidate is, and no matter how tight the job market is, we still need to be rational when it comes to shaping an offer. So until employees are hired at auction, we must think like accountants, not collectors.

Take Action

- *Start with base salary.* Some pay rates, such as those for entry-level fast-food jobs, jobs covered by collective bargaining agreements, and most government jobs, are fixed. But most are not, which puts the burden on you to figure them out. If you work in a large organization, you probably have established salary grades, which give you a head start. If there aren't published grades, at least you can look to salaries for precedents.

  In a smaller organization, you have more options and therefore more work. If you're filling a job that already exists (hiring a second retail clerk, for example), use existing salaries as a guideline. If it's a new job, or one that's unique in your organization, be sure you know the going rate for comparable jobs. You may get a good sense just by asking candidates about their current salary during the interview process, but if you're unsure, look at a salary survey. Certain companies specialize in salary surveys, and trade associations and consulting firms also conduct them. You'll probably have to pay for the data, but it's worth it. Just be sure that the data is current and that you understand what's included in the figures. (Some surveys, for example, report base salaries only, while others report total pay packages.)

Once you know the general parameters, you can set a specific salary. The rate shouldn't be arbitrary. Base it on the following:

- The education, experience and skills the candidate brings to the job
- The job's responsibilities (for example, two retail clerks may have essentially the same job, although one has responsibility for opening the shop)
- Hardship (you may offer a shift differential, for example, to people who work nights)

  Correlate salary with experience and responsibility. That said, in a tight labor market, it's self-defeating to pay at the bottom of the range. You should also avoid offering salaries at the top of the range. If you start at the top, you'll have nowhere to go if you need to negotiate to close the deal, and you'll have a harder time giving the employee a raise if he excels. So where does that leave you? In the middle. Just to make the math easy, assume a job has a range between $20,000 and $30,000. Offer someone with less experience $22,000 and someone with more $27,000. Whatever you decide, be sure you have objective reasons to explain it.

  An ethical aside: Don't ever bring in someone new with the same or less experience at a higher pay rate than a current employee. If you find that you have to move to a higher rate to compete for talent, then adjust the rate of your current employee as well.

- *Look at variable pay*. Base pay compensates people for their skills, consistent job performance, and value in the labor market. Variable pay has become a popular way to compensate for specific results. It may include bonuses, profit sharing, stock options, and commissions, for example. If a new hire will be eligible for such variable pay, you should present it as part of the offer.

Most variable pay is linked to specific business goals and is *not* something to create or amend when determining an offer. This rule has a couple of exceptions, however: signing bonuses and commissions.

If you discover that established salaries in your company are more than 10 percent below the market, you can't compete for talent. In those cases, negotiate with your HR department or, if there isn't one, with the CEO for a signing bonus to boost the package. The signing bonus should bridge the gap between the salary you're offering and market pay rates. (After the hire, push to have the grades revised.)

Signing bonuses are sometimes used deliberately to bring in new hires at market rates or above without raising salaries of existing employees. In effect, it's a technique to "hide" unfair disparities. It's a bad idea, though. Not only is it dishonest, but it sets a poor precedent. What will you do the following year to keep the new employee at the higher overall rate?

The other variable pay to determine at this stage is sales commissions. Any job offer to a salesperson should be explicit about the commission structure. Be sure to address these issues:

- What is the basic commission rate?
- Does the rate apply to all sales, or is commission higher on some sales (such as new accounts, accounts "stolen" from competitors, or accounts of a certain size)?

- When are commissions paid? When the sale is made or when the client pays?

- Are any commissions shared (as in shared territories or split accounts)?

- When does the salesperson begin earning commission? (Does he earn commission on sales that he services but were actually made by his predecessor?)

- Are there house accounts that do not earn commission?

- What happens when the employee leaves the job? Does he earn commission on business sold at that time even if the transaction hasn't yet happened (standing orders, for example) or only on transactions complete when employment ends?

  If the commission plan is not in writing, it should be. It should address exactly what the salesperson must do to earn the commission. It also should state that customers and territories can be assigned and reassigned at the employer's discretion and that the plan itself is subject to change. Consider reiterating your at-will policy and stating that disputes about commission will be resolved by arbitration.

- *Remember benefits.* When is a $30,000 job not a $30,000 job? When it's a $30,000 job. That's because salary is only the beginning. The employer's actual cost also includes payroll taxes, the employer's contribution to Social Security, and benefits. Those expenses generally add 30 percent to the total package. In other words, a job with a $30,000 salary actually costs the company $39,000.

Get the figures on how much your company spends per employee on benefits and include this in your offer. Health insurance, vacation pay, 401(k) matching funds, and other perks are part of *total compensation.* A $39,000 job is easier to sell than a $30,000 job.

- *Spring for relocation expenses.* Not so long ago people applied for jobs within a half-hour of home. Today they apply for jobs anywhere. That means that you may be faced with deciding whether to help a candidate relocate from across the state or even across the country.

There are no rules dictating how much you should subsidize a move, but these are the things to consider:

- *Home-finding trips:* Candidates and their families need time to find housing, and the sooner they find it, the sooner they can be fully productive. Many firms pay for trips before the relocation to facilitate the process.

- *Moving expenses:* Include packing, moving, and storage.

- *Real estate costs.* Some firms will make up for any loss taken in selling a home. Some also pay for expenses related to buying a new home, such as inspections or title searches.

- *Cost of living differentials:* Many candidates turn down out-of-town job offers when they realize the financial implications of the move. For example, someone moving from Kansas to Southern California will have less disposable income even with a higher salary because housing is much pricier in California. Some companies address that by offering a one-time payment to help bridge the gap.

Those are the basics, but employers have been asked to pay for everything from moving a hothouse full of expensive orchids to docking fees for a sailboat.

Where do you draw the line? If you have corporate policies about relocation, turn to those first. After that, it comes down to the return you'll get on your investment. If you're hiring for a job that demands unique skills and the *only* good candidate for the job is out of state, you may be over a barrel. Think hard about whether the work needs to be done in your office, though. It may be cheaper to let the candidate stay where she is and telecommute.

On the other hand, if you're choosing between two strong candidates, do the math. Sometimes people pursue top candidates with missionary zeal and stop thinking rationally. Let's say, for example, that your top choice is out of state, but your second choice is local. Most people, naturally, will pursue the top choice. By the time you add relocation expenses to the deal, however, the top candidate could end up costing 40 percent more. Is the top candidate really 40 percent better than your second choice?

- *Decide a start date.* The final part of the offer is the job's start date. Think about what you really need. Is the job tied to a project with a distant deadline? Or do you want someone in the office yesterday? Remember that you need to give the candidate time to make the transition. People who are leaving jobs usually require more time that those who aren't working, for example.

Stay Out of Jail

- *Be sure that your offers aren't arbitrary.* Don't expose yourself to discrimination charges by appearing to play favorites or basing pay on subjective factors. Tie pay to experience and responsibilities.
- *Make sure that people in comparable jobs earn comparable pay.* Be careful, for example, that women aren't being offered lower salaries than men.

Manage Up

Take responsibility for closing the deal. Find out in advance what maneuvering room you have in shaping an offer. If you run into trouble, look for solutions. Don't whine, "Our pay scale is too low. I can't hire anyone." Instead, present research proving that your salaries are out of step. Be prepared to make cuts in other parts of your budget if your boss can't just throw money at the problem.

MAKING THE OFFER: HOW TO PRESENT A DEAL CANDIDATES WANT TO ACCEPT

Know the Issue

When's the last time you went to a nice restaurant and food was just dumped in a heap on your plate? It's probably been a while, as heaps have made way for triangular towers of polenta, artfully placed herb sprigs, and colorful swirls of raspberry and mango puree. That's because top chefs know that presentation counts.

That's a good principle to keep in mind when making a job offer, too. If a candidate isn't excited about the offer, all the hard work that led up to that point may be wasted. So how do you generate excitement? With enthusiasm and clarity (and a little legal savvy).

Take Action

- *Timing is everything.* Once you've decided whom to hire and put your offer together, you're probably chomping at the bit. But impatience can backfire. Not many candidates will really listen carefully to an offer that comes while someone is listening to the conversation.

    Call the candidate to make an appointment. Ideally, you should present the offer within a couple of days; if you delay, all your top choices will have been snapped up. Try to present the offer face to face, so that you can convey interest and gauge the candidate's reaction. If that's not possible, at least arrange to have the candidate's undivided attention during a phone call.

    Friday is the best day to make an offer because it gives people the weekend to talk with family and friends and to think without the distraction of their current job. And, yes, that means that Monday is the worst day.

- *Put it in writing.* Even a face-to-face offer isn't enough. Your offer should also be in writing. A written offer gives the candidate something to review (because she won't be able to remember everything), leaves less room for misunderstanding, and offers you some protection if there's a dispute later.

The written offer should include the following:

- Job title, location, proposed start date, and duties and responsibilities
- The job the position reports to
- Base salary
- Specifics of any variable pay (including sales commission if appropriate)
- Employment benefits (include dates when employees become eligible for specific benefits, such as health care coverage)
- Special considerations (such as reimbursement for moving expenses or signing bonuses)
- Dates when the employee's performance will be reviewed
- Any legal documents that will be required (such as proof of eligibility to work)
- Any contingencies to the offer (such as passing a physical)

The letter also should cover certain legal ground:

- If you are an at-will employer (and you should be), the offer is the place to say so. The concept is simple: *at-will employment* means that either the employer *or* the employee can end employment at any time for any reason. Make it clear that the employment offered is at will and not for any definite term.
- State that no promises have been made other than those in the letter.
- If you call for arbitration to resolve disputes (and more and more employers have concluded this is a must), have the applicant review that language as well.

Finally, the offer also should include a written copy of the employee handbook or policies and procedures manual and be clear that the employee will be bound to the terms of the handbook if she accepts the position.

- *Keep the meeting upbeat.* If you're having a bad day, don't carry that baggage into the offer meeting. Convey your enthusiasm about the company, the job, and the future. Talk about ways in which you think the candidate can contribute and make him feel wanted.

  During the meeting, the offer letter and attachments may seem intimidating to the candidate; with its legal details, it may feel like a contract from a police state, but don't apologize. Explain that it's comprehensive so there won't be any surprises later.

  Allow time for her to ask questions, and make yourself available should she have questions later.

- *Give the candidate time to think.* Accepting a new job is a big decision that affects not only the candidate, but also her family and the people at the job she would leave behind. Allow the candidate a few days to consider the offer, but don't leave the door open indefinitely. (One candidate asked if he could have a month to think about it. A month is long enough to lose *all* your other prospects for the job if he turns you down.)

- *Be prepared to negotiate.* The candidate probably won't see the offer as an all-or-nothing proposition. Expect to negotiate. (See pages 155–160.)

Stay Out of Jail

- *Be consistent in presenting offers.* Although the terms will vary from job to job, the format should be consistent.

- *Don't say anything that could be construed as a promise other than that which is expressly set forth in the offer letter.* Such comments as "we've been very successful in the past two years and fully expect to continue to be successful" and "we expect to go public in the next year" and "we always pay more than our competitors" and "there will be stock options" have led to lawsuits.

- *Be specific about exactly what benefits are included in the offer package.*

- *Double-check before you make the offer that the need still exists for the new hire and that you still have the authority to fill the position.*

- *If you don't know the answer to a question, say so and get the answer.* Don't make something up.

NEGOTIATING THE PACKAGE: HOW TO RESOLVE DISAGREEMENTS ABOUT THE OFFER

Know the Issue

We Americans like choices. Lots of choices. When we shop, choice becomes a birthright: "What other colors does this come in?" "Do you have a larger size?" "Which one is unscented?"

There's no switch to shut off that consumer mindset. So where *you* see a job, candidates see a purse. Or a tie. Or a box of detergent.

"I'd really like to be earning more than that." "Would it be possible to work a different schedule?" "Hmm . . . couldn't my medical coverage kick in before then?"

Welcome to the world in which candidates are choosy buyers looking for the best offer they can get. Gone are the days when your top choice would eagerly accept the job as offered. Today, odds are high you'll have to negotiate something —if the candidate accepts at all!

So don't take a deep breath. Know your limits. You want to hear a yes, but not at any price.

Take Action

- *Set a money ceiling.* If the candidate wants to negotiate money, know your limits going in. Remember the range you set at the outset. Resist all temptation to exceed the range. Although you may "win" in the short term, in the long term, it won't be worth it. (One executive eventually had to raise the salaries of every secretary in the firm after he broke down and hired one for a salary outside the established range.) If you've left yourself some room, you can bump the offer up somewhat if you think the candidate's experience warrants it. Sometimes all candidates really want is a good-faith gesture.

    Don't get suckered into making promises that will haunt you. Too often, managers buckle in the heat of the moment and promise big raises in the future. Unless you have a crystal ball, don't do it. There are too many unknowns, starting with how the candidate will actually perform.

- *Be careful with benefits.* Candidates think you have control over benefits, but often you don't. Insurance carriers usually decide the eligibility requirements for health care coverage, and company policy often limits you in other ways. In rare cases, it's possible to get around the rules, but don't try to negotiate without checking *first.*

- *Little things count.* All candidates want to be wanted. Although we often think the grand gesture or big bucks are the only way to show our interest, smaller gestures are often enough. If you can't meet some demands, ask what else a candidate might like. Managers have landed top talent with cell phones (around $300), membership fees in airline clubs (around $400), or software. You don't want negotiations to become "Let's Make a Deal," but a little creativity can go a long way.

- *Focus on flexibility.* You usually have more room to negotiate with things that cost little or nothing. For example, one manager won the bidding war for a graphic artist when she offered to let the artist work earlier hours. The candidate had another offer with a higher salary, but the flexibility cut her commute time and let her spend more time with her kids. Ultimately, those benefits were more important than money. Look to flex hours, telecommuting, and other options that might help close a deal.

- *Look for other money.* You've topped out on salary? Get creative and hunt for other money. One candidate was enrolled in a master's program, for example. The manager couldn't offer a higher salary, but he did have money in his training budget to help offset the candidate's tuition. Another manager found out that a candidate's family lived near the host city for the industry's trade show; he tagged money in his travel budget and offered to send her on a trip home as long as she attended the conference while she was there.

- *Listen to the candidate.* What does the candidate really want? It's one thing if he's genuinely trying to strike a reasonable deal, but sometimes a candidate's true motivation surfaces only during the negotiation stage. Is he really interested in the job, or in meeting his own agenda? Listen for
  - Whether the candidate is trying to find a way to take the job or a reason to turn it down.
  - Whether he's interested in a career move or a financial windfall. If all the questions are about perks and none are about job challenges, he may not be the passionate employee you're hoping for.
  - Whether the candidate can see beyond the next six months. Does she have the patience to earn the long-term rewards of the job?
- *Go back to basics.* During negotiation, it's easy to get distracted by the trees and lose sight of the forest. Remember, the candidate initially was interested in the *job,* before she even knew about the salary, benefits, and so forth. Focus your energy on what excited her initially: job challenges, increased responsibility, the chance to work with cutting-edge technology, or whatever it might be.
- *Don't meet counteroffers.* Once a candidate accepts your job, he may call to say that his current employer has made a counteroffer. A few things might have happened. The candidate

may be a stellar employee, and his current boss may be stricken at the thought of losing him. It's also possible the candidate initiated a job search expressly to get a raise in his current job. Or the candidate might be "auctioning" his services to the highest bidder. Whatever's going on, don't match the offer.

By this stage of the process, you've negotiated a fair package and the candidate wants the job. To squabble about money again smacks of extortion. It may be good for the candidate, but not for your business. The bidding war often doesn't stop after one round either. The current employer may best your counter to the counteroffer, and so it goes. Where will it end?

A good pre-emptive strategy is to raise the issue of counteroffers yourself. Warn the candidate that he may get one, and remind him of all the reasons he sought your job in the first place. Counteroffers rarely address the root issues. (Recruitment guru Robert Half says that seven of 10 people who accept a counteroffer from their current employer have left that company within a year precisely because the root problems are still there.) If candidates are prepped to expect a counteroffer, they're more likely to reject it.

- *Revise the offer letter.* If you negotiate any changes to the offer, revise the offer letter. You and the candidate both need an accurate one.

Stay Out of Jail

- *Remember, once again, not to promise anything that you can't deliver.*

Real Life Example

The candidate had impeccable qualifications and he seemed to have people lining up to offer glowing references. He had so much going for him that the manager decided to fly him from the Midwest to California for an interview. During his visit, he won over everyone he met and the manager offered him a job. But after thinking about it over the weekend, the candidate turned it down. He didn't want to uproot his family. The manager was crushed.

Then, two days later, the candidate called. He was reconsidering. After accepting another offer in his hometown, he learned that he would have to wait six months for medical coverage. His wife was undergoing treatment, and he couldn't wait six months. Could the manager in California get him coverage any sooner?

Yes, the manager in California could have him covered in 90 days. "But I thought about it long and hard," the manager said, "and then I called him back and told him I couldn't help him. He had decided against our job for some profound reasons, and now it was all about medical coverage. None of his other thinking had changed. I ended up hiring my second choice. Her qualifications weren't as impressive, but she really wanted the job. That counts for something."

NONCOMPLETE AGREEMENTS: HOW TO BE SURE YOUR TOP CANDIDATE CAN ACCEPT YOUR OFFER

Know the Issue

It was 1415 and King Henry V was on the throne. A guild sought to enforce an agreement to keep a dyer from working in a particular town for six months. Not only did the judge in the case refuse to uphold the agreement, he (we know it had to be *he* because centuries would pass before the world was ready for Judge Judy) found it so offensive that he threatened to fine the man who sought to enforce it.

That was the first time that an employee's ability to work as he chose was tested, but it was hardly the last time. Today the concept is so prevalent that we even have a name for the restrictions: non-compete agreements.

It's easy to see where the notion comes from. Sweet young Duncan is hired as an apprentice in your dying business. You teach him everything there is to know about the craft: how to get that perfect red, how to make the dye permanent, how to care for those really delicate fabrics. Then, just when he's learned it all, the backstabbing cur bolts and opens his own dying business across town and tries to steal your customers.

As the guy who gave Duncan the Dyer his start, you want him stopped. It's hardly fair for him to compete in such an underhanded way. But as in all things, there are two sides. Suppose you were so awful to work for that you drove Duncan out. Or suppose Duncan had to leave for some perfectly non-nefarious reason. Is it really fair that he be prevented from earning a living at the only thing he knows how to do?

Generally, the courts have said that people should be allowed to pursue their livelihood, which means that non-compete agreements are a bad idea. In fact, in California they are all but unenforceable. Still, enough companies are out there requiring employees to sign them that when hiring from within your industry you can't be cavalier. Since you can't always beat 'em, at least be prepared to deal with 'em.

Take Action

- *Find out whether a non-compete is an issue.* Ask candidates whether they have an agreement with their current or former employer that includes a non-compete clause. If the answer is yes, ask to see the agreement and have a lawyer look at it. Many noncompete agreements are written in ways that are not enforceable or will not hold up in court. Your lawyer can advise you about this, but even if the agreement is not enforceable, you need to decide if this candidate is worth the risk of possibly having to argue the agreement in court. If the agreement *is* enforceable, your prior knowledge of it will be a liability in court.

- *Be careful that nothing you do can be construed as unfair competition.* The courts generally have left the definition of *unfair competition* open-ended because "unfair or fraudulent business practices may run the gamut of human ingenuity and chicanery." That means you must rely on basic ethics and common sense. Historically, the courts have frowned on people misrepresenting themselves, as when a medical supplies salesman left his job and then sold supplies that looked very much like the originals without ever telling his customers that they were no longer buying from the same firm. Ah, details. That case was back in the '40s. Since then, the courts have also considered employees who formed new businesses even before resigning their jobs, solicited their former employer's customers by using confidential information, and disparaged their former employer's products, among other forms of chicanery.

If it sounds unfair, looks unfair, and smells unfair, it probably *is* unfair.

- *Have new hires acknowledge your intentions.* You may have no intention of doing anything unfair, but it's important that your new hire and his former employer understand that, too. Have an attorney draft a statement stating that you don't want the new hire to compete unfairly with a former employer, breach any agreement with a former employer, or use any confidential information of a former employer while employed with your company. Ask the employee to sign it.

Stay Out of Jail

- *Don't ask a new hire for any confidential information, trade secrets, client lists, or other sensitive data.* If an employee offers it, decline.
- *You can't control who applies for jobs in your firms.* But you may run into trouble if you actively solicit applications from your competitors' employees.

CLOSING THE HIRING PROCESS: HOW TO TURN A CANDIDATE INTO AN EMPLOYEE

Know the Issue

The star athlete was wooed by every college big enough to have a team and he's chosen yours. You can already count the money that will pour in from alumni. Maybe this is the year for a berth in the

NCAA tournament. Now that the press conference is over, all that's left is for him to show up. Or is it?

Not quite. There's still all that pesky paperwork: registering for classes, getting a parking permit, getting a dorm assignment, and on and on.

So it is with your star hire. She accepted the offer. Now, shake her hand, shout "Hallelujah!," and get back to your real job until she starts, right? Not so fast. Hiring is a complex process that doesn't just *stop*; you need to *finish* it. You also need to take a few steps to make sure that nothing goes wrong between now and the hire's start date.

Take Action

- *Get it in writing.* Just as you need to make the offer verbally *and* in writing, the candidate should accept verbally *and* in writing. The offer letter also should make clear that he's read your company policies and employee handbook, understands them, and agrees to abide by them. Have the candidate sign the offer letter; his signature indicates that he understands and accepts the offer.

   You and the candidate should keep signed copies of the letter. Put your copy in the candidate's brand-new personnel file.

- *Tie up loose ends.* If employment was at all conditional, make sure the conditions are met. If you require a physical, for example, make sure the candidate gets the physical and that you (or someone in HR) has a copy of the report.

- *Three groups of people are lawfully permitted to work in the U.S.:*

- U.S. citizens
- Permanent resident aliens (green card holders) who have an unlimited right to work in the U.S.
- Other non-U.S. citizens who have some type of time-limited work authorization (which may or may not be limited to a specific employer)

In a large organization, HR will make sure that all employees are legally entitled to work. In smaller organizations, it's probably up to you. This is not a trivial concern. The penalty for knowingly hiring unauthorized workers is as great as $10,000 per employee and six months in prison. Fortunately, the law includes a mechanism to help protect you. It requires that every new employee complete a Form I-9. Have the candidate complete the form when he accepts the job. (For details on how to comply, see "Form I-9: A Primer," pages 168–169)

Everything should be in order *before* the candidate's first day.

- *Notify the other candidates.* Once you've made an offer and someone has accepted it, let the other candidates know that the job has been filled. Notify them in writing. (Other candidates includes *all* other candidates. Even if you choose not to interview an applicant, she deserves an acknowledgement of her interest. It's easiest to send letters as you eliminate people from consideration, but if you haven't already done so, do it now.)

  The letter should thank people for their interest. If you interviewed them, or they completed an assessment of some sort, thank them for their time. *Do not* offer other information about why a candidate wasn't hired.

If you would consider them for a future opening and you think such an opening may exist, say so. Otherwise, don't raise false expectations.

Keep all the rejected applicants' cover letters, resumes, tests, and so on in a file for at least three years. (How long you're required to keep the material varies from state to state; check with HR or an attorney if you're unsure.) Cumbersome? Yes, but this protects you in case a rejected candidate sues for discrimination or your decision is otherwise challenged.

- *Don't share too much information.* Candidates often want to know why they weren't hired. If they got far enough in the process that they were seriously considered, you probably like them and are tempted to help. *Don't.* Sharing your perception of their weaknesses invites hurt feelings and arguments about why you're wrong. Some disgruntled candidates might even make a complaint. Besides, the information isn't as helpful as candidates think it is. Something you considered a weakness in comparison to other candidates for that job may be irrelevant in the eyes of another boss hiring for a different job. Don't share anything about the hiring process either. One young manager called her favorite applicant to tell her that she had wanted to hire her, but that she had been overruled by her boss. The manager's impulse was probably to help the candidate feel appreciated. That's a nice idea, but such a call may leave the candidate with the feeling that she was most qualified for the job and was discriminated against. At a minimum, she might call the boss to argue; she could go further and file a complaint. Sometimes silence is golden.

Stay Out of Jail

- *Be sure all offers are accepted in writing and include the candidate's signature.*
- *Make sure all conditions of employment have been met.*
- *Verify eligibility to work.*
- *Be sure the applicant agrees in writing to be bound by the employee handbook and company policies* before *actually being hired.*
- *Don't make comments about information supplied on the I-9.* If something doesn't look right, ask about it and postpone hiring until it's clarified.

Get More Information

Form I-9 is available on the Internet at **www.ins.usdoj.gov/index.html**.

BEFORE THE FIRST DAY: HOW TO HELP EMPLOYEES HIT THE GROUND RUNNING

Know the Issue

Imagine this vacation: Instead of going to work one morning, you drive to the airport. You buy a ticket for the first available flight. When you arrive, you hunt for a place to stay and then ask the concierge for suggestions of what to do and where to eat. Dinner is fabulous and life is great, until you reach into your wallet and realize you've left your credit card at home.

Form I-9: A Primer

Employers face substantial penalties for knowingly hiring unauthorized workers. Therefore, they are required to have all new hires complete a Form I-9 and to review documents that substantiate an employee's right to work. The *Immigration and Naturalization Service* (INS) periodically audits I-9 forms, so it's important that they be completed and stored properly.

Who Should Complete a Form I-9?

All new hires. This includes anyone who gets paid for work performed on a regular schedule. (Technically, the law requires homeowners to verify the status of the kid who mows the lawn once a week.) I-9s are *not* required for independent contractors.

When Should It Be Completed?

On an employee's hire date, which the INS defines as "the actual commencement of employment for wages or other remuneration."

Is an Employee's Statement That He Is Eligible to Work Enough?

No. In addition to attesting under penalty of perjury that he is not an unauthorized alien, the employee must produce documents to prove his identity and authorization to work. Employees may choose a single document to prove their identity and eligibility, or may prove each separately. The INS lists more than 20 acceptable documents, ranging from the obvious (a U.S. passport) to the obscure (INS Form I-688A). (Employers may not insist that employees choose a specific one.) Most people will produce a passport or green card. If you're unsure about which other documents to accept, check with the INS.

continued

So It's All up to the Employee?

No. The employer must look at the documents. The law doesn't require that employers be experts in fraud or counterfeit documents; it only asks employers to use their best judgment as to whether the documents seem genuine. The employer must then, within three business days, complete section two of the form.

Should Copies of the Documents Be Included with the Form?

The law says that copies *may* be attached to the form, but don't have to be. Employers must be consistent, though. If they attach copies to one form, then they should attach them to all.

What Happens to the Form when It's Complete?

Employers should keep the forms in their files. (The forms should be kept separately from personnel files.)

Forms should be kept for three years or until one year after termination of employment, whichever is longer.

If an employee is hired when he has a temporary permit to work in the U.S., who is responsible for verifying that the permit has been renewed at the appropriate time?

The employer.

Sound like fun? To a few spontaneous souls, perhaps, but most of us like to plan ahead. Anticipation can be half the fun, and there's some comfort in knowing we have a place to sleep.

Yet many of the same managers who make absolutely sure they never leave home without their American Express card don't give a moment's thought to preparing for an employee's first day. The attitude seems to be, "She's hired, she'll show up, what's to do?"

There's nothing to do if you don't mind employees being frustrated, unproductive, or even literally lost. But if your goal is to have energetic, focused employees who are making a contribution, then you can take certain steps before a new employee shows up for work.

Take Action

- *Send paperwork in advance.* Wouldn't it be great to spend the first day of your Hawaiian vacation in a windowless room filling out paperwork? There'd you be, form after form related to all the cool stuff you're *going* to do —signing up for a massage, choosing a tee time on the golf course, and so on. It doesn't sound at all fun—you want to get to it. Yet the most common image there is of the first day at work is, yes, paperwork.

  Take a tip from many cruise lines and send the paperwork in advance. Yes, there may be some benefit enrollment forms that employees can't complete until they have a chance to ask questions (and even then, you could hook them up with someone in your HR department or front office). But most forms, which capture emergency contact information, tax withholdings, and so on, can be filled out any time. Let employees arrive the first day with the forms completed.

  Note: In some states, you may have to pay employees for the time spent filling out the forms, even if they do it at home. Even so, it may be worth it to help give them a running start.

- *Make access easier.* If the new hire needs a security badge or a parking permit, try to take care of it before the first day. It's more welcoming and makes it easier for the hire to be fully productive.

- *Set up a work area.* You've just arrived at the resort of your dreams only to find that your room isn't ready and you'll have to cool your heels in the lobby instead of changing into your tennis shorts and heading for the court. Or worse, you're sent to a room that looks like it hasn't had maid service in two weeks. Not exactly what you signed up for, is it?

  Having nowhere to work, or getting a workstation that has no supplies or is still full of someone else's junk, isn't what employees signed up for either. At a resort, you may at least get upgraded to a better room if you complain enough. At work, your best bet is usually to pilfer from other work stations or to bond with the keeper of supplies. Either way, it's time spent *not working*.

  Personal space is important. Having a clean, functional, well-stocked work station ready when an employee walks through the door is the best thing you can do to help him feel he belongs.

  Don't stop with a working telephone, a comfortable chair, and a few paper clips. Be sure to organize paper files and delete unneeded files from the computer. One secretary spent much of her first day trying to make sense of letters to God left on the hard drive by her predecessor.

- *Let existing staff know that the new employee is coming.* Which situation will leave you feeling better about the hotel you chose: The desk clerk who says, "I'm sorry, sir, I don't have a reservation under that name," or the clerk who says with a smile, "Oh, yes, Mr. Jones, we've been expecting you. Welcome!"?

New employees will begin wondering immediately whether they can really make a contribution if their position is so unimportant that no one even knows they're starting. Take time to let your existing staff know

- That you've made a hire
- When the person starts
- The nature of the person's job duties (especially if the job is new or has been changed since the previous person left)
- Something about the person's qualifications (don't share personal information, but give people an idea of what you think this person can contribute)

  It's best to make this announcement in person, so that you can convey your enthusiasm and answer any questions. Remind people the day before that the new employee is starting.

- *Don't get too hung up on the calendar.* You've agreed on a start date for your new hire. Now don't get tunnel vision about that date. Suppose your annual planning meeting falls before that date? Give the new hire the chance to attend the meeting. Just be sure that hires for non-exempt jobs get paid for that time.

- *Arrange your schedule around the new hire.* The worst thing you can do on an employee's first day is not be there. The next worst thing is to be so busy that you can't take any time with the person. New employees deserve at least some of your undivided attention on the first day. If something comes up that you absolutely *must* be out, call to arrange an alternate start date.

- *Have an orientation program in place.* Don't wait until an employee shows up to decide to teach him the ropes. Work out the program—content, timing and participants—*before* the first day (see "Orientation," pages 174–179).

Stay Out of Jail

- *Employee information is confidential.* If new hires complete forms in advance, ask them to mail them directly to HR or to bring them directly to you on the first day. Don't take a chance that the forms will end up where anyone in the office can see them.

Real Life Example

The work station assigned to the new employee had been empty for a few months, and no one had thought to look through it. As the new employee got assignments, information, and back-up material, she looked for somewhere to put it. The file drawers in her work station were full. When she asked about it, she was told to "make room." So she did; she threw out most of what was in the files. Only weeks later, when someone came looking, did it become apparent that she'd thrown out work samples, invoices, and contracts. Oops.

Do at Least the Minimum

- *Be there the employee's first day.*
- *Be sure the employee has a work station ready.*
- *Tell existing employees to expect a new co-worker.*

Get More Information

Love 'Em or Lose 'Em: Getting Good People To Stay, Beverly Kaye
and Sharon Jordan-Evans, Berrett-Koehler Publishers, Inc., San
Francisco, 1999.

ORIENTATION: HOW TO LAY THE GROUNDWORK FOR SUCCESS

Know the Issue

There's nothing haphazard about boot camp. The process of turning
a new recruit into a Marine is a deliberate, consistent process that's
been proven effective for decades.

But the Marines spend more time on the right way to make a
bed than many companies spend on the entire orientation process.
Perhaps this scenario sounds familiar: A new employee hangs out in
the lobby until someone realizes he's there. Then he's shown his office
or cubicle and given a pile of forms to complete. Sometime around
noon someone (perhaps the boss) will show up and take him to lunch.
Welcome to Consolidated Behemoth. You're on your own now!

What a wasted opportunity. The Marines understand that the
first few days and weeks lay the groundwork for everything to follow. Although you needn't have your new employees crawl through

the mud, they'll appreciate it if finding the bathroom isn't the biggest accomplishment of their third day. After all, you never get a second chance to make a first impression.

Take Action

- *Introduce the new employee yourself.* Take time to introduce the new employee to as many co-workers as possible. Doing so shows respect for the new employee and for your current employees. It also makes it clear that the new employee is important. Don't delegate this task to someone else who has "more time."

- *Review expectations.* You've spent a lot of time writing a job description and thinking about the expectations you have for new employees (see "Setting Expectations," pages 42–54). Now don't forget to share them!

- *Develop an orientation program.* After any length of time in a job, we forget how much we know. That's probably why so many orientation programs just scratch the surface. A good orientation program should cover three key areas: the organization, the product (or service), and operations. Within each of those areas are specific issues to address. (See the "Orientation Program Overview" on pages 108 and 181 for a list.)

- *Don't go it alone.* You're probably thinking, "Yeah, I'd love to orient my new employees, but I don't have the time." Well, who said you've got to do it all yourself? You might want to do the goals and strategies sections yourself, but assign other sections to seasoned employees and/or teams. (In fact, asking employees who are about to complete their first year to give a portion of the orientation to *you* is a great way to test how much they know.)

This strategy will save you time and offer other rewards as well. New employees will meet their co-workers, they'll get different points of view, and veterans will value the chance to help new employees succeed.

- *Schedule the orientation.* Once you've developed the program and assigned "teachers," don't just hope that the plan gets implemented. Assign dates for each part of the program and determine who should teach that part of the program. Work all your new hires into the schedule.

- *Don't rush.* People can only absorb just so much information at a time, so it doesn't make sense to try to tell people everything in 48 hours. Orientation works best when you allot several hours each week for the first month. That frees up most hours for employees to focus on their jobs.

- *Give employees the schedule.* On an employee's first day, give him the dates and times for each part of the orientation. Make it his responsibility to follow through, and hold other employees accountable for meeting their commitments as scheduled.

- *Be consistent.* Once your orientation program is developed, use it for every new hire. Don't cheat and decide that some employees are smart enough to get along without it, or that because of a pressing deadline you'll do the orientation "later."

- *Take advantage of support materials.* If you're in a large organization, your HR department may have materials (such as videos) to help in the orientation process. If not, use product

brochures, catalogs, annual reports, and other material to sup-
plement your information.

- *Assign a buddy.* As your new employees' manager, you're
  their number one source of information, and that's great
  when it comes to sharing overall department goals. But
  because you're the boss, new employees won't come to you
  about many things, either because they don't want to look stupid or because they think you're too busy. Assigning a buddy
  gives them another resource.

Choose employees who have been around at least a year. If
you can, select people who are outside the employee's immediate work group. Logic might tell you to choose someone *in*
the work group, since those people are closest to the work,
but new employees will interact with those people anyway.
Having a buddy further removed will expose him to other
parts of the company and gives him someone to talk to about
his co-workers ("What's the best way to approach Henry?
Does he prefer email or should I talk to him in the coffee
room?").

Buddies are also information resources. They can answer
everything from "Is there anywhere nearby where I can drop
off my dry cleaning?" to "What's the best way to present
ideas?" Most of the buddy time should be informal and spontaneous, but give them structured time, too. Buy them lunch
once a month for the first six months so they can get away
from the office and talk.

And don't put any limits on what they can talk about, including you. Current employees are the best source of insight on

how to work with your quirks. (Yes, you do have some.) Don't ask buddies to share what they hear from new employees; nothing will undermine the buddy system faster. (The only exception should be situations you really *need* to know about, such as threats by a new employee.)

Real Life Examples

A thorough orientation is important, but it's possible to go overboard. Just ask new employees at Diedre Moire Corporation, a New Jersey-based recruiting firm. CEO Steve Reuning has all new employees copy the company's 244-page Standard Operating Protocol three times over in longhand. It can often take 100 hours.

The Protocol is *quite* specific, witness the section that includes hair and grooming tips:

1. Follow reasonable convention, as dictated by the managerial members of society.
2. Bring hair spray, brush or comb, and other grooming devices as necessary. Plan for wind conditions, and so on.
3. Brush your teeth, carry mints, and/or breath freshener.
4. Control body odors.
5. Groom nails appropriately.
6. Keep pores clean.

Employees must also pass 12 oral exams, covering everything from motivational psychology to desk decor to how to shake a client's hand.

All this orientation and order isn't everyone's cup of tea. Half of those thinking about working for Diedre Moire head for the door when told about the protocol requirements. Of those who stay, about one in five lasts beyond a year. Recruiter Don Klein spent nine months at Diedre Moire several years ago and calls it more structured than the basic training he received at Fort Dix.

Those who stick around say that there's a "comforting efficiency" about the organization.

For another sample orientation program, see "Gen X," pages 218–219.

Source: "Employees Feel Comforting Efficiency in Stephen Reuning's World of Order," by Dan Morse, *The Wall Street Journal*, October 4, 2000.

THE 90-DAY REVIEW: HOW TO DECIDE WHETHER THE EMPLOYEE SHOULD STAY—OR GO

Know the Issue

The offers for trial subscriptions to magazines arrive in your mail by the pound and every one promises a risk-free experience. If, after three (or six or nine) issues you aren't completely satisfied, just write "cancel" on your invoice and owe nothing.

But at some point you have to decide whether to subscribe and write the check. And so it is with new employees. At some point, you have to decide whether they have become a fully functioning member of the team (ready to be managed like everyone else) or whether they are not performing and need to be replaced.

If only it were as simple as writing "cancel" on an invoice. It isn't, of course. If the employee has done well, you must meet with her to say so and set goals for the coming months. If she hasn't done well, the decision has profound implications for her, of course, but it

Orientation Program Overview

A good orientation program gives new employees a thorough overview of the organization, its operations, and its products or services. Here are some areas you should be sure to address:

The Organization (Allow about six hours)

Company history
Key stakeholders
Organization chart

- Roles and responsibilities of each department

Corporate culture
Corporate goals

- Immediate
- Long-term

Revenue

- How does the company earn money?
- What are key expenses?

Policies and procedures
The benefit plan

- Components
- Enrollment procedures

Products and Services (Allow about eight hours)

Your industry/market

- Brief history
- Overall size

continued

Projections

- Is the industry growing? By how much?

Regulatory issues
Market or industry lingo or vocabulary
Specific products produced or services provided

- Their relative importance to the company

Strategy for key products
Market position

- Chief competitors
- Who are they?
- What do they produce?

Operations

Facilities

- Tour
- Hours
- Security

Handbook review
Time cards
Communication

- Mail and fax processes
- Telephone system
- Voice mail
- Email

Schedules and deadlines
Operating processes and procedures
Workflow
How departments interact

also has implications for you and your company. The prospect of beginning the hiring process again can be daunting and costly; if the situation isn't handled right, it can lead to legal problems. You may feel that as a manager you've failed, and word may get out that your company has terminated new employees.

To postpone the decision as long as possible, employers have long relied on probationary periods. Probation—usually 90 days, but sometimes six or even 12 months—is a term that suggests two things: 1) that a new employee must prove herself, but that once probation is over her employment is secure, and 2) probation gives employers a legal out, a period in which they can fire an employee without the risk of lawsuits.

Unfortunately, both of these ideas have seen their day, for we live in an era of at-will employment. At-will employment is a legal concept that says either the employer or the employee can end employment at any time for any reason (or no reason). At-will employment is increasingly popular because, as long as employees are told they're working at will from the outset, employers have more latitude (refer to "Making the Offer," pages 151–155). But at-will employment and probation are redundant. If employment can end any time for any reason, what status does an employee assume when he "passes" probation?

So where does this leave you as a manager? You still must decide whether a new employee should stay, and the end of 90 days is a good time to do so. Once you've made it, meet with the employee, she deserves to know where she stands.

Take Action

- *Don't call the first few months probation.* Avoid using the word probation, especially if you have an at-will employment policy (and, unless a collective bargaining agreement prevents it, you should). New employees need to know that employment is never guaranteed. If you insist on a similar concept, use the phrase "introductory period." Just be sure that the introductory period is tied to something other than the employee's at-will status, such as her ability to earn or use vacation time or to qualify for portions of the benefit plan. Even then, the downsides may outweigh the benefits of a defined period because delaying vacation accrual or benefits enrollment may hurt your recruitment efforts.

- *Assess performance.* Evaluate the first 90 days. If the employee is doing well, consider her a successful hire. If performance problems have been an issue from the start and still haven't been resolved, however, then it's probably time to fire her. (Note: If the employee has significant performance problems, meet with her as early as 30 days after the start date so the employee has time to improve *before* you get to the 90-day mark.)

In rare cases, you may want to postpone the decision another 30 days, but don't take that step just because the decision is uncomfortable. Prolonging the decision can make it more difficult to terminate the employee in the future. Postpone the decision only if the employee has shown substantial progress and you think the employee will succeed given more time.

You may also postpone the decision if the employee did very well the first few weeks, but you've seen a sudden decline in her performance. (If that happens, you're back to setting targets and monitoring performance). In any case, you *owe it to the employee and your company* to make a decision within 120 days.

- *Set new goals.* After an introductory period, employees should move into the standard performance review period. That's usually annually, assuming they stay in the same job. Now is the time to set goals for the next nine months, even if the goal is as simple as meeting the expectations outlined in the job description.

  There's no point twisting yourself in contortions to find goals for employees, particularly nonexempt employees whose jobs are focused and routine. However, professional employees who have career paths need incremental goals to keep them challenged and growing.

- *Meet with the employee.* If an employee is succeeding, let her know that you're pleased with her performance. Identify areas of particular strength, and take time to celebrate her accomplishments. Share the goals you have for her, and give her the chance to share any goals she may have for herself. Make sure that her goals won't conflict with yours, distract her from your goals, or demand resources that you can't commit.

  If an employee is not succeeding despite the reviews and warnings we've described, then you need to make a change. If your company has an HR function, review the termination with them in advance. When you meet with the employee, treat her with respect (see "Termination," pages 315–324). Don't begin your search for a replacement until you've let her go.

- *If you hired through an agency, pay attention to your contract.* Most agencies guarantee the placements they make, meaning that if the hire doesn't work out within a specified time, they will either refund the placement fee or apply the fee to a new search. Be mindful of the guarantee period when making a decision.

Stay Out of Jail

- *Be consistent.* If you give employees a 90-day review, be sure that *all* employees get the review.
- *Document performance.* Be sure your comments (pro and con) are in writing. Include a space for the employee to add comments, if any. Have the employee sign a copy to indicate that he got the review and understands it. Keep a copy in the employee's file.
- *Keep performance issues confidential.* An employee's performance is between you and the employee and, if appropriate, HR; others don't need to know

Manage Up

After 90 days, let your boss know how the new employee is doing. If the new employee is doing well, let your boss know what she's accomplished and how she's contributing. If you fire the employee, let your boss know that it's happening and share your plan for replacing her. Take responsibility for the situation, especially if it is a hire that didn't succeed.

8

Today's Diverse Workforce

Employees beginning third careers in their sixties, parents working flextime to attend Little League games, domestic partners enrolled in the benefit plan, and 27 languages spoken in a single company cafeteria. No other workforce in history has had such varied experiences and brought them all into the workplace. No wonder there has been so much misunderstanding.

Yet all of this diversity offers us unparalleled opportunity—to solve problems using multiple perspectives, to relate to customers in their native languages and cultures, to improve communication, and to turbocharge creativity. This is "two heads are better than one" at an exponential level.

To move from misunderstanding to productivity, we must stop *talking about* diversity and start *taking advantage of it.* How much would the United Nations have accomplished if its delegates were still playing villains and victims? The U.N. doesn't have time, and neither do we.

187

CULTURAL VALUES: HOW TO GET PAST RACE AND ETHNICITY

Know the Issue

Don't do diversity training! (Well, not the way it's done most often.)

For a decade now, American business has had an obsession with diversity. We've spent millions on diversity training. People have trudged across the country to attend conferences. Books on the subject have flown off bookstore shelves. All of this has been well meaning, but much of it has been misguided. Why? Because too often, race, ethnicity, and gender have been shoved front and center, and that's the last place they should be. Instead of examining people's external characteristics (where they come from and what they look like), we need to explore their *underlying values* because the real reward in diversity training is learning to work effectively with people who *think* differently than we do.

Consider this: native-born Americans generally value directness. We tend to "tell it like it is." As managers we're encouraged to be straightforward and offer constructive criticism. Well, if we're managing people with that same value, this is no problem. But suppose we're managing people who value indirectness. To them, saving face can be very important; straightforward criticism, even politely offered, can be humiliating. It can even undermine your suggested changes. You'd be far more effective if you offered a subtle suggestion: "When Mary tried it this way, she had great success." Perhaps that seems uncomfortably vague, but that's only because you're probably an acculturated American.

Be wary of the stereotypes, however. Consider Latinos who have lived in the U.S. for a decade. Are their values Latino? American? Or a blend? And what are "American" values anyway? Any presidential candidate will tell you that the core values of Jews in New York City aren't much like the core values of Louisiana Creoles. Ultimately, each of us has values all our own.

Understanding those values and observing the behavior that reflects them will make you a better manager. The better you can see another person's point of view, the better you can communicate with her. You'll get the results you need, and people will feel respected. What better retention tool could you have?

Take Action

- *Learn the core values.* There are 13 basic, or core, areas in which people's points of view determine much of how they function in the world. Do you feel you have a lot of control over your life, or do you believe that what happens to you is fate? This question has no "right" answer. Most people's view is somewhere between the two extremes. The same is true for each of the 13 core values (described in "The Values Continuum," pages 192–193). Getting familiar with the list will begin to give you insights into yourself and your employees.

- *Learn basic American business values.* No articulation of values applies across the board to every member of a group, but some basic values are generally accepted in American business (see "The Values Continuum"). Learn what they are, not because they are absolutes, but because they'll offer a framework for understanding differences.

- *Identify your own values.* Think about what you really believe. Place yourself on the continuum. How does your perspective affect how you manage? Think of ways in which you reflect values without even thinking about it.

- *Identify your employees' values.* Where do your employees fall on the continuum? It's helpful to look at them individually. Are there places in which their values are different from the American norm? If you aren't sure about their values, ask. Keep the conversation respectful. Don't make assumptions ("You people don't really care about being on time, do you?") and don't ask employees to speak on behalf of a group ("What do people from your country think about this?").

- *Where appropriate, ask employees to respect the business values.* Employees want to do a good job. If people fall short of your expectations, it may be a reflection of differing values. For example, if an employee is chronically late, she may have a different value about time. Share the American business value of timeliness. Be respectful and make it clear that her values are not "wrong." Ask the employee to respect your values while at work. (These are complex discussions; if employees aren't fluent in English, consider using a translator.)

- *Meet employees half way.* When it's a matter of policy or business necessity, asking employees to adapt is reasonable, but in other cases, making the effort to respect other values is a gracious thing to do. For example, if an employee's values make it difficult for her to accept praise on public, adjust your style and offer praise privately.

- *Offer training.* If you have a large number of employees with different cultural backgrounds, offer training in the underlying values of American business culture. Make sure that *all* your employees are trained, not just those from different backgrounds.

Stay Out of Jail

- *Don't make hiring, promotion, or work assignment decisions based exclusively on employees' values.* For example, don't assume that someone who values being indirect can't succeed in sales. Explain what the job entails and let people make choices. Then hold them accountable for their performance.

Get More Information

Managing Multicultural Work Environments, Robert B. Ericksen, 1995.

Patterns of American Culture, Dan Rose, University of Pennsylvania Press, 1989.

The Values Americans Live By, Robert Kohls, San Francisco State University, San Francisco, 1988.

EMOTIONAL INTELLIGENCE: HOW TO ASSESS AND DEVELOP EMPLOYEE APTITUDES

Know the Issue

What would you say about these employees?

Every day, employees said "good morning" or "hi" as they passed their co-worker in the hall or saw her at the coffee pot, and every day they were greeted with silence. No one ever heard "good

The Values Continuum

People's views in each of these areas determine much of how they function in the world. Where do you fall on each continuum? Where do your employees fall? Where does your company fall? In most American organizations, the dominant values are those on the left side of the continuum.

I have control over the environment; what happens in my life is up to me.	1 : 2 : 3 : 4 : 5 : 6 : 7 : 8 : 9	What happens in my life is fate; I'm living out my destiny.
Change is progress; it's a good thing.	1 : 2 : 3 : 4 : 5 : 6 : 7 : 8 : 9	Tradition is our strength.
I control my time; being late is rude.	1 : 2 : 3 : 4 : 5 : 6 : 7 : 8 : 9	I don't control time. If I meet a friend on the street, I must stop to honor the relationship; I'll get where I'm going when I get there.
We're all equal, and I try to be fair to everyone.	1 : 2 : 3 : 4 : 5 : 6 : 7 : 8 : 9	I show my respect to people of higher rank or status and I expect respect from those of lower status.
It's every person for him- or herself; I do what's best for me.	1 : 2 : 3 : 4 : 5 : 6 : 7 : 8 : 9	We're all in this together; I do what's best for the group.
If I work hard, I can do anything and get anywhere in life.	1 : 2 : 3 : 4 : 5 : 6 : 7 : 8 : 9	My place in life will reflect my birthright.

continued

I feel good when I win.	1 : 2 : 3 : 4 : 5 : 6 : 7 : 8 : 9	I feel good when I help others.
I'm focused on a better tomorrow.	1 : 2 : 3 : 4 : 5 : 6 : 7 : 8 : 9	I honor the past.
It matters what I do; I need to get things done.	1 : 2 : 3 : 4 : 5 : 6 : 7 : 8 : 9	It matters who I am; I value each day.
I'm informal; it's friendly and democratic.	1 : 2 : 3 : 4 : 5 : 6 : 7 : 8 : 9	I prefer formality; it shows respect.
I tell it like it is; honesty is the best policy.	1 : 2 : 3 : 4 : 5 : 6 : 7 : 8 : 9	I am not direct; it's important to people to save face.
I do what I need to do to get the job done.	1 : 2 : 3 : 4 : 5 : 6 : 7 : 8 : 9	I follow the best proven method for getting a job done.
Success is a big house and a nice car.	1 : 2 : 3 : 4 : 5 : 6 : 7 : 8 : 9	Success is inner peace and contentment.

Source: Adapted from *The Values Americans Live By,* Robert Kohls, San Francisco State University, San Francisco, 1988

morning" in response, or even made eye contact as she strode by, eyes to the floor.

An employee did as she was asked and decorated the office for Christmas. Several co-workers told her how much they enjoyed the decoration, but the boss said, "They're nice, but the color scheme doesn't match the office. The lights should have been purple and blue, but we've had too many expenses this month so it will do. My Christmas theme at home is white and blue. You should see it; it's so beautiful."

An employee told her colleague that she was going to be out for a few days, explaining that she was going to get married. "OK," said her co-worker. "You might as well get your first marriage over with."

What would you say about these people? "They just don't get it" is one possibility and you'd be right—they don't. These are people no one wants to supervise. Although it would be easy to write them off as hopeless jerks, don't. Most likely, their emotional intelligence isn't all that it might be.

Emotional intelligence is a range of skills that influence one's ability to cope. It can be both measured and improved. This means that you can hone your own skills as you listen and observe, and adjust your style to help your employees achieve their best. You can also help your employees improve *their* emotional intelligence. Through thoughtful coaching and exercises, employees can learn to better handle stress or to solve problems more effectively. Those changes will boost productivity at work and help them at home, too.

Take Action

- *Understand the basics of emotional intelligence.* There are five broad areas of emotional intelligence: intrapersonal, interpersonal, adaptability, stress management, and general mood. (See "What Is Emotional Intelligence?" pages 200–202.) No one is equally strong in all areas; in fact, the population has a broad range of skill levels. Understanding these skills will help you see your employees' strengths and weaknesses. You may see them with greater empathy, too. (One employee might easily manage stress levels that would overwhelm another, for example.)

- *Identify which skills are most important for your employees.* Just as no individual is equally strong in all five areas, few jobs require strength in every area. Interpersonal skills are less important to accountants than to salespeople, for example. Problem-solving skills are more crucial for engineers than for valet parking attendants. Review the five areas that define emotional intelligence and decide which are most important for the jobs you supervise.

- *Assess skills.* Once you know which skills are most important for specific jobs, assess employees. Begin informally. Let's say you're supervising an airline gate agent. The potential for stress in that job is about on par with being Bill Clinton's PR rep, so it's important that employees in that position can handle stress. How do employees react when flights are delayed or canceled? How do they respond to several passengers talking to them at once? What happens if angry passengers yell? Watching these situations will tell you whether employees need help. You may also take a more formal approach. You can measure emotional intelligence using the BarOn Emotional Quotient Inventory or EQ-i (see "Values Testing: A Primer," pages 94 and 95). Using the EQ-i tool is more objective and probably more credible to employees, particularly if you believe they may need improvement in some areas. The EQ-i score also gives you a benchmark against which you can measure improvement. (You may also assess your entire work group and then address the composite group profile, as opposed to focusing on individual employees.)

- *Coach to reinforce the appropriate skills.* Once you've focused on key skills, help employees hone those skills. When you see them effectively use the skills, point it out and praise them. If they miss opportunities, take a moment (privately) to ask them to suggest some other ways they might have handled the situation. If they don't have other ideas, suggest some of your own and discuss whether they'd be comfortable trying other approaches. Don't force the issue; emotional intelligence can be coached, but it can't be imposed.

- *Reward improvement.* Although improving emotional intelligence is possible, it isn't easy. When employees improve, reward their efforts. Rewards can range from a note in their annual review to free movie tickets or even promotion to another job. It all depends on how important the skill is to a job and how much improvement you see. Watch for sustained improvement.

- *Keep emotional intelligence in perspective.* There's a difference between emotional intelligence and personality disorders. For example, being assertive is not the same as being aggressive. Although you might offer coaching to an employee who seems to have a negative attitude, you can't let employees get away with being abusive or disruptive. In those cases, employees need discipline.

Stay Out of Jail

- *Don't make hiring, promotion, or work-assignment decisions based on an employee's real or perceived emotional intelli-*

gence. Consider it only as one of the tools you have to assess performance and coach for improvement.

- *Focus on work-related behavior.* Don't ask employees to make generic improvement ("You need to be more flexible"). Instead, explain why being flexible is important in their job, and offer examples of what flexibility looks like when performing their job tasks.
- *Be sure any test you use is legal.* The test
  - Should not invade privacy (questions in the test should not request information about personal feelings and beliefs that one would generally not want to divulge publicly)
  - Should not reveal protected information about someone's mental or physical health
  - Should be validated and test what it professes to test (presumably something work-related)
  - Should not disproportionately limit the hiring, promotion, or retention of employees in a protected class

    Ask the test publisher to address those concerns. If you still have concerns, ask an attorney.
- *If you formally assess an employee's emotional intelligence, keep his scores confidential.* (In fact, don't expect to see the actual scores yourself. Most certified administrators of the tool give results only to the person assessed. Instead, you might get a summary report showing overall strengths and opportunities for improvement.)
- *If you formally assess individuals or a group, be sure to follow the administration guidelines provided by the instrument's publisher.*

Real Life Example

In 1996, the U.S. Air Force had a serious problem with its recruiters —the same people charged with getting young people to join the service. Recruiter turnover was at 50 percent, and every bad hire cost the service $30,000.

Lieutenant Colonel Rich Handley, head of the recruitment project, thought that emotional intelligence might hold they key to solving the problem. Almost 1,200 recruiters were assessed using the EQ-i to see if there was a correlation between their EQ-i scores and success on the job. The results showed that 45 percent of the recruiters' self-reported success was accounted for by their EQ-i scores. When compared to their objective performance, the recruiters who scored highest in the five factors most likely to translate into success (assertiveness, empathy, happiness, self-awareness, and problem-solving) were 2.7 times more likely to succeed than the average. Of the 262 recruiters who scored the highest, 95 percent met or exceeded their quotas.

In response, the Air Force changed its recruiter-training program to address the success factors identified through the EQ-i assessment. In addition, the selection process was modified to include the EQ-i; responses of prospective recruiters are compared to the scores of the original 1,200 respondents. Candidates also participate in structured interviews to explore the results.

A follow-up study a year later found that retention of recruiters had increased 92 percent, which saved the Air Force $2,700,000 that year alone. The Army and Navy are now exploring similar use of emotional intelligence assessment.

Manage Up

Have your own emotional intelligence measured. Identify areas in which you could improve. Develop a plan for improvement and share it with your boss. If you think your boss has the skills you're seeking to improve, ask for coaching help.

Get More Information

Emotional Intelligence, Daniel P. Goleman, Bantam Books, 1995.

Emotional Intelligence at Work, Hendrie Weisinger, Ph.D., Jossey-Bass, 2000.

The EQ Edge, Steven J. Stein, Ph.D. and Howard Book, M.D., Stoddart Publishing, 2000.

Working with Emotional Intelligence, Daniel P. Goleman, Bantam Books, 1998.

The BarOn EQ-i

Multi-Health Systems Inc.

3770 Victoria Park Ave.

Toronto, ON Canada M2H 3M6

800/268-6011

www.mhs.com

PARENTS: HOW TO HELP EMPLOYEES BALANCE WORK AND FAMILY

Know the Issue

The singular anguish of being a working parent takes many forms: getting to that important meeting and finding the morning's peanut

What Is Emotional Intelligence?

Psychologists and social scientists began discussing something they called "social intelligence" as far back as the 1920s. In the decades since, the idea has been called "emotional factors" and "personal intelligence" among other things. In 1980, psychologist Reuven Bar-On, who had been studying the idea, coined the phrase "emotional quotient." Finally, in 1990, John Mayer of the University of New Hampshire and Peter Salovey of Yale coined the phrase "emotional intelligence" and defined it.

It was Daniel Goleman's best-selling book *Emotional Intelligence* that popularized the idea. Two years later, Toronto-based Multi-Health Systems published the EQ-i, which was developed by Dr. Bar-On. It's the only scientifically based and validated measurement of emotional intelligence.

Mayer and Salovey define emotional intelligence as "the ability to monitor one's own and other's feelings and emotions, to discriminate among them, and to use this information to guide one's thinking and action." Bar-On defines it as "an array of noncognitive capabilities, competencies, and skills that influence one's ability to succeed in coping with environmental demands and pressures." In developing the EQ-i, Bar-On captured emotional intelligence in five areas, with 15 subsections or scales:

Intrapersonal

Emotional self-awareness: The ability to recognize and understand one's feelings and emotions, differentiate between them, and know what caused them and why.

Assertiveness: The ability to express feelings, beliefs, and thoughts, and defend one's rights in a non-destructive way.

Self-regard: The ability to look at and understand oneself, respect and accept oneself, accepting one's perceived positive and negative aspects, as well as one's limitations and possibilities.

continued

Self-actualization: The ability to realize one's potential capacities and to strive to do that which one wants to do and enjoys doing.

Independence: The ability to be self-reliant and self-directed in one's thinking and actions, and to be free of emotional dependency; these people may ask for and consider the advice of others, but they rarely depend on others to make important decisions or to do things for them.

Interpersonal

Interpersonal relationships: The ability to establish and maintain mutually satisfying relationships that are characterized by intimacy, and by giving and receiving affection.

Empathy: The ability to be attentive to, to understand, and to appreciate the feelings of others; being able to "emotionally read" other people.

Social responsibility: The ability to demonstrate oneself as a cooperative, contributing, and constructive member of one's social group.

Adaptability

Problem solving: The ability to identify and define problems, as well as to generate and implement potentially effective solutions.

Reality testing: The ability to assess the correspondence between what is experienced (the subjective) and what in reality exists (the objective).

Flexibility: The ability to adjust one's emotions, thoughts, and behavior to changing situations and conditions.

Stress Management

Stress tolerance: The ability to withstand adverse events and stressful situations without falling apart by actively and confidently coping with stress.

Impulse control: The ability to resist or delay an impulse, drive, or temptation to act.

continued

> ### General Mood
>
> *Happiness*: The ability to feel satisfied with one's life, to enjoy one-self and others, and to have fun.
>
> *Optimism*: The ability to look at the brighter side of life and to maintain a positive attitude, even in the face of adversity.
>
> Source: Multi-Health Systems, Toronto.

butter on your tie, brushing the jelly beans and Barbie clothes off the front seat before your client can get in the car, or discovering that the minutes from yesterday's meeting made an excellent canvas for your toddler's masterpiece. However, being a working parent is more than living gags right out of "Baby Blues." The real anguish is loosening the arms of a screaming child and walking out the door of a preschool, or sitting alone in a hotel room while your first grader appears in her first school play. Those are the situations that make life tough for parents and their managers.

Most parents have jobs outside the home. Parents of young children face daunting emotional and financial duties. We can either pretend that it isn't our problem (which is about as easy as pretending that the children screaming at the next table in our favorite restaurant aren't there) or we can accept the fact and find ways to make the situation work for both sides.

Take Action

- *Be flexible.* Parents learn that they really don't have control over their time. Inevitably, there is an overlooked homework assignment, a bout of chicken pox, or a lost pet to screw up a schedule. Every incident is stressful, and running your department like the German railway system does nothing to ease that stress.

- *Lighten up.* When job duties permit, give parents the latitude to come in late, leave early, take time out of the middle of the day, or work at home. Stop worrying about *when* an employee gets work done and focus instead on the quality of the work. When you do that, you can stop worrying about people abusing the system.

  Of course, many jobs require people to be at work during certain hours, but there may still be room for creativity. At a large hotel, for example, several resignations had put pressure on the housekeeping staff and replacements were hard to find. Rather than just buy bigger brooms or extend the workday, the manager asked the housekeepers for ideas. To his surprise, they proposed taking turns caring for each other's children; just eliminating the challenge of finding reliable childcare enabled them to get more done.

- *Be reasonable.* A few gestures can go a long way toward making life easier for parents. Whenever possible, for example, avoid scheduling meetings for first thing in the morning or last thing in the afternoon; it's more difficult for parents with children in childcare facilities to be flexible at those times of day. If you schedule all-day meetings, build in breaks that allow parents to check in with their child care providers. Ask your employees if there are other easy things you can do to reduce their stress.

- *Respect time at home.* Many parents take work home to make up for time out of the office. Don't add to that burden by calling parents at home with questions that can be answered just as well the next day. Also, try to permit parents to get home at a reasonable hour. Be careful that you don't reward only those employees who join the gang for an after-work drink or a weekend trip to the beach. If you do, you're sending the signal that sacrificing personal time is a requirement for getting ahead.

- *Don't make kids invisible.* Just acknowledging employees' kids goes a long way toward helping parents feel supported. If you sponsor social events for employees, include their children occasionally and plan activities for the kids. (If children's activities are about as familiar to you as a state dinner for the ambassador from Botswana, ask the parents in your office.) When kids show up at the office (and they will!), smile and talk to them. No one's asking you to audition for a job on Sesame Street, but watch morale plummet if you pretend you don't even see the kids. Better yet, set aside a free office or a corner somewhere where kids can entertain themselves for short periods.

- *Don't overdo it.* Do what you can to help parents, but be careful not to do it at the expense of employees who don't have kids. (See "Employees Without Children," pages 207–211)

Stay Out of Jail

- *Don't make hiring, promotion, or work-assignment decisions based on whether employees are parents.* It has no bearing on their ability to do the job.

- *Giving employees flexibility is easiest when they are exempt.* With nonexempt employees, you run the risk of violating overtime laws. Be sure that nonexempt employees accurately track their time in the office and that you approve any work schedule changes *in advance.* Note the approval in writing so there is no disagreement later.

- *Allow children to visit occasionally, but be sure children are not allowed anywhere that might be dangerous, such as near an assembly line or in an auto-repair bay.*

- *If you have an area where children may spend time in the office, be sure it's childproof and that it's secure.* Have parents sign a release stating that they are responsible for their children. (An attorney or your legal department can draft the release.)

- *Remember the Family Medical Leave Act (FMLA).* If your company is covered and the employee is eligible, the law protects the employee's right to miss work to care for an ill child, parent, or spouse under many circumstances. Furthermore, if the employee is eligible for family leave, you will want to notify the employee of that fact so the company can deduct the time taken from the employee's annual allotment.

Real Life Example

Wonderware, an Irvine, California-based developer of software for manufacturing firms, is a very parent-friendly place. Most employees set their own schedules. That means that some arrive as early as 6 A.M. so they can have more time with their children after school. No one frowns if parents leave the office for school conferences or doctor appointments.

When parents get in a child care bind, they're welcome to bring kids into the office. The Kid's Rooms (each of the company's four buildings has a room) are stocked with standard office supplies (paper, staplers, pens, pencils, crayons, rulers, tape), a TV, a VCR, and several older computers. The kids are also welcome to the free food: vending machine items, fresh fruit, string cheese, hard-boiled eggs, celery sticks, carrots, and a drink refrigerator that includes milk, fruit juice, and sodas. A telephone in the room makes it easy to reach Mom or Dad.

At Wonderware, kids are considered part of the company "family." At the annual picnic, they play on an inflatable mountain, a large slide, and a human Foozball field. They participate in the hula hoop endurance challenge, water balloon tossing, and sack races, and also enjoy the hired juggler/mime. Other annual family activities include an Easter egg hunt, a summer kickoff barbecue, and a Christmas crafts evening at which kids visit with Santa, frost cookies, and decorate mugs, glasses, and ornaments.

All of that makes the company an appealing place for parents to work. It's great for recruitment and retention, and it goes a long way toward building commitment.

Manage Up

If your boss has children, learn their names and ages. Say hello if they visit and make a point to ask about them occasionally.

Do at Least the Minimum

Don't pretend that parents aren't parents and make their lives difficult (by letting a meeting run long past normal hours, for example) just because you can.

Get More Information

Ask the Children: What America's Children Really Think About Working Parents, Ellen Galinsky, William Morrow & Co., 1999.

The Working Parents Handbook, June Solnit Sole and Kit Kollenberg with Ellen Melnikoff, Fireside, 1996.

EMPLOYEES WITHOUT CHILDREN: HOW TO REAP REWARDS BY RESPECTING PERSONAL LIVES

Know the Issue

Max is Julie's prize teddy bear. He has his own wardrobe in her closet, his own place at the kitchen table, and a favorite chair for watching TV. Julie even buys Max a seat when they fly. So if Julie asks for a day off because Max needs her, would you let her take it?

Before you answer, consider some other situations. What if Max were her golden retriever? What if Julie is a Meals on Wheels volunteer and Max is a housebound elderly man? Would you give Julie the time if Max were her five-year-old nephew? Her grandfather? Her boyfriend? Her 10-year-old son?

These situations are at the center of workplace skirmishes that threaten to erupt into full-scale warfare because most employers will only give Julie the time if Max is her son, and employees without children resent that. "Our company says it wants to help balance the demands of work and personal life," John says, "but they seem to think that *personal life* is the same as *children*. I'm tired of watching the parents walk out of here at five to pick up their kids while the rest of us stay here and work. It isn't fair."

This is a highly emotional issue. Parents argue that juggling work and family is tough. They face childcare crises, doctors' appointments, and family situations that require them to take time off. They say that their co-workers don't see the time they work at home after the kids are in bed. Besides, they argue, *someone* has to raise the next generation.

Fair enough, say those without children, but we're tired of feeling that our personal lives don't matter. "I get asked all the time to help out so someone can go to his kid's soccer game, or whatever," John says, "and I do it. But when I ask them to return the favor so I can do something that's important to me, they're always too busy." John also complains that his manager never interferes when employees need to do something for their kids, but subjects everyone else to the third degree when they want to take time off or alter their schedule. He adds that parents are asked to travel less often, they are forgiven for missed deadlines, and they earn the same money for working fewer hours.

As with most divisive issues, there is truth on both sides, which is a manager's nightmare. Ignoring the issue won't make it go away. (You might as well write job requisitions to fill the empty jobs you're about to have and start packing rations so you'll be ready for the open warfare.) You *can* make the whole problem go away by putting the focus back on job performance.

Take Action

- *Flexibility is flexibility is flexibility.* Let's assume you're managing exempt employees. If you're a cool boss who lets people slip out early or come in late occasionally, give everyone the same flexibility. Resist the temptation to ask what they'll be doing. If you give people time to deal with their personal lives, it doesn't matter whether they spend that time taking their kids to a soccer game, volunteering in a homeless shelter, or going to an antique show; it's *their* business, not yours. Measure whether work is completed on time and done well; don't log every time Jane comes in late or leaves early.

- *Give people maneuvering room.* Even if you are a cool boss, it's tougher to give people in nonexempt jobs the flexibility to just cut out early. Often the work they do can only be performed on site (and not at home, for example), and you must also contend with overtime law. Still, we're talking about a job, not a prison camp. If your company policies allow it, let people use vacation or personal leave time in small increments (such as a half-day at a time) provided they request the time in advance so you can plan. Track the hours used.

- *Accept that there will be emergencies.* Crises happen in everyone's life; treat them all equally. Don't reassure parents that "everything will be fine here, just go" and then make it tough for others to get away.

- *Don't make assumptions.* Don't assume that employees without children are more willing to travel, or that parents can't stay late. Make decisions based on who is best suited to the job.

- *Monitor work hours.* No one's asking you to track every hour exempt employees are at work, but watch general trends. Employees might leave at different times for many reasons. But if those leaving on time or early are *always* the same people, it's time to step in and coach them about sharing the burden.

- *Hold people equally accountable.* Once deadlines are determined, decide the consequences for not meeting them and hold everyone to the same standard. Don't cut parents extra slack.

Stay Out of Jail

- *Don't make hiring, promotion, or work assignment decisions based on whether an employee is a parent.*
- *Remember the Family Medical Leave Act (FMLA).* If your company is covered and the employee is eligible, the law protects the employee's right to miss work to care for an ill child, parent, or spouse under many circumstances. Furthermore, if the employee is eligible for family leave, you will want to notify the employee of that fact so the company can deduct the time taken from the employee's annual allotment.

Real Life Example

Cancer patients often have extended hospital stays, and during that time they get to know the nurses and other members of the staff. The team at one California hospital helped that process with a bulletin board on the oncology floor. Each employee was invited to post something about him- or herself, which patients and their families could then look at. Although some people chose to post pictures of their children, the board was *not* just an oversized "Hey, look at my kid display." Some employees posted pictures of their spouse or significant other; others pinned up photos of themselves busy with their hobby or charity work. "I like the board because it shows we're all real people with real lives," one nurse said. "We're not just nurses or just parents."

Do at Least the Minimum

Don't routinely pick on employees without children to work late or take out-of-town trips.

OLDER EMPLOYEES: HOW TO TAP INTO EXPERIENCE

Know the Issue

"We don't trust anyone over 30."

If you're around 40 (or older), you may not know that Jack Weinberg first used the phrase in an interview about free speech in 1964, but you surely recognize it as the watchword of the 1960's counter-culture movement that it became.

If you're around 30 (or younger), the phrase may sound like a manifesto for the dotcom economy from Fast Company or Red Herring.

Therein lies the generation gap for the new millennium. This time it isn't about clothes, music, or drugs (well, OK, maybe it is a little). Mostly it's about business management and culture.

To those of you who are younger, anyone over 40 (and certainly over 50) may seem rigid, stuffy, and tired. They've seen everything and haven't had a new idea in 20 years. But they're sure *your* new idea will never work. Right?

If you're older, you're mad that experience doesn't count for anything and fed up with assumptions that you can't turn on a computer without help. At least you have reliable transportation and understand office protocol. Right?

We're not going to choose sides in this one, but we will point out that demographics are on the side of the over-40s. The median age in the U.S. was 28 in 1970. Today it's 35 and will be 40 by 2010. By 2006, just 36 percent of the workforce will be 34 or younger. In other words, "oldsters" are the majority of the workforce. Already 63 percent of companies responding to a 1999 survey by the Society for Human Resource Management (SHRM) say they are hiring retirees as consultants or temporary employees.

So why is this group so beleaguered? Often, they're ignored; two-thirds of all companies say they are not actively recruiting older workers for regular jobs and almost half aren't trying to retain older workers. A surprising 81 percent of companies don't offer any provisions or benefits designed specifically with older workers in mind. If older workers aren't being ignored, they're being discarded; they're filing age discrimination suits in record numbers.

None of which makes good business sense. To stay competitive, no one can afford to squander talent.

Take Action

- *Don't believe the negative stereotypes.* If you believe that sitcoms mirror real life, then you believe that anyone over 40 can't learn anything new, is computer-illiterate, and probably can't remember how to get to work every day. Judge people on their performance. Don't make assumptions based on their age, young or old.

- *Respect experience.* No, people over 40 don't know everything. At the outset, they may not know much about your business. But they do know *something*—and often a lot. Draw on their expertise. If possible, create a structure for them to offer their insight and experience. Mentor programs pairing older workers with younger ones are particularly effective.

- *Don't let them rest on their laurels.* Yes, experience counts, but the question "What have you done for me lately?" is valid, too. It's not a good sign if all you hear about is the good old days. A woman over 50 told WorkingWounded.com that she doesn't hire peers who lack energy, a spark in their eye, and a willingness to take risks. It's reasonable to expect employees over 50 to have passion for their work, too.

- *Advocate for benefits.* As a manager, you probably don't have much control over which benefits your company offers, but you can still do two things. First, be sure that all employees understand the benefits they have. Don't assume a correlation between an employee's benefits needs and her age. Many people are raising their grandchildren, for example, and may value dependent-care benefits. Second, advocate that your employer not overlook benefits that may appeal to older employees, such as long-term care insurance and retirement plans.

- *Whenever possible, be flexible.* Most employees report that they prefer easing into retirement by cutting back on work hours, rather than going cold turkey. Work within your company's policies to allow productive older workers to scale back gradually. Just be equitable in making the effort (don't extend the offer only to your favorite employees), and don't burden younger workers in the process. For example, don't trim a 40-hour job into a 35-hour job and add the five hours to someone else's job.

- *Offer training.* Training is a cheaper alternative than finding new employees. And, yes, employees over 40 can learn just as well as anyone else.

Stay Out of Jail

- *The Age Discrimination in Employment Act prohibits dis-criminating against employees aged 40 or older.* Don't make hiring, firing, promotion, or work assignment decisions based on an employee's age.

Real Life Examples

- "I've had some great mentors who trained me to look at each candidate based on his own sense of worth and need for ful-fillment," says David Barrett, president of BearCAT Productions in Oakland, California. "In making a case for those applicants over 40, I've found they generally need to share the highlights of their careers in a meaningful way, to pass the baton to the next generation. They have something to teach. I encourage that because it promotes stability and makes for a stimulating culture.

  "The average age in our company is the late 40s, and I'm convinced that experience leads to better judgment. And though I want them to teach, I also want them to learn, so I foster an environment that encourages experimenting without worrying about mistakes."

- On his first day, the new 30-year-old CEO called everyone over 50 into his office. He told them that he didn't believe that older people have any sense, and added "You'll have a tough time proving to me that you can fit in with my 21st century philos-ophy. Time to get some new blood into this stodgy business!" For the next several months, the CEO questioned whether older workers could do the job. During a single meeting, he presented the 55-year-old loading-dock supervisor with a cane and a walker, called another older executive "Methuselah," and suggested an afternoon nap time for all of the "old codgers." The CEO also encouraged younger employees and supervisors to taunt the older workers with remarks about their age. At the end of four months, all the workers over 50 had quit, and the prejudiced, insensitive, and overly talkative CEO was the key witness in some costly lawsuits.

Source: "Age Discrimination," part of the Equal Employment Opportunity Commission (EEOC) Technical Assistance Program. May 1999 (Revised).

GEN X: HOW TO BRIDGE THE GENERATION GAP

Know the Issue

Remember when you were a teenager and those clueless adults didn't understand a thing about you—not your clothes, not your music, not your humor? Not even your vocabulary? That was then. Now, as an adult yourself, you can see that those adults understood more than you gave them credit for; they just didn't *like* what they understood.

If you remember the feeling, you know how most Gen X employees feel all the time. The only difference is that Gen X employees (defined by Neil Howe and William Strauss, authors of the book *Generations*, as the 57 million people born between 1965 and 1980 now in the workforce) really *are* misunderstood. How else can you explain the huge disparity between the popular image of Gen Xers as lazy, fickle, disloyal slugs who want everything *right now* and the altogether different image that experts see?

"It could be that organizations just don't know how to harness this techno-savvy, info-addicted, thrill-seeking group of talented

young idealists," says Rebecca S. Morgan, a consultant and expert on Gen X.

Morgan says that Xers have been unfairly maligned ("More than 75 percent of media coverage about Generation X is negative," she says) and she has plenty of data to back her up. The Bureau of Labor Statistics says that Xers work almost four hours longer per week than the average employee. A Marquette University/University of Michigan study found that Xers are responsible for 70 percent of all start-up firms in the U.S. A CNN/Time poll found that three out of every five Xers aspire to be their own bosses. All of which probably contributed to *Forbes* magazine branding Gen X as "the most entre-preneurial generation in American history."

Clearly, hanging on to the idea that Gen Xers are couch-potato scoundrels will only result in a waste of talent. "The average Gen Xer changes jobs every 18 months. That turnover is a slow, steady blood-letting of human capital," Morgan says. "It cripples productivity and growth. Finding replacements swells recruiting budgets. You can reduce turnover, but you have to be willing to learn from the New Economy employment playbook."

Heed the playbook. For better or worse, Gen Xers are here to stay, and right behind Generation X is Generation Y (also known as "Nexters," "Echo Boomers," or "Millenials"). Gen Y is even more technically savvy, demanding, and creative!

Take Action

- *Earn their trust and respect.* Previous generations were taught to respect their elders and love their country, but Gen X came of age during Watergate, Iran-Contra, the Challenger explo-sion, and soaring divorce rates. "The result is a generation of young people who don't talk to strangers and rely on themselves," Morgan says. "They are skeptical." But they are not unreasonable. Don't tell them to respect you; give them reasons why they should.

- *Set clear expectations and then get out of the way.* This is America's first generation of latchkey children; 40 percent of them were raised in single-parent households. They learned to rely on themselves to set the VCR, set the table, and set the agenda for quality time with Mom and Dad. They are adept at thinking for themselves. Let Gen Xers come to you with questions, rather than micro-managing them. Morgan says that one of the most frequent complaints she hears from Gen Xers is that they don't feel that they have autonomy. Let them be entrepreneurs within their departments. (Hint: This is pretty good advice for managing *most* people.)

- *Give a lot of feedback.* Take a few minutes every day (not once a year at review time) to talk with Gen Xers. To make it easy, Morgan says make it QUIC: Quality (brief, specific), Immediate, and Constructive (for example, say "this is what you can do better, this is how this project is tied to your longer term goals").

- *Get to the point.* Baby Boomers had three black and white networks. Previous generations had the public library and radio. Xers grew up with hundreds of TV channels, video games, and computers so they're adept at sifting through data, and more responsive to short e-mail and memos with bullet points than to a treatise.

- *Offer professional and personal development opportunities.* So an employee wants to leave early on Mondays to take a

T'ai Chi class? Let her! Xers learn four or five software programs per year; they thrive on stretching themselves. As long as the employee's work doesn't suffer, support professional *and* personal development for Gen Xers.

- *Foster an "alumni" program.* The single best source of new employees is former employees. So, if a Gen Xer leaves to pursue a new opportunity, Morgan urges that you don't burn that bridge. Send him an occasional e-mail, ask him to train his replacement (on a contractual basis, of course), and let him know when you have positions available. The former employee may realize the grass is not greener on the other side and return to the fold. "Boomerang" employees are among the most loyal, so this is a talent pool no one should overlook.

Stay Out of Jail

- *Don't make any hiring, promotion, or work-assignment decisions based on an employee's age.*

Real Life Example

One technology firm has figured out that getting Xers up to speed ASAP helps in hiring and in retention. The process begins when a manager makes a hire. The manager completes an online form that captures the new employee's bio, start date, position, salary, and bonus structure. The manager also identifies the technology and workspace requirements for the job, and requests a mentor for the employee and pass code.

The form is e-mailed to the COO, who coordinates the workspace, orders the right technology, processes the passwords, recruits a mentor, and posts the new employee bio online so everyone can welcome her aboard when she starts.

One week before the new employee starts, she receives a bouquet of flowers, a welcome note from the president and senior staff, and a packet of forms from HR that she is asked to complete and bring on her first day. On the first day, the new employee has breakfast on-site with her mentor. The mentor shares her story and talks about future opportunities for growth. They agree on goals for the mentoring relationship.

The mentor takes the new employee on a tour. They set up e-mail and voice mail accounts, and visit the corporate library where on-site training takes place. The new employee receives a workbook filled with questions about the company, its products and services, and the policies and procedures. This workbook must be completed within two weeks.

The new employee lunches with her manager, who shares the new employee's job description and first project assignments, and asks for feedback. They talk about how success is measured, and agree on an appointment for the two-week employee review. The manager explains her "open door" management principle: when you need help, ask. By the end of the day, the new employee has the tools (technology, job description, project assignment, policies, and procedures, and a mentor) to hit the ground running as a full member of the project team.

"Time after time, Gen Xers refer to this orientation as one of the things that attracted them to this firm," Morgan says.

Get More Information

Ca$h in on Generation X: How to Get the Best from Young Talent, Rebecca S. Morgan, www.keepyoungtalent.com, 2001.

Managing Generation X: How to Bring out the Best in Young Talent, Bruce Tulgan, W.W. Norton & Co., 2000.

The Manager's Pocket Guide to Generation X, Bruce Tulgan, Human Resource Development Press, 1997.

The Productivity Path, Rebecca S. Morgan et al, www.keepyoung-talent.com, 2000.

RELIGION: HOW TO RESPECT ESTABLISHED PRACTICES

Know the Issue

It's a paradox of American society that discussion of our deepest private feelings is most often limited to the most public forums imaginable. We know more about sex between President Clinton and Monica Lewinsky than between any people we actually know, and we know more about Senator Joseph Lieberman's religious beliefs than we likely know about the beliefs of our neighbors.

This paradox is evident at work, especially regarding religion. On the one hand, religious beliefs are among the least-discussed topics at work, so as a manager you're unlikely to face the issue. On the other hand, when the issue *is* raised, it can affect several very public elements of work, ranging from schedules and job duties to dress and appearance standards.

Happily, managing this aspect of diversity is less complex than it seems. We'll share some of the specifics, but there's really just one simple rule: do your best to respect established religious practice.

Take Action

- *Make a reasonable effort to accommodate a range of religious beliefs.* Title VII of the Civil Rights Act prohibits discrimination on the basis of religion. That sounds broad enough to be intimidating, but over time, the Supreme Court and the EEOC have clarified what it means.

The Court first said that those who have an "orthodox belief in God" are clearly protected. Later, it expanded the definition to protect moral and ethical beliefs that have the function of a religion in someone's life. This opened the door for the EEOC to state that the law's protection is not limited to traditional religion and religious practices. For example, a teacher won a judgment against a school district after she argued successfully that she was fired because of her New Age beliefs.

Having said that, the law distinguishes between what a religion *requires* and what people simply *prefer*. For example, a former employee sued a department store after she was fired for going on a pilgrimage during the store's busy holiday season. The employee lost the case because although she "felt called to go," her religion didn't require it and there were pilgrimages at other times that she could have attended.

In another case, an employer required its salespeople to live in the same area as their customers. A Jewish applicant was offered a sales job and accepted it. Later, he asked to move 40 miles away because the town had no Jewish community. The company denied his request, and he sued for religious discrimination. He lost the case because the Jewish faith doesn't require living in a Jewish community, and he admitted that part of his motivation was to enroll his children in a better school district. The court found he simply *preferred* to live in a Jewish community.

The courts only ask that employers make a *reasonable* effort to accommodate religious beliefs; the courts specifically protect employers from *undue hardship.* As a manager, your job is to decide what's "reasonable" when it comes to scheduling, job tasks, appearance, and so on. Obviously, this decision can't and shouldn't be made in a vacuum; the courts and the EEOC have provided the framework.

- *Don't sacrifice business interests.* No accommodation should imperil your business. For example, an employer working to meet a deadline hired welders to work at least 10-hour days, six days a week to finish the project. One welder sued after he was fired for refusing to work Saturdays on religious grounds. The employer won after proving that it had a shortage of welders and had been unable to hire welders for just one day per week. Short one welder, the company would have missed delivery on contracts that included penalties for being late. The court concluded that giving the man Saturdays off would be a hardship for the whole firm.

- *Don't impinge on the rights of other employees.* After being offered a job as a sheriff's deputy, a woman told the department she was unable to work on her Sabbath. She withdrew her application and sued when she was told that she would have to work on those days. The department explained that work assignments were based on seniority. The woman lost her case because the court said that the department's seniority system was fair and accommodating her would have impinged on the rights of other employees.

- *Explore the options.* The law requires that you consider how to accommodate an employee's religious beliefs. A temporary Department of Agriculture border inspector sued when he didn't get a regular position because his religion kept him from working Saturdays. The Department argued that giving him Saturdays off would burden his co-workers and complicate scheduling. The employee won because the Department had not considered any options, such as shift trading. The court also found that co-workers would not be burdened because the man was willing to work other undesirable shifts, relieving co-workers from having to do so. (Beware, however, that the decision might have been different if scheduling was influenced by a collective bargaining agreement or an established seniority system.)

Stay Out of Jail

- *Don't make any hiring, promotion, or work assignment decisions based on someone's religious beliefs.*
- *If the only way to accommodate a religious belief is to break the law, don't do it.* Yes, it does come up. At one company, an employee believed that his Social Security number was the "mark of the beast" and refused to disclose it; he asked his employer to create one for him. At another company, a Sikh employee refused to wear the hard hat mandated by OSHA because his religion requires wearing a turban. Because both

accommodations were illegal, employers didn't have to make them.

- *Don't permit religious harassment.* Allowing employees to advocate for their religious beliefs at work can create a hostile environment. Three examples illustrate this point:

  - A bailiff who was a Jehovah's Witness read passages from the Bible to prisoners and in public areas of the courthouse.
  - A police chief advised a dispatcher about her prospects for salvation; his conduct escalated to the point that eventually he suggested to her that suicide would be preferable to the sinful way she was leading her life.
  - An employee sent letters to her co-workers asking them to accept Jesus and criticizing aspects of their behavior.

Remember, just as employees have freedom of religion, they also are entitled to freedom *from* religion.

Real Life Example

Sometimes, the best way to deal with a religious issue is on its own terms. Take, for example, the case of the farm workers and the devil. Several women who picked crops were asked to use the portable restroom facilities provided. For a time, they did, but then they began crossing the street to use the facilities at a neighboring gas station. That was dangerous, took them much longer, and angered the station owner. When they were asked why they weren't using the restrooms provided, they explained that the devil was living in it. They knew this for a fact because they could see his boots while they were in the stalls. No amount of logic persuaded them that the devil was elsewhere. Finally, the manager decided to deal with the issue head on:

he called a priest to perform an exorcism on the facility. Problem solved.

DISABILITIES: HOW TO HELP PEOPLE WITH DISABILITIES GIVE THEIR BEST

Know the Issue

What comes to mind when you picture an employee with a disability? Perhaps because of the ubiquitous blue-and-white handicapped symbol, many people see someone using a wheelchair, but in today's workplace, that image is far from complete.

To even begin getting the complete picture, you also have to consider vision and hearing impairment, epilepsy, multiple sclerosis, cancer, heart disease, HIV, diabetes, and depression. Then there is chronic psoriasis, Crohn's disease, bowel disorders, and high blood pressure. Some employees have claimed (largely unsuccessfully) that sleep disorders, menopause, fainting, and injuries sustained in car accidents are disabilities. Even all of these disabilities barely scratch the surface.

Of course, people have faced most of these health issues for as long as people have been working. However, the passage of the *Americans with Disabilities Act* (ADA) in 1990 put the question of what constitutes a disability and how it should be managed at work in an entirely new framework. Now disabilities are as much a legal matter as they are medical and social concerns.

The ADA is actually rather vague. In a nutshell, the law defines "disability" as an impairment that limits one or more major life activities. However, the law doesn't specify which activities, so those are being determined in court. Furthermore, one of its key points—that employers should make *reasonable accommodations* on behalf of employees with disabilities—has been interpreted differently from one job to another. Those facts make managing employees with disabilities perhaps the most complex issue that supervisors face today.

ADA compliance is a full-time job for many attorneys, so there isn't any way that we can explore every nuance of the law. But we can offer you some fair, sensible guidelines to handle most situations.

Take Action

- *Review the basics of the law.* Not every ailment or injury is a disability, and not every proposed accommodation is reasonable. Review the basics of the law (see "The ADA: A Primer," pages 230–233) so that you're comfortable recognizing situations in which the ADA is probably pertinent.

- *Work to make reasonable accommodations.* Many employers get into legal trouble because they make no effort to accommodate a disability. Yet most accommodations are not difficult or expensive. Peter Blanck at the University of Iowa did a study in which he found that the average cost of an accommodation is less than $50, and that 75 percent of all accommodations cost less than $100. Do everything you can to make a reasonable accommodation. It's the best strategy for keeping good people, too.

- *Focus on the accommodation, not the disability.* Once we hear someone's diagnosis or the nature of his injuries, it's easy to become an amateur doctor and decide what he can or can't do. *Don't.* A diagnosis or injury report actually tells you nothing because different people in different situations have different capabilities. Beyond that, you're actually better off *not* knowing an employee's diagnosis because then there's no risk you'll breach his privacy. All you really need to know is whether an employee can perform the core job functions, with or without a reasonable accommodation.

For example, suppose a doctor says an employee is unable to lift more than 15 pounds. It makes *no difference* whether the employee's limited because of a lower back injury, arthritis, medication that causes dizziness, or any of 20 other possible reasons. You must decide whether, on behalf of the company, you should ask for a second opinion. If you decide against making that request, then you must decide whether the limitation impacts a core job function and, if so, what reasonable accommodation to make. (You don't have to make the "most" reasonable or "best" accommodation, only a reasonable one.) If you can't make any reasonable accommodation, you don't have to retain the employee. (Just remember that you can't fire an employee because of a limitation that doesn't affect a core job function, whether you can make an accommodation or not.) Remember this mantra: ask *what* employees can do, not *why*.

- *Educate employees to focus on accommodation, not the disability.* Some employees value their privacy and won't even admit that anything is wrong. Others want to share every detail of their doctor visit. Neither extreme is helpful. If you've been told that an employee's performance of a core job function is limited by an ADA-covered disability, what you need to do is have a good-faith conversation to decide whether you can make an accommodation and, if so, what it will be.

Explain to employees that you need their help to protect their privacy and to accommodate them, and that accurate information about what job duties they can or can't do is the key. Suggest that employees ask their doctor to omit a diagnosis from any information you receive. Be sure to document your attempts to arrive at a reasonable accommodation.

- *Don't let employees practice medicine.* Some people decide their own treatment without a doctor's advice. Don't accept an employee's explanation that she can't lift a certain weight, or needs extra breaks because of her disability. Ask to see a doctor's recommendation. If the employee hasn't seen a doctor, explain that everyone involved needs accurate medical information. (Likewise, require that employees who have been out for medical reasons present a doctor's release stating that they are fit to return to work.)

- *Monitor employee behavior.* Sometimes employees don't ask for an accommodation; they simply make one of their own. If you see that, don't assume that everything is OK. If, for example, an employee begins delegating work that they "can't do" to a co-worker, then you need to step in and find out whether the employee really has a protected disability. Even if he does, you may prefer a reasonable accommodation that does not involve other employees directly.

You should also keep in mind that a disability and a workers' compensation claim can overlap. Generally, workers' comp applies to injuries sustained on the job. However, such injuries can aggravate existing disabilities, lead to long-term disability, or result from disabilities that were not accommodated.

Stay Out of Jail

- *Be consistent when accommodating employees.* Don't decide whether to make an accommodation based on the disability an employee has.
- *Keep information about an employee's disability confidential.*
- *Don't discriminate against employees known to have a relationship with a disabled person.* For example, it's illegal to discriminate against someone because he or she associates with someone who has HIV infection or AIDS.
- *If you're unsure whether an employee's situation is covered by the ADA, don't guess.* Consult your company's HR, legal department, or an attorney.
- *Document your attempts to reach a reasonable accommodation.*

Do at Least the Minimum

- *Take disabilities seriously.* Meet your obligation to the company and employees.

Get More Information

Accommodating Employees with Psychiatric Disabilities: A Practical Guide to ADA Compliance, Allen Smith and Don Montuori, Thompson Publishing Group, 1998.

The Americans with Disabilities Act: Hiring, Accommodating and Supervising Employees with Disabilities, Mary Dickson and Kay Keppler, editors, Crisp Publications, 1995.

The ADA: A Primer

Even attorneys who specialize in the ADA struggle to master the nuances of the law. However, it's easy to grasp the basic concepts. If you know them, you'll know when you need a doctor to suggest an accommodation, and when you need legal advice.

Which Employers Are Covered by the ADA?

The ADA applies to all employers with 15 or more employees. However, the ADA sets minimal standards of protection. Many state laws are more stringent and cover employers with as few as two employees. If you're unsure, check with an attorney or with your state employment department.

Which Employees Are Protected?

The ADA protects *qualified* individuals with a disability. With respect to an employee, the law defines a disability as:

- A physical or mental impairment that substantially limits one or more major life activities (defined not exclusively as caring for oneself, performing manual tasks, walking, seeing, hearing, speaking, breathing, learning, working, and participating in community activities). The Supreme Court has ruled that a person is not impaired under Federal law if medication, prostheses, eyeglasses, and so on can eliminate the effects of the employee's medical condition.

- A record of such impairment (this provision is intended to protect people who have a history of disability but are no longer impaired, such as cancer patients in recovery)

- Regarded as having such an impairment (this provision protects people whose impairments don't actually limit major life activities, but who are treated by an employer as if they have such limitations).

continued

However, the ADA doesn't require an accommodation if an impairment limits someone in performing only a particular job or a narrow range of jobs. For example, an auto body welder developed carpal tunnel syndrome and was no longer able to do repetitive factory work. Her employer was not required to accommodate her in a welding job because her education, skills, and training made her eligible for many other positions. In order to qualify for an accommodation, an employee must show that her ability to perform a broad range of jobs is limited.

You may *choose* to accommodate a worker when it isn't required, but if you do so, be consistent—don't just accommodate the employees you like.

If the ADA Protects Qualified People, Who Is Considered Qualified?

Determining whether someone is qualified under the ADA requires two steps. First, he must meet the necessary prerequisites for the job, such as education, work experience, training, skills, licenses, certificates, and other job-related requirements (for example, has the ability to work with other people).

Second, you must determine whether a reasonable accommodation would permit him to perform the essential functions of the job. (See "Job Descriptions," pages 42–48) For example, if someone is qualified to work with people as a counselor, but can't type documents, you need to decide how essential typing documents is to the job and, if it is essential, how the inability to type can be accommodated.

What's a Reasonable Accommodation?

Any effective accommodation that an employer can make without undue hardship is reasonable. It may include

- Making existing facilities readily accessible to and usable by people with disabilities

continued

- Restructuring jobs
- Modifying work schedules
- Reassigning a disabled person to a vacant position
- Acquiring or modifying equipment
- Adjusting examinations, training materials, or policies
- Providing qualified readers or interpreters
- Making other similar accommodations.

The ADA does not require an employer to modify or change a job to accommodate an employee if the employer can show that the change would alter the essential functions of the job. For example, a romantic, candle-lit restaurant need not change its ambience by putting bright lights in the dining area to accommodate a server with poor eyesight. However, the same restaurant may have to install the very same lights in the kitchen as a reasonable accommodation to a chef with poor eyesight.

Are Accommodations Limited to Job-Specific Functions?

No. Accommodations may have to be made to address issues beyond the employee's job duties, such as access to

- The facility
- Restrooms
- General communications (such as memos)
- Break and dining areas
- Company social events

What Is an Undue Hardship?

An undue hardship is anything that would require significant difficulty or expense. You should consider

continued

- The nature and cost of the accommodation needed
- The overall financial resources of the facility
- How many people are employed at the facility
- The effect on expenses and resources, and the impact on the operation of facilities
- The overall financial resources of the organization
- The overall size of the business
- The number, type, and location of its facilities
- The type of the company's operations
- The composition, structure, and functions of the workforce

In other words, undue hardship includes any action that is unduly costly, extensive or substantial, or that would fundamentally alter the operation of the business. Generally, larger employers are expected to make greater efforts than small employers to accommodate employees.

Beware, however, that the EEOC and the courts are very reluctant to conclude that an undue hardship exists. Both have defined the term very narrowly.

SEXUAL ORIENTATION: HOW TO INCLUDE THE INVISIBLE MINORITY

Know the Issue

Do your co-workers have pictures of their spouses and children on their desks? Do people talk about their weekend plans at the water cooler or in the elevator? Does the company host social events that include spouses? Has anyone ever stopped by your desk to collect money to send a gift to a newlywed colleague or the parents of a new baby? If the answer to any of those questions is yes, then sexual orientation is an issue in your workplace.

This issue can be either a big positive or a big negative. If it's a positive, people feel included and respected. They are more productive and more committed. If it's a negative, people feel excluded and disrespected. They are less productive and far more likely to quit and go work for your competitor. They're also more likely to file potentially costly harassment lawsuits.

Huh? How did we get from baby gifts to turnover and lawsuits? Here's how: your heterosexual employees take for granted that they can comfortably share important elements of their private lives at work. All those normal activities from pictures to weekend plans are reflections of that comfort. That's as it should be.

In most work places, however, gay men, lesbians, and bisexuals do not feel comfortable sharing anything of their private lives. Although they may have been with a partner for years, they do not have any pictures on their desk. If they talk about weekend plans at all, they probably talk about "I," but never "he" or "she" and probably not "we" because it invites too many questions. They probably attend social events alone, or they come with a friend of the opposite sex. In short, while their heterosexual colleagues have one life, they have two lives: work life and personal life.

OK, but how is this your problem and not something for the U.N. Human Rights Commission to address? It starts as a productivity issue. Gay men, lesbians, and bisexuals still in the closet at work expend an enormous amount of psychic energy protecting their secret. If you doubt it, try this experiment: go an entire day without saying or doing *anything* that reveals your sexuality. You'll see

"Don't Ask, Don't Tell" in a whole new light. Odds are that you'll be exhausted at the end of the day. You'll have devoted a lot of thought and energy to protecting yourself that would have been better served solving a work problem.

So, if it's that much work to stay in the closet, then why not just be honest? Many gay people are afraid to be honest, and for good reason. Gay men, lesbians, and bisexuals know too many friends who've been passed up for promotions or fired or worse. They know people who've been called names, robbed, beaten up, and splashed with acid. Yes, at work. What started as a productivity issue has become much more.

People faced with quiet indignity or violent hostility have three choices. They can put up with it, fight back, or leave. Fewer gay men, lesbians, and bisexuals are putting up with it. Many take the issue to court. Others leave for jobs where they are accepted. Can you afford to fight a lawsuit or have good people walk out the door?

You may have religious beliefs that homosexuality is wrong, or you may simply be uncomfortable with the idea. We're not asking you to change those beliefs, but we are asking you to recognize that as a manager it's often your job to set aside personal feelings and treat people fairly. That's good business sense. Here's how to do it.

Take Action

- *Look at your company policies.* Most large organizations (and many smaller ones) have nondiscrimination policies. If yours is among them, does the policy prohibit discrimination based on sexual orientation? If so, be sure you follow the policy. If not, suggest to HR or senior management that the policy be expanded. A clear policy is an important foundation for everything else you do.

- *Review your benefit plan.* Most employer-sponsored health care plans offer dependent coverage. Usually, however, dependents are defined strictly as spouses and children. A growing number of companies, however, offer health coverage to domestic partners as well. If your plan offers such coverage, be sure your employees know about it. (Tell everyone about the coverage, not just those you think may be gay, lesbian, or bisexual.) If not, advocate to HR or senior management that such coverage be offered. Having it offers a competitive advantage (Microsoft, IBM, Disney, and General Motors are among the many companies that now offer the benefits). It's also a matter or fairness; married people are effectively earning more for doing the same work if health coverage is provided to their spouses without cost. Don't worry about costs either. Numerous studies have shown that only a small number of employees accept the benefits (many partners are covered by their own employers) and the claims made by unmarried partners generally cost less than those filed by spouses.

- *Don't permit a hostile environment.* Most people wouldn't think of telling a racist or sexist joke at work. Telling jokes about gays, however, is more often still accepted. It shouldn't be. If you overhear such a joke, take the employee who told it aside and make it clear that such humor is unacceptable. Don't allow cartoons or images that impugn gay men, lesbians, or bisexuals to be posted. And by all means, don't allow any derisive or hostile remarks to be made to employees known or suspected to be gay. If an employee tells you about such behavior, investigate promptly and confidentially. (For more information, see the section on "Sexual Harassment," pages 368–381.)

- *Use inclusive language.* If you or the organization is hosting a social event for employees and their families, be sure that invitations include "partners" or "significant others," and not just spouses. If employees attend these events with partners, be sure you introduce yourself and welcome the employee's guest. If you have policies allowing employees to take time off to care for an ill spouse (and in many cases the FMLA mandates that you do) or for bereavement leave, be sure that partners or significant others are covered by the policy. An employee who loses a partner of 20 years should not have to be at work the next day because his partner "didn't count." It's happened.

- *Be consistent.* If some employees have photos of their spouses or children on their desks, don't tell gay, lesbian, or bisexual employees that photos of their partners are not allowed. (Yes, it happens.) If winners of a sales incentive program are sent on a trip to Hawaii with their spouses or significant others, don't tell gay, lesbian, and bisexual employees that their partners have to stay home. If . . . well, you get the idea.

- *Hold everyone accountable.* You won't tolerate off-color jokes, obscene photos, or lewd behavior from straight employees. Don't tolerate it from gay employees either. Gay people are entitled to equal treatment, but not special treatment.

Stay Out of Jail

- *Don't discriminate.* Currently, no Federal law prohibits job discrimination based on sexual orientation. However, such discrimination *is* illegal in several states and many cities. Congress has considered a Federal law barring discrimination based on sexual orientation, and most experts expect it to pass at some point. (Most Americans support the proposal.) To be prudent, do not make decisions about hiring, promotion, overseas assignments, or other work-related issues based on someone's actual or perceived sexual orientation.

- *Don't ignore harassment.* Harassment law from any perspective is complicated (see "Sexual Harassment," pages 368–381). However, when it comes to issues related to sexual orientation, it becomes particularly complex.

  Two types of harassment are at issue here:

  1. *Sexual harassment of an employee*: There are two forms of such harassment: demanding sexual favors or relations in exchange for promotion, job security, or other work-related actions (known as *quid pro quo* or economic harassment) or allowing an environment in which sexually explicit language, humor, images, and so on are present (this can be seen as harassment because some employees feel they are working in a *hostile environment*). This kind of harassment is illegal no matter who does the harassing or is harassed; men harassing men or women harassing women is no more acceptable than men harassing women or vice versa.

  2. *Harassment based on sexual orientation*: Sometimes employees are harassed based on their sexual orientation.

In such cases, the harassment generally has nothing to do with sexual favors. Instead, employees are taunted, humiliated, or even physically abused *because* they are gay, lesbian, or bisexual (or perceived to be). Such harassment is similar to name-calling or threats to African-Americans, Latino, or women because of their race or gender. Currently, there is no Federal law against harassment based on sexual orientation, but it is illegal in some states and cities. And it's always bad business.

The prudent thing is to protect employees from harassment and promptly investigate any claims.

Real Life Example

Gays were frequently the butt of jokes. Disparaging comments were common. No one at the office was "out" so the salesperson at the high-tech company decided not to let anyone know she was a lesbian. "I truly believed that if I came out, I could lose my job," she said. "At a minimum, I wondered about the territories I would get."

So she lived in the closet. She never mentioned the partner she went home to every night, the one offering encouragement, a sympathetic ear about difficult clients, and occasionally a shoulder rub. She never talked about her weekends or holidays. She often had lunch alone.

But professionally she was excelling. She surpassed sales goals and earned a bigger territory. The promotion required travel and, because everyone assumed she was single, she was asked to travel on weekends. Soon she was among the company's top salespeople. And the lying began.

Her job performance caught the attention of the CEO, who invited her to his home for dinner. In a panic, she called a good friend, a gay man with a partner of his own, and asked him to go with her as her "date." After that, her friend was her date for all company social events. People even began asking when they were going to get married.

Then she won a sales contest. The prize was a trip to the Caribbean. She took the trip with her friend; her partner stayed home. But that trip put a strain on her relationship and on her friend's home life. She was the company's top salesperson, producing more revenue than anyone else, but she quit; the strain had gotten to be too much.

"My boss never knew why I left," she says. "He still calls once in a while and tries to get me back. I loved that job, but I could never go back. Life is too short."

Do at Least the Minimum

Don't allow gay, lesbian, or bisexual employees to be treated with less respect than other employees.

Get More Information

Straight Jobs, Gay Lives: Gay and Lesbian Professionals, The Harvard Business School and the American Workplace, by Annette Friskopp and Sharon Silverstein, Touchstone Books, 1996.

Today's Diverse Workforce: A Glossary

The issues of workplace diversity and affirmative action are often hot buttons, and the emotions they elicit are often based on misunderstandings, so you and your employees may find these basic explanations helpful.

Affirmative action describes an effort to achieve equality in employment. President Johnson introduced the idea in 1965 when he signed Executive Order 11246. The order requires employers that do business with the Federal government to "develop affirmative-action plans to assure equal employment opportunity in their employment practices." Initially, that meant simply that companies pledged to take steps not to discriminate. To ensure that Federal contractors comply with the order, those employers are now required to monitor applicant pools to make sure they include women and minorities. Employers evaluate the data themselves (though reports are subject to government audit), and when they spot problems, they establish employment targets to ensure that women and minorities are represented in all segments of the work force. Some employers that are not Federal contactors elect to develop affirmative action efforts to improve the diversity of their workforces.

Equal Employment Opportunity Commission (EEOC) is the agency charged with enforcing Federal anti-discrimination laws.

Quotas are commitments to hire or promote a specific number or percentage of people in protected classes. Quotas are often seen as part of an affirmative action plan, but they are not. In fact, quotas are illegal. The only exceptions are when quotas are imposed as the outcome of a legal dispute in which an employer is found guilty of active discrimination. (Only judges may impose quotas.) In such cases, the quotas must be met.

Set-aside programs set aside some government contracts in a pool for minority- and women-owned businesses. They allow such businesses to win contracts even if they don't submit the lowest bid.

continued

Diversity is a concept that recognizes that many kinds of people are in today's workforce. It is often misused to suggest only race or race and gender. In reality, there are many other kinds of diversity. They include age, religion, varying abilities and disabilities, sexual orientation, education, and so on. As opposed to affirmative action (which addresses the workforce yet to be hired), diversity generally refers to employees already in place. Some people speak of *managing diversity,* a phrase that experts generally discourage because it suggests that diversity is a problem that somehow must be contained. A better phrase is *valuing diversity,* which describes a process of recognizing and appreciating differences, and using those differences for the benefit of the whole organization. It sees diversity as an opportunity, not a problem.

Reverse discrimination is phrase that describes a situation in which someone outside a protected class (a young white male, for example) is passed over for a job or promotion in favor of someone less qualified from a protected group. Such cases can attract a lot of attention, but actually they are rare; between 1990 and 1994, less than three percent of Federal discrimination cases were filed alleging reverse discrimination.

9

Managing Performance

A company or a department with low morale is about as cheery as a seedy nightclub in 1930s Berlin. When you look around, everyone you see looks angry or depressed. You hear cynical comments and caustic laughter coming from the lunchroom. Cubicles sport posters that say, "You obviously have mistaken me for someone who gives a damn." People are out "sick" in epidemic proportions. People get to work late and leave early. It's ugly.

It didn't get that way overnight. Low morale is the inevitable result of a lot of bad management. Decisions are second-guessed, mistakes are repeated, blame is assigned, poor work is ignored, training and performance reviews are not done, and recognition is overlooked. In short, low morale is a collective statement that employees feel adrift, ignored, and uninvolved.

Fortunately, high morale is within any manager's reach. It takes respectful leadership and a willingness to support employees. It takes

sincere recognition of work done well, and finishing fair performance appraisals on time. It also takes giving employees the help they need when they need it.

Maybe that sounds like common sense. If so, you're halfway home.

LEADERSHIP: HOW TO VARY YOUR STYLE TO GET RESULTS

Know the Issue

Good chefs need knives—many knives. They need knives with long and short blades that are serrated and smooth, and heavy and light. Good chefs know when and why to use each knife, whether they are slicing carrots or bread, boning fish, or spreading frosting.

Good leaders need different styles of leading: demanding and mobilizing, harmonious and consensus-building, driven and developmental. Good leaders know when and why to use each style. One style works best in a crisis whereas another helps forge a new vision; one helps heal and another builds competencies for the long-term.

Becoming a good leader who can use varied styles isn't easy. The only learning is trial and error. Good leaders are resilient and they look for options, so if one style doesn't work in a given situation, they try another. As they learn which style they're best at and which people respond to, they can draw on them as needed.

Getting to this point requires self-awareness, discipline, and a willingness to take risks. Ultimately, the leaders who are most comfortable with all six leadership styles are the leaders who get the best results. Isn't that what leadership is all about?

Take Action

- *Know the six styles.* It used to be that good leadership was like good art: no one could define it, but everyone knew it when they saw it. Recent research by the consulting firm Hay/McBer, however, has clarified what good leadership really is. The research drew on the experience of more than 3,800 executives worldwide and found that there are six basic leadership styles: coercive, authoritative, affiliative, democratic, pacesetting, and coaching. (See "Leadership Styles: A Primer," pages 247–251)

  Each style reflects underlying emotional intelligence competencies (see "Emotional Intelligence," pages 191–199). Empathy, self-awareness, and the ability to develop others are the foundation of the coaching style, for example. Each style works best then when deployed in the appropriate circumstance and doesn't work at all when used inappropriately. Using a coercive ("because I said so") style, for example, is disastrous when consensus is needed.

  Each style also has an impact on the organization's climate. Two of the six styles are negative.

- *Know yourself.* After even a quick review of the six styles, one style will probably feel right. That's the style that comes most naturally to you. Now pay attention to how you interact with your staff. Do you use solely that style, or do you use others as well? Do you use varied styles on your own, or only when your boss forces you to? Which style gets the best results, or does it depend on the situation?

- *Ask your employees.* Ask a few of your employees which leadership style you use because it's hard to see yourself objectively. Ask employees who you trust to be truthful, even though they are not necessarily your favorite employee. You want honesty, not fawning.

- *Observe your staff.* Just as we all *use* different leadership styles, we also *respond* to different styles. Someone with an affiliative personality, for example, won't feel warm and fuzzy toward a pacesetter-style leader. Which styles do members of your staff respond to? It's unlikely that your employees all respond to the same style.

- *Challenge yourself.* Think about situations in your department that might benefit from different leadership styles and work at using some of the emotional intelligence skills required in those situations. If your style is affiliative, for example, work on your collaborative skills to forge a more democratic style, or work at developing the potential in your employees to become better at coaching. Stretching yourself is important because even generally positive styles can become negative if they're used in every situation. Too much of an affiliative style, for example, can leave a group feeling rudderless. The group might feel good about each other, yet still fail.

  If your style is naturally coercive or pacesetting—the two leadership styles with negative impacts—you'll want to balance your approach with more positive styles.

- *Find mentors.* You can easily identify the leadership style of anyone you know. Pay attention to other people in your organization or even outside it. Single out those who use the styles you'd like to learn and observe them. Look for examples of how they get things done.

- *Experiment.* In the end, thinking and observing will get you only so far. To grow, you must take the plunge and actually try different styles in different situations and see what works for you in your company. Be bold. As William James once advised, "To change one's life: start immediately, do it flamboyantly—no exceptions."

Manage Up

Observe your boss's style. What can you learn from her? Help your boss by using styles that complement her style. If your boss is a pacesetter, for example, being an affiliator can help balance this style and improve productivity and morale. Just don't do it in a way that undercuts your boss.

Discuss your leadership style with your boss. Then share your plans to develop other styles and ask for candid feedback about your attempts.

Leadership Styles: A Primer

Recent research by the consulting firm Hay/McBer found six basic leadership styles, though the most effective leaders use all the styles at least occasionally. Daniel Goleman, a Hay/McBer consultant and author of *Emotional Intelligence and Working with Emotional*

continued

Intelligence, has analyzed the six styles to determine their strengths and weaknesses, the situations in which they work best, and their overall impact on the climate of an organization or department.

Coercive

Basic Approach: Demands immediate compliance

Catch phrase: "Do what I tell you."

Underlying emotional intelligence competencies: The drive to achieve, initiative, self-control

Strengths: Willing to make tough decisions; can break failed business habits; can shock people into new ways of working

Weaknesses: Kills new ideas on the vine; people feel disrespected; sense of responsibility evaporates; damages the rewards system; employees become resentful.

When the style works best: In a crisis; when kick-starting a turnaround; with problem employees

Overall impact on climate: Negative; it is the least effective of the six styles.

Authoritative

Basic Approach: Mobilizes people toward a vision

Catch phrase: "Come with me."

Underlying emotional intelligence competencies: Self-confidence, empathy, change catalyst

Strengths: Helps people see how their work supports the broader mission; maximizes commitment; standards for success are clear, as are rewards; people have the freedom to innovate and take calculated risks.

Weaknesses: Leader may be seen as pompous or out-of-touch; the spirit of effective teams can be undermined.

continued

When the style works best: When changes require a new vision; when a clear direction is needed

Overall impact on climate: Strongly positive; it is the most effective of the six styles.

Affiliative

Basic Approach: Creates harmony and builds emotional bonds

Catch phrase: "People come first."

Underlying emotional intelligence competencies: Empathy, building relationships, communication

Strengths: Has a markedly positive effect on communication; flexibility rises; people get ample positive feedback; people have a sense of belonging.

Weaknesses: Poor performance may go uncorrected; employees may feel that mediocrity is tolerated; employees must figure out how to improve on their own and may feel rudderless.

When the style works best: To heal rifts in a team; to motivate people during stressful circumstances

Overall impact on climate: Positive

Democratic

Basic Approach: Forges consensus through participation

Catch phrase: "What do you think?"

Underlying emotional intelligence competencies: Collaboration, team leadership, communication

Strengths: Builds trust, respect, and commitment; drives up flexibility and responsibility; people tend to be very realistic about what can and can't be accomplished.

continued

Weaknesses: Endless meetings; consensus remains elusive; critical decisions may be postponed.

When the style works best: To build buy-in or consensus; to get input from valuable employees

Overall impact on climate: Positive

Pacesetting

Basic Approach: Sets high standards for performance

Catch phrase: "Do as I do, now."

Underlying emotional intelligence competencies: Conscientiousness, drive to achieve, initiative

Strengths: Sets extremely high standards and exemplifies them; obsessed with doing things better and faster; demands a lot from people and replaces those who don't rise to the occasion.

Weaknesses: Employees feel overwhelmed; morale drops; people second-guess what the leader wants; flexibility and responsibility evaporate; work becomes routinized.

When the style works best: To get quick results from a highly motivated and competent team.

Overall impact on climate: Negative

Coaching

Basic Approach: Develops people for the future

Catch phrase: "Try this."

Underlying emotional intelligence competencies: Developing others, empathy, self-awareness

Strengths: Employees understand their unique strengths and weaknesses; employees set long-term career goals; plentiful instruction and feedback; excellent at delegating

continued

Weaknesses: May focus on long-term development at the expense of work-related tasks; fails if the leader lacks expertise

When the style works best: To help an employee improve performance or develop long-term strengths.

Overall impact on climate: Positive

Source: "Leadership That Gets Results," Daniel Goleman, *Harvard Business Review,* March-April 2000.

MANAGING 101: HOW TO BE THE BOSS TODAY'S EMPLOYEES NEED

Know the Issue

True, Microsoft's Bill Gates is smart and GE's Jack Welch is dynamic, but our management role model is Glinda, the Good Witch.

Glinda? Yep. Think about it: Not only did Dorothy get home, but ultimately *she* figured out how to do it. Along the way, she found strength and resourcefulness in herself she had never seen. She learned from her mistakes. She faced challenges with courage, and relied on her friends for support.

Yes, Glinda got results, but she was no micromanager. She simply pointed Dorothy in the right direction ("Follow the Yellow Brick Road"), gave her the resources she needed (the Ruby slippers), and removed a few obstacles (such as the Wicked Witch of the West's sleeping spell) when it was judicious to do so.

Swatch workers would be thrilled to work for Glinda. You can learn from her example.

Take Action

- *Expect the best.* No one goes to work to do a bad job. Teachers, directors, coaches, and generals will all tell you the same thing: people do what's expected of them. If you give an assignment and then stand back to wait for the screw-up, you won't have to wait long. On the other hand, if you give an assignment that seems just beyond an employee's reach, people usually rise to the occasion.

  People occasionally fall short of their best, and when that happens they disappoint themselves and you. But people almost never fail intentionally. Give them the benefit of the doubt. As Abraham Lincoln observed, "It's better to trust and be disappointed occasionally than to distrust and be miserable all the time."

  If you really believe that your people aren't capable, ask yourself two questions: are they in the wrong job? Are you?

- *Put work in context.* People perform best when they feel they are part of something. Help people understand how they contribute to the overall mission and goals of the company. Do hotel laundry workers just wash sheets, or do they play a vital role in the guests' overall experience? Employees who don't see that connection wonder why it's important to do a good job.

  Once they know the overall mission, set goals to help them achieve that mission: how many guests do they need to please today?

- *Be clear.* When making those assignments, be clear. One boss routinely made assignments by scrawling instructions on scratch paper and leaving the scrawls on an employee's chair or in his in-box. Inevitably, employees would take the scrawl to a co-worker for help in deciphering it. Sometimes large groups worked together to decode the messages.

  Why didn't they just ask? Because if they did the boss would snatch back the assignment and yell, or she would tell them that they were paid to figure it out. It never seemed to occur to her that *none* of her staff could decipher what she wanted, and that an incredible amount of time was being wasted trying to figure it out or redoing tasks they'd misinterpreted.

  If you write instructions, read them to yourself slowly. If you followed them literally, could you do what you're asking the employee to do? If you aren't sure, have someone else read them. If you give instructions verbally, ask employees to repeat them to you, and ask whether they have any questions.

- *Give employees the resources they need.* You wouldn't send a Boy Scout on a weekend camping trip without a sleeping bag, a canteen, and a compass. Don't ask employees to do a job without the resources either. Consider

  - Are enough people assigned to the task?
  - Have you allowed enough time?
  - Do people have the appropriate equipment?
  - Do they have enough information?
  - Do they know where they can go for help?

- *Let employees do the work.* Once employees know the goal and have the resources they need, get out of their way. Resist any temptation you may have to micromanage. Nothing can be gained by standing over someone's shoulder, and a lot can be lost. Yes, employees will do it differently than you would. That's OK.

- *Remove obstacles.* Twelve Parisian streets come together in a star formation at Place d'Etoile. In the center is the Arc de Triomphe, and if you stand on top of it for five minutes you're guaranteed to see at least one traffic accident. From that vantage point, you can see the big picture and anticipate where the accidents will happen. If you could somehow communicate with the drivers below, you could prevent many fender benders.

   As the boss, you *can* communicate with the drivers if you see an accident ahead. Do it! But as a boss you can do better than that. You have more clout in the organization. Use it! Picture yourself as a traffic cop in d'Etoile. You can stop lanes of traffic, block cars from entering, or make drivers slow down. Do what you can to help your people maneuver through the traffic to get where they're going.

- *Don't give employees the answers.* Employees will come to you for help, and if you're busy or tired you'll tell them what to do. Don't. Every time you do it, you encourage them to come to you with the next problem. After all, it's easier to get the answer than it is to figure it out.

   But no one learns anything by getting the answer. Instead, ask employees what they've tried. Explore why it didn't work. Ask them what options they've considered. What do they see as the pros and cons of each? If they're not seeing some things, ask questions to gently open their eyes. Challenge sloppy thinking or miscalculations, but don't just tell employees what to do.

If employees get to the solution themselves, they'll take greater responsibility and have greater ownership.

- *Vary your style.* We're not all the same. Not exactly a head-line ripped from this morning's newspaper is it? Yet many managers continue to treat their people as if they are all the same; everyone receives the same instruction, the same way, every time.

  Manager Gilbert G. Bendix told WorkingWounded.com that it helps to think of employees as chefs. "One employee is like the chef who doesn't need a cookbook," he says. "Give him oral instructions once and know that the job will be done and done right. But another worker forgets simple instructions by the time he reaches his workstation. He needs different help: a detailed recipe with all the ingredients listed at the top."

  Match your style to what employees need.

- *Don't stereotype.* We all know some stereotypes about per-formance: white men can't jump, women aren't good at math, or older people are forgetful. Even though they're only occa-sionally accurate, and more often just plain wrong, that hasn't diminished their ubiquity. Still, you should be careful to avoid them.

  In a landmark study, Stanford University psychologist Claude Steele showed that it's the targets of a stereotype whose behavior is most affected by it. Steele and his colleague Joshua Aronson observed that stereotypes make people so painfully aware of how they're seen that the knowledge affects their performance.

For example, the University of Arizona's Jeff Stone found that women who were reminded of their gender even in the subtlest ways before taking an exam scored significantly lower than women who didn't get the reminder. Furthermore, stereotypes seem to affect star performers most strongly.

Avoid stereotyping employees—even in a positive way and even in jest. There's nothing funny about a stereotype.

- *Let employees fail.* If we all had to be perfect the first time, no one would ever have seen a circus trapeze act. Sometimes employees fall. The solution is not to keep them from trying to catch the trapeze. The solution is to be sure that they have a net beneath them and the confidence to climb the ladder and try again.

- *Help employees learn from their mistakes.* When employees screw up, count to 10 and resist the urge to get mad. Instead, use these talking points to help employees learn:

  - What went wrong?

  - When did it go wrong? Could they have seen the problem earlier?

  - Why did it go wrong? Was the mistake inevitable, or the result of a freak incident?

  - When did they notice something was wrong? Did they take action then or hope it would get better? Did they ignore their gut or warnings from others?

- Were they lacking information? If so, where could they have found the information?
- Does the incident remind them of any other mistakes they've made?
- What will they do differently next time? Why?

- *Don't play favorites.* It's only natural to like some people better than others, but this is work, not dating. Don't make work decisions based on your personal feelings. Ask yourself who is best qualified to do the work. Be consistent in making assignments and bestowing privileges. (Don't take your favorites to lunch to talk about tasks while others get an email.)

- *Think "we."* Here are some words to strike from your vocabulary: I, me, my, mine. (Put a quarter in a jar every time you use them and give them to your employees at the end of the year.) Don't refer to management as "us" and to employees as "you."

  Remember, you're all in this together. Talk about what *we* will do, what *our* customers expect and so on. Never set yourself above or apart from the team.

  Don't stay above the fray either. If there's work to be done and you can do it, pitch in and help. Employees resent bosses who won't get their hands dirty stuffing envelopes, answering phones, or making copies occasionally. Is the work important, or isn't it?

Stay Out of Jail

Mistakes may be inevitable and excellent learning opportunities, but that doesn't mean you should avoid written warning and discipline in all cases. Think of discipline as a form of education. Failure to take disciplinary action can lower the bar as to employee expectations and lead to more mistakes.

Real Life Examples

- When Kelly was appointed acting director of an emergency medical services coordinating system, her first challenge was dealing with the department's secretary, Rose. Rose was often seen painting her fingernails; she resisted deadlines and instructions; and she generally was seen as unwilling or unable. "No" was her favorite word.

  Given her reputation, Kelly was surprised when Rose mentioned that she had figured out how to do mail merge on an outdated computer system with barely 64K of memory. Because Kelly was replacing the antiquated system, she asked Rose if she would like to have the new computers in her office. Rose's face lit up. "I saw that I was on to something," Kelly says.

  They talked about rearranging the office to accommodate the new system. Kelly asked Rose where she thought everything should go and how it all should be arranged. "I took her advice on everything," Kelly says, "which apparently no one had ever done before. She became another person: willing, hard-working, dependable, totally 'with it.' She went from being an employee everyone barely tolerated to one who should have been employee of the year. It really taught me a lesson about managing people. The manager's true job is to serve those that work for her, in the sense that you give them the power and the assets they need to do their job, and permission to do it pretty much their own way, and you get happy, hard-working people who exceed all expectations."

- The CEO of a software firm called a meeting of the technical support department and proceeded to lecture them on what a poor job they were doing with his customers. "He actually used the phrase 'my customers' several times during this diatribe; in his mind, we clearly weren't part of the team," says Steve, an employee who was in the meeting. "He capped it off and lost any remaining respect we had for him when he told us that none of us cared about his customers. Now, you can tell me I have a thing or two to learn and I'll likely go along with you. You can even tell me I need to work harder —no one is 100 percent efficient. But don't tell me I don't care about the people I've been doing my best to help for more than a year, despite getting very poor training."

Years later, the employees who were there—now working elsewhere—still talk about that meeting.

INFORMAL RECOGNITION: HOW TO KEEP PEOPLE MOTIVATED

Know the Issue

It starts with the gold star on a kindergarten drawing. As we grow older, there are Twinkies passed between friends at recess, notes written in yearbooks, and boosts onto the team's shoulders after scoring the winning touchdown. We are endlessly inventive at finding ways to recognize each other.

Except, it seems, at work. In researching this book, we heard hundreds of stories—good and bad—about what really happens on the job. It's telling that recognition was the issue that came up most often. People feel their work is largely unrecognized, or that it's recognized in ways that actually do more harm than good.

That's disappointing for many reasons, not least of which is that recognition is one of the easiest, cleanest, and least expensive things a manager can do. Almost nothing offers as much bang for the buck, yet we parcel out praise as if we had a very limited supply.

Break the mold. Dole out recognition with the fervor of a Swedish welfare worker, not the parsimony of Ebenezer Scrooge. Find reasons to recognize people, not reasons not to. Get creative like a kid with the Big box of Crayolas. Then watch your employees surpass your greatest expectations.

Take Action

- *Decide what you want to encourage.* Any recognition you offer sends a message to employees, so be sure you're sending the right message. In her book, *Management Would Be Easy . . . If It Weren't for the People,* Patricia Addesso talks about a software firm that recognized employees who eliminated bugs from a program. It was a great idea until employees started putting bugs *into* programs just so they could get rewarded for taking them out. It would have made more sense if the company had offered to reward employees who created bug-free programs in the first place.

- *Think small.* We're all ready to recognize the employee who cures cancer or puts a man on Mars, but those career-making events happen about as often as the Cubs win the World Series. Recognize the incremental step, the deadline beaten by days, the customer kudo, or the embarrassing error caught in time. The recognition needn't be much; a simple "thank you" or a chocolate bar on someone's desk makes a big difference.

- *Be relentless.* Saying thanks once or twice a year is nice, but it won't have a big impact on your group's culture. Make recognition a habit. Don't recognize people just to do it (recognition should always be earned), but do it at least often enough that people still remember the previous time.

- *Keep your personal feelings out of it.* Be careful not to recognize only those employees who are most vocal or who you like best. Recognize people strictly for their work performance.

- *Make it personal.* Any recognition means more if it's personal and therefore special. If you know something about an employee's hobbies or interests, try to tie what you do to those interests. You might give a can of tennis balls to a tennis nut, or movie passes to someone who wouldn't dream of missing the Oscars. One boss had an employee who collected postcards, and made a point of sending her one whenever he traveled, each one praising her for something she'd done.

  Be sensitive in your choices. Don't give a big box of candy to someone on a diet, for example.

- *Be prompt.* To make the most of recognition, offer it as close to the accomplishment as possible. Make it seem spontaneous. Belabored recognition offered weeks or months after the fact isn't as meaningful. (But yes, late is better than never.)

- *Remember the team.* Sometimes it's tough to single out just one person. When that happens, recognize everyone. Send the group to lunch or bring them all breakfast. Let people know you recognize a group effort.

- *Don't get in a rut.* Vary the recognition you offer to keep it fresh. Create a bank of ideas and then use them all. Recognition that becomes rote isn't too motivating.

- *Be creative.* Recognition is one big opportunity to have *fun.* Let your imagination run rampant and use all the tools at your disposal:

  - *Time*: Can you let people off early? Give them a longer lunch hour? Let them sleep in? Offer a day off?

  - *Money*: Cash is nice, of course, but so are gift certificates, movie passes, frequent flyer miles, and so on.

  - *Food*: Everyone has to eat. Consider lunch out or bringing lunch in. Bring in a gourmet coffee bar or have ice cream sundaes one afternoon. There are also the old reliable doughnuts, popcorn, cookies, and Thanksgiving turkeys.

  - *Gifts*: The number of small gifts you can offer is limited only by the number of catalogs and Internet shopping sites you can find.

  - *Presentation*: Say thanks in a handwritten note or with a card. If your employees speak English as a second language, have notes translated into their native language occasionally. Recognize people with balloons or flowers. And don't get your head stuck in the office; surprise a star salesperson by having champagne waiting in her room the next time she hits the road.

- *Offer at least some recognition privately.* Business Analyst Louis Ratcliffe points out that if you recognize people in staff meetings, but always take someone into your office to chew them out, then everyone knows what's happening anyway: it might as well be a public reprimand. If you praise privately, nobody knows what's being said and the dignity of the people receiving reprimands is saved.

- *Remember that not all accomplishments are equal.* Some achievements are a big deal and the recognition you offer should also be a big deal. (See "Formal Recognition," pages 266–271)

- *Accept that you'll screw up.* Eventually, you'll overlook someone who felt he really deserved recognition. It happens. Apologize and move on. Employees will forgive you if you make a consistent effort. If most employees feel recognized most of the time, consider your efforts successful.

Stay Out of Jail

- *Keep your recognition work-related.*

Real Life Examples

- Wayne Hartrick is CEO of Verus Group International, a public relations consulting firm in Vancouver, British Columbia. Hartrick believes in rewarding employees and he also has a sense of humor. Consequently, the company gives several annual awards that recognize that life at work is rarely perfect or easy:

  - The Corkscrew Award recognizes funny screw-ups that have happy endings. The award takes its name from an incident in which simultaneous celebrations at 10 different bank branches were held up while Verus employees searched frantically for corkscrews for the wine. It turned out that the employee who bought the wine had thoughtfully chosen bottles with screw tops. The event was a huge success, so today winners receive a plaque with a corkscrew.

- The Baker Street Award is also a plaque. In honor of Sherlock Holmes, this award is emblazoned with a magnifying glass and a mouse. It's given to employees who use research most effectively.

- The Spin of the Year Award is for the top accomplishment in the firm.

The awards are consistent with the Verus culture, which includes rainy Monday breakfasts and beer and pizza on Fridays after an especially busy week.

"Little things like that really help keep morale high when everyone is busy and a bit short-tempered because of the underlying stress of finishing a project on time," says Juanita Odin, Executive Assistant to the CEO and president. "And it encourages everyone to do well."

- "Although programming was my primary responsibility, there were times I helped the documentation team by writing the more technical sections of manuals," says Catherine, a software engineer. "I considered it just part of my job, and even when the writing team won a national award for one of the manuals, it didn't cross my mind that I deserved any recognition. My manager, however, thought otherwise and gave me an American Express Gift Check in a large denomination!

I was overwhelmed by his thoughtfulness and his desire to make sure I was also rewarded."

- Priscilla Ware is a boss who likes to break up the routine. She and another manager stage monthly "unexpected" days. They dress in goofy clothes (cheerleader outfits or feather boas, for example) and have a related treat to hand employees during the day. On Mardi Gras Day, they passed out beads all day and had Cajun food brought in for lunch. "Our employees can't wait to see what we'll do next," Ware says. "The laughter breaks up an otherwise boring job."

- Employees had been working for months to solve a problem that jeopardized the company's biggest contract. Nothing had worked, and it looked like the company wouldn't meet its commitment and would pay stiff penalties. One evening an exhausted employee took a break and went to a movie. During the movie, he had a brainstorm and rushed back to the office. He shared his idea, and employees who were still there offered to help him test it. The test worked, and his idea saved the contract. Soon after, the employee was called into the CEO's office. He thought he would hear "thank you," but instead he was reprimanded for working overtime without authorization and for distracting people from their assigned duties. Today, the employee is sharing his brilliant ideas with another employer.

Do at Least the Minimum

Say "thank you" for a job well done. And say it like you mean it.

Get More Information

1001 Ways To Reward Employees, Bob Nelson, Workman Publishing Co., 1994.

Love 'Em or Lose 'Em: Getting Good People To Stay, Beverly Kaye and Sharon Jordan-Evans, Berrett-Koehler Publishers, Inc., 1999.

Management Would Be Easy . . . If It Weren't for the People, Patricia Addesso, Amacom Books, 1996.

FORMAL RECOGNITION: HOW TO CELEBRATE MILESTONES

Know the Issue

Sally Field will never live it down. Accepting her second Oscar, she blurted, "You like me! You really like me!" She's been teased and parodied ever since, but it was an unguarded response to a moment she had worked her whole life to achieve: the acclaim of her peers before family, friends, colleagues, and a billion strangers. (And a chance to wear a cool dress, too.)

Few of us get moments quite like that, but that doesn't mean that we don't long for and deserve public recognition. True, you don't want to throw a party every time one of your employees straightens up his desk or even does a good job, but your company, your department, your teams, and your individual employees all achieve milestones worthy of star-studded recognition:

- New product or service launches
- New patents

- Personal development (earning a graduate degree, for example)
- Opening an overseas market or office
- Meeting earnings or profit goals that were a stretch
- An IPO
- Promotions
- Outside recognition (winning a national award, for instance)
- Maintaining a safety record for an extended period
- Meeting specific long-term business goals (increasing the percentage of flights to arrive on time, for example)
- Retirements

Take advantage of these milestones to create formal recognition ceremonies. These ceremonies can recognize individuals, teams, or entire departments. They can be lavish, whole-company affairs or small staff meeting presentations. The important thing is to make the recognition sincere, appropriate, and public.

Take Action

- *Make the reward reflect the winner.* Recognize personal milestones with trophies, plaques, or merchandise. (Cash is usually a poor choice because it is quickly spent or banked and therefore has a short afterlife. Trophies, on the other hand, are kept, and remind employees of their accomplishments.) It's OK to reward individuals during other events, such as staff meetings. When recognizing teams or groups of employees, create events that allow the team to celebrate together (such as a chili cook-off or a party).

- *Tell employees how to win.* Although informal recognition is actually enhanced if it's a surprise, formal recognition is another matter. If something in your company is important enough to merit formal recognition, employees need to know ahead of time what that thing is and what they have to do to earn it.

  Create and share a structure for achieving the recognition:

  - What must one do to be recognized?
  - Who decides who gets recognized?
  - When will the recognition be made?
  - What are the rules? (For example, are employees on disciplinary probation eligible?)
  - What form will the recognition take? (A trophy? Money? A new car?)
  - Is it a one-time event, or will it be annual?

    Make sure the recognition is fair and objective; don't play favorites.

- *Remember presentation counts.* One employee was startled to see his award slid under the stall partition in the men's room because that's where he happened to be when his boss decided it was time to present it. Somehow, the presentation undercut the impact of the award.

  Employees should feel that the recognition is something special, not an afterthought. You can't always bust the budget with a lobster dinner for 500, but do what you can to make the occasion memorable. Even cheap trimmings (balloons and streamers) can turn a presentation at a staff meeting into a ceremony. If you can afford more, do it. (One CEO flew his entire staff and their families to the Caribbean for a week.)

As you plan, keep your efforts in scale. Don't make an event to honor a single employee splashier than the ceremony recognizing the company-wide milestone.

- *Reflect your culture.* Events work best when they mirror the prevailing culture. If you're in a freewheeling start-up company, a black-tie dinner may not be what gets employees most excited. On the other hand, swing night at the roller rink might not be the best choice for commercial bankers. Events should feel like a natural (albeit special) extension of the workplace. If you're unsure what would most appeal to employees, ask.

- *Don't attach strings.* One boss complained that employees never thanked her when she recognized them. She likened the recognition to Christmas or birthday gifts and said she expected comparable thank-yous. She decided to solve the problem when she recognized employees who worked on a new product launch. She sent them all notes letting them know they would be recognized at a staff event and instructed them to prepare a thank-you speech. She included a list of elements each speech should include. "I didn't feel like I got an award," one employee said. "I felt like I got punished."

Recognition is not a gift—it's something that's been earned. Recognition is about *them,* not *you.*

- *Make it personal.* Occasionally, employees may win an award or otherwise be recognized outside the company (by a national trade association in your industry, for example). That kind of recognition is priceless, but employees want to know that it mattered to you, too. Send them flowers or a gift certificate to express your congratulations.

Stay Out of Jail

- *Tie any recognition to the work.* Don't play favorites.
- *Make sure recognition is warranted; don't do it just to make people feel better.* If an employee claims unlawful discipline or discharge, expect to see a trophy as Exhibit One of her worthiness. Did she deserve it?

Real Life Examples

- Only a handful of employees ever earn one of the highest honors the company bestows. Colleagues nominate recipients for exemplifying the company's values the best. A panel reviews the nominations, and the employees' managers are consulted. Mike was lucky enough to win one, and his co-workers were thrilled; no one deserved it more. But when the day came to present the award, Mike's manager was out. Rather than wait for her to return, the company asked another manager to make the presentation—a manager Mike barely knew. Not only was Mike disappointed, the manager missed her chance to publicly recognize her star employee, his co-workers missed the chance to have a group celebration, and the company missed an opportunity to make a coveted award mean all that it might have.
- Because of changes in the company, the team had had five managers in nine months. Understandably, many things fell through the cracks, including Carla's 10-year pin. Several of her co-workers, who had started at the company just weeks earlier than she had, had been invited to an elegant luncheon,

but Carla had missed the cutoff date. The next 10-year luncheon never happened, and so neither did the presentation of her pin. Months had passed by the time someone noticed the oversight. No one offered a luncheon, but they did tell Carla she would get her pin. When the moment came, one of the managers making the presentation looked at the other and said, "Now, what trick should we make her do to get this?" Carla had had enough. "Never mind," she shouted. "Keep your damn pin!"

Get More Information

1001 Ways to Reward Employees, Bob Nelson, Workman Publishing Co., 1994.

Love 'Em or Lose 'Em: Getting Good People to Stay, Beverly Kaye and Sharon Jordan-Evans, Berrett-Koehler Publishers, Inc., 1999.

DOCUMENTING PERFORMANCE: HOW TO BE FAIR, COMPLETE, AND LEGAL

Know the Issue

We're good at documenting many things:

"He leads the league in late-in-the-game stolen bases against left-handed pitchers."

"That's the fourth-best movie opening ever for a non-comedy in October."

"The stock closed at its highest price since May 9, 1993, when
it was buoyed by a higher earnings projection . . ."

Unfortunately, job performance isn't one of them. If it were,
we'd find personnel files with notes like this:

"Joan had the sixth-best day of her tenure today when she
processed more checks than on any post-holiday Tuesday
since our merger with GigantiCorp . . ."

OK, it's a bit much, but it's better than the familiar alternatives,
which are inaccurate or incomplete documentation or no documentation at all.

There is a happy medium: consistent, objective, honest, and
thorough documentation of milestones and key conversations.
Although that sort of record won't give you the cocktail party cache
of sports stats, it will make for better performance reviews, better
management decisions, and a better defense in court.

Take Action

- *Keep track of the big stuff.* You can't document everything,
  or that's all you'd ever do, but you can and must document
  key management decisions and the events that influenced
  them. So, what is the big stuff?
  - Counseling and other conversations that could be important
    in the future regarding discipline, pay, transfer, promotion,
    demotion, and so forth. Include meetings that you initiate
    (such as counseling an employee about tardiness) and meet-
    ings initiated by the employee (such as conversations in
    which she expresses interest in a transfer or promotion).

- Discipline, including verbal warnings, written warnings, suspensions, and demotions
- Evidence of training the employee received
- Changes in employment (such as raises, promotions, transfers, and commission agreements)

If there's ever a question about employee performance, you want an accurate record of what was expected, the rewards for meeting those expectations, the consequences for not meeting them, and the training and other support offered to help employees. You also want a record that you will be proud to show to a jury—one that is professional, concise, and based only on work-related issues. You *don't* want things to degenerate into "he said, she said" finger pointing with nothing to back you up. If that happens, it will cast doubt on your management ability.

Most interaction with employees is conversational, so it's lost unless you make a record of it. Document what was said (not word for word, but generally) by both of you. Note the outcome of the conversation. For example: "I pointed out to Julie that she has been tardy six times in the last month on the following dates: August 9, 15, 17, 24, and September 3 and 5. She had no protected reason for the tardiness. This number of absences clearly exceeds what our policies permit. I told Julie that if she's late again during the next 30 days without a valid reason (such as a necessary medical appointment) that I will give her a written warning that will go into her file, and that if she's late two or more times in the next 30 days she could face further discipline, including suspension. Julie explained that she had been having car trouble, but said that she understood and made a commitment to get to work on time."

If a problem gets to the point that a written reprimand is required (see "Discipline," pages 310–315), then a copy of the reprimand, signed by you and the employee, should be part of your documentation.

- *Be prompt.* No matter how well intentioned you are, you won't remember the details of your conversations. Notes made weeks or months after the fact aren't as credible as notes made right away. Do your documenting as soon as possible and date whatever you write.

- *Be open.* Give the documentation of the conversation to the employee. Have the employee sign it to acknowledge that he received it. *Always* allow a place (and sufficient space) for the employee to reply.

- *Keep the documentation.* All documentation should go into the employee's personnel file. That way you can find it when you need it.

- *Limit access to the documentation.* Keeping documentation in the file also keeps it confidential. The only people who should see it are the employee, you, members of the HR staff, and senior management. Even then, no one should see it unless there's a specific management reason to do so.

- *Don't forget informal documentation.* In addition to the formal documentation we've discussed, it's also helpful to keep informal documentation. Many reviews suffer from focusing only on recent events because that's what managers can remember. You can avoid that if you keep notes when employees do something well, or if you notice opportunities for improvement. Because the notes are for you, use any format that works, but keep them brief (for example, "Lillian found a billing error that saved us $10,000") so you aren't discouraged from doing it.

Stay Out of Jail

- *Be absolutely honest.* Don't sugarcoat the truth, or praise employees if you aren't sincere (in hopes of motivating them, for example) or the compliment isn't relevant to their job performance. If a performance problem arises, documentation should prove it, not refute it.

- *Stick to the facts.* Don't speculate. Avoid hearsay and don't express generic opinions. For example, don't just write "I have lost confidence in this employee's judgment." Explain specifically what happened that caused you to lose faith in his or her judgment.

- *Stick to work-related facts.* Employees' personal lives, beliefs, race, religion, pregnancy status, marital status, and so on are irrelevant to job performance and therefore have *no place* in documentation.

- *Verbal discipline isn't worth the paper it isn't written on.* Employees intentionally and unintentionally recall the praise and ignore verbal criticism.

- *Remember that documentation can be a double-edged sword. Never* put anything in writing you would feel uncomfortable having read to a jury slowly, in detail, and while projected on a PowerPoint slide. According to at least one expert, poor, incomplete, dishonest, and inaccurate documentation is the single most common reason that employees file and win employment-related lawsuits.

Real Life Example

The manager pulled no punches when he called the VP of HR. "I can't stand it anymore," he said. "I have an employee who has a bad attitude, who's chronically late, and who makes a lot of mistakes. She's not doing a good job. She needs to be fired. Preferably today."

The VP of HR agreed that if the employee really had that many performance problems she should be terminated. He offered to look at the facts in the case and develop a plan.

When he went to the file, however, the VP of HR was stunned: everything in it was positive. There was no mention of a bad attitude, tardiness, or poor work.

He called the manager to ask how long there had been a problem. "Ever since we hired her six years ago," the manager said.

"But there's nothing in the file except reviews saying she's been doing a good job," the VP said.

"Well," the manager snapped, "everyone *knows* this employee is a problem."

Everyone, apparently, except the employee herself. The VP of HR explained that there was no way to fire the employee without risking a wrongful termination suit, and even if it were possible it wouldn't be fair.

Instead of firing the poor performer and hiring the young star he had lined up to replace her, the manager began the long and painful process of documenting all the problems "everyone" knew about. The process was made longer and more painful because of the years of running away from the problem instead of doing the employee and the company the favor of addressing and possibly changing the behavior.

PERFORMANCE REVIEWS: HOW TO KEEP EMPLOYEES ON TRACK

Know the Issue

There are all those needles: for blood tests, flu shots, and some of unknown purpose. There are urine samples, cold stethoscopes, and lots of time to catch up on old (really old) magazines while sick people cough all around you. Fun, isn't it? No wonder that despite the fact that annual physicals have proven health benefits, many of us avoid them.

There are proven benefits to annual performance reviews, too. Yet as many, or more of us avoid them, too. It requires all that paperwork. Employees argue about what's written or, worse, cry. You're unlikely to get any rewards from your own boss for doing reviews, let alone doing them well. No wonder they're one of the least popular responsibilities managers have.

Although reviews often settle at the bottom of a manager's to-do list, almost nothing bugs employees more than reviews that are late, inaccurate, or never happen. Employees are right—reviews *are* necessary. You may believe that employees "know how they're doing," but in fact they often don't know. Even if they do know, they want their perceptions validated. Without objective reviews, many of your decisions about raises, promotions, and so on may seem (or even be) arbitrary and unfair.

There is no magic to make reviews stress-free, but you can take certain steps to make them valuable development tools, to enhance your credibility as a manager, help keep you out of court, and help you and your company if one of your decisions is tested by a lawsuit.

Take Action

- *Make reviews a priority.* Block out time on your calendar to write them and to meet with employees. (Share the date with employees so that you have an incentive to do the review. Then hold to the date unless you have a really good reason not to.) If need be, take time out of the office to focus on writing the review. If doing reviews is right up there with filing a tax return on your list of favorite tasks, reward yourself for getting them done on time with a nice lunch, a sundae, or a round of golf.

- *Tie reviews to something.* Some business gurus now argue that reviews should be detached from raises, promotions, or other rewards. The theory is that if the two are linked, then employees pay attention only to the amount of the raise and ignore the feedback about their performance. We disagree. We see just the opposite: reviews measure progress against goals and expectations. If the goals are met, employees should be rewarded. (The reward doesn't have to be a raise—it might be a chance to work on a really cool new project, or other perk.) What sort of work would students produce if they had no idea whether their efforts would earn an A, a D, or no grade at all?

Having said that, you may want to detach cost-of-living increases from reviews. Such increases are generally given to all employees to keep pace with inflation. They aren't tied to performance, but people may believe they are if they are discussed during the review. (It's a mistake to give any discretionary raise to an employee at risk of being terminated for poor performance.) Although detaching cost-of-living raises from reviews may mean that people get smaller boosts, they may get raises more often. (For example, Dorothy may get a three percent cost-of-living raise in April when the company's fiscal year begins and a two percent merit increase in September on her employment anniversary, rather than a five percent increase all at once.)

- *Be consistent.* Reviews are not an improvisational art form. They demand a consistent format, especially for all employees in the same job. Your company may have forms that you can or must use. If not, you can buy standard forms or software from management supply firms. You also can create your own form and then use it consistently. There is no "right" format, but be sure you're reviewing behavior and skills related to the position.

- *Be thorough.* Most review forms use a scale, such as "excellent, good, fair, poor" or "far exceeds expectations, exceeds expectations, meets expectations, does not meet expectations," or a numerical scale. Whatever format you use, use the scale as a means and not an end. *How* does the employee exceed expectations? Existing forms likely rely on very general performance issues, such as decision-making or judgment. Those are certainly good things to consider, but go back to the job description and expectations you drafted, and be sure that the review addresses every key responsibility and task. Be specific, and use objective data whenever possible. If you were reviewing a teacher, for example, you could refer to test scores, parent comments, and the percentage of students promoted to the next grade. Offer examples of behavior that you'd like to see more of or that needs improvement.

Also be sure that the review includes examples from throughout the review period. Many reviews inadvertently focus only on the 90 days or so preceding the review because that's what managers remember. Don't deprive people of credit for great work done during the early part of the review period, or overlook major problems during that time.

If you're creating your own form, consider

- Attendance
- Cooperation and teamwork
- Communication skills
- Compliance with safety requirements
- Compliance with company or department policies

    Your mission is not to write *War and Peace*, but a review is an important document, and it shouldn't fit on a cocktail napkin either.

- *Don't play games.* Some reviewers withhold top ratings in the theory that "no one is perfect" or "if I give the top rating, then there is nowhere for the employee to go." Bad idea! Unless you can offer concrete ways in which an employee can do better in a given area, she should get the top rating. Anything less discredits the whole process and your skills. Likewise, never rate an employee higher than he merits to avoid hurting the employee's feelings, having a confrontation, or discouraging him. Our rule for reviews: be totally honest and professional.

- *Don't spring surprises.* Reviews should summarize and validate; they should not shock. Don't wait until the review to let an employee know he's at risk of being fired. Serious performance issues should be addressed promptly, but employees also shouldn't get good news (such as a promotion) during a review unless you've discussed the possibility in advance and they understand that a decision is pending. Reviews should be just one of many conversations you have about performance.

- *Consider other opinions.* Far more creative energy has been directed at airline fares than at review formats, so most reviews package one manager's assessment of one employee. In most cases, that's appropriate, but when an employee has many constituencies, getting other perspectives may be helpful.

For example, suppose you're managing managers. A manager may be well respected by her employees, but not by managers of other departments she must work with (or vice versa). Or a key employee may be an expert at managing up (keeping you happy) while alienating everyone else. One way to get at that information is through multi-rater feedback, sometimes known as 360-degree feedback.

Multi-rater feedback is becoming increasingly popular because it can yield richer, more accurate feedback. Of course, no system is perfect, and critics claim that multi-rater feedback opens the door to hearsay and politicking. To mitigate those risks

- Include at least five people in the rating. With any fewer, it's too easy to figure out who said what, which discourages people from being candid. There also are fewer benefits to expanded feedback from such a small pool.

- Seek to include raters from all levels. Limiting feedback to an employee's peers misses the intent of multi-rater feedback, which is to get a complete picture of an employee's performance.

- Keep the feedback anonymous. If names are attached to ratings, people won't be candid. You also run the risk that the people being rated will retaliate against people who say less than positive things.

- Be consistent. If you use multi-rater feedback for one employee, use it for all employees in the same job.

- Look for patterns. Focus on areas where many raters agree. This limits the number of issues the employee must address and minimizes the impact of feedback given with a personal bias.

  Using multi-rater feedback is a complex process. If you plan to use it, partner with your HR department or contact a professional firm that specializes in such reviews.

- *Get employee input.* A review is an opportunity for dialogue, not a one-sided information dump. Encourage employees to rate their own performance. Most will be honest, and they may raise issues that surprise you. (See "Self Reviews: 12 Questions" page 288 for conversation starters.)

  Always leave space on the review form for employees to respond to their review.

- *Set a course for the future.* A good review is almost as much about the future as it is about the past. It should give an employee a good idea of what's next. How can he earn another raise? Is training available that the employee needs or can opt for? Are there deficiencies that the employee must address? Are there problems that can result in discipline or termination? What opportunities exist for promotion, and how are they earned? What goals do you have for the employee in the coming year? If you don't foresee any significant changes in the employee's job, she deserves to know that, too.

- *Meet with the employee.* A review is an opportunity for discussion, so just handing an employee his review isn't enough. Sit down with the employee and talk through the year's accomplishments and the next year's goals. These meetings work best if you
  - Set aside at least 30 minutes for a meeting.
  - Make an appointment.
  - Give the employee a copy of the review during your meeting so he or she can to ask questions or comment.
  - Get a copy of the employee's comments so you can review them.
  - Meet in private and deflect interruptions.
  - Meet in a neutral place (such as a conference room).
  - Spend at least as much time listening as talking.

- *Review the job description.* If an employee's job has changed enough that her job description is no longer current, now is a great time to update it and review it with the employee.

Stay Out of Jail

- *Focus on job performance.* Reviews should be fair and objective, so your personal feelings about the employee are irrelevant. Everything in the review should relate directly to job issues. Don't comment on an employee's religion, politics, marital status, or other characteristics. Don't guess at the motivation for behavior.

- *Stick to the facts.* Include objective data whenever possible. When the review is subjective, draw conclusions yourself and base them on specific work-related incidents or behavior. Don't rely on hearsay or gossip.

- *Be honest.* Tell it like it is. If the employee is excelling, say so, but if there's a problem, be candid. Document the problem and outline the steps you expect the employee to take to improve. Don't rate an employee higher than she merits to "encourage" her, reward good intentions, "help" her through a tough personal time, or because you like the employee. Remember, a review could end up in court. It should be the truth.

- *Keep the review.* Copies of the review should go in the employee's file. Have him sign the review to indicate that he received it and understands it. (Include a space for his comments, if any.)

- *Keep it confidential.* The contents of a review should be between you and the employee (and in some cases the human resources department). Don't share the contents of a review with anyone else—even if the review is positive.

- *Avoid common mistakes.* The road to a good review is studded with land mines. To avoid them

- Measure an employee's performance against the standards for the job, not against the performance of other people in the job.

- If no one is performing well, then everyone is falling short of expectations. Poor performance is still poor performance, not average or acceptable performance.

- Don't let your review of one employee affect your review of others. For example, don't let a superstar or poor performer raise or lower your standards when reviewing the next employee.

- Don't mistake kindness, favors to you, or loyalty to you for good performance.

- Don't write reviews at 10 p.m. or when you're out of town. Be awake.

- Don't spend less than 30 minutes on any one review, don't do all your reviews in one sitting, and don't set a goal to do a set number of reviews at any one time.

- Go over and proofread your review at least one day after you write it, and don't check reviews in the same order in which you wrote them.

Real Life Examples

- Dave's review was months late, but his manager assured him that he would "get to it." Then, as the six-month mark approached, the manager gave notice that he was leaving. Still, there was no review. Finally, on the manager's last day, he asked Dave for a ride home. As they pulled into the manager's driveway, Dave finally got his review: three lines scribbled on the back of scratch paper.

- The HR department acknowledged John's five years with the company by giving him his five-year pin, but he didn't get a review. Weeks passed, then months, then his anniversary date. When he finally got his review, along with another five-year pin, it was more than a year late. No one mentioned the entire sixth year he had also worked. "Either I worked my fifth year twice," John said, "or the sixth year doesn't count."

- Madeline had been with her company for more than three years, and it was time for her annual review. It was, as always, positive. Then there it was, in the last sentence on the last page: promotion to manager of her department. Surprise! No one had ever asked Madeline whether she wanted to be a manager. No one had told her that she was being considered for the job, or shared what the job entailed. No one had in any way prepared her for the responsibility she had just been handed.

- Her supervisor put off doing Mary's review because she wanted to identify all the work-related problems she was having with Mary and develop a performance plan to correct them. Months went by and the problems persisted. Then Mary announced that she was pregnant. Two weeks later, Mary made another mistake like those that Mary's boss had intended to discuss during the review. Feeling that the mistake was the last straw, the boss went to HR with her decision to fire Mary. But HR was surprised that the boss didn't see how her decision seemed to be based on Mary's pregnancy. After all, there was no review to suggest that Mary had performance problems—and certainly not ongoing ones. Mary stayed.

Do at Least the Minimum

- *Do reviews on time.*
- *Put your comments in writing.*
- *Be accurate and honest.*
- *Meet with employees to discuss the review.*

PERSONNEL FILES: HOW TO KEEP YOUR RECORDS USEFUL AND LEGAL

Know the Issue

The story goes that when L. Frank Baum was looking to name the setting of the children's book he was writing, he looked up at his file cabinet—specifically at the drawer labeled O-Z.

Your files may not provide such inspiration, but they should provide the first line of defense against miscommunication, misunderstandings, and legal complaints. Of course, this assumes that the files have been kept current and the right material has been kept in them.

Take Action

- *Start at the very beginning.* Begin a personnel file for each employee as soon as he or she is hired. From the outset, the file should include
  - The employee's completed application
  - The employee's resume and, if applicable, cover letter
  - Material used in deciding to hire the employee, such as assignments, test results, or material provided by an employment agency

Self-Reviews: 12 Questions

An employee's insight into his or her own performance can be invaluable. Use these questions to jump-start the conversation.

1. Of all the things you've done during the past year, what's the one accomplishment you're most satisfied with? Why?
2. Of all the things you've done during the last year, what's the one accomplishment you're least satisfied with? Why?
3. Based on what you've experienced during the last year, what's a situation you'll handle differently when you encounter it again? How is this new approach better?
4. What have you learned about your job that you didn't know 12 months ago?
5. What have you learned about yourself that you didn't know 12 months ago?
6. When it's time for your next review, what's one thing you would like to have accomplished? Why?
7. In working toward that goal, what resources do you feel are available to you? That is, what here will help you meet your goal?
8. In working toward that goal, are there any obstacles (for example, time, money, lack of expertise) that you feel you face? If so, how can you overcome them?
9. How can I, as your manager, help you meet that goal?
10. What has been your biggest job-related frustration during the past 12 months?
11. What ideas do you have for alleviating the frustrations?
12. How are you more valuable to the organization than you were 12 months ago?

- The offer letter, signed by the employee
- A signed statement that the employee received and understands the policy manual

- *Keep the file current.* Files should reflect an employee's complete work history, including raises, promotions, transfers, and discipline. To do that, include
  - All documentation (see "Documenting Performance," pages 271–277)
  - Performance reviews
  - Evidence of training completed
  - Development plans (if you use them)

- *Don't put just anything in the file.* Some things are *not* appropriate for a personnel file. They include
  - Information relating to an employee's medical condition or disability (Keep that in a separate, secure, confidential medical file.)
  - Letters to or from the company attorney
  - Legal claims (such as workers' compensation claims, overtime claims, and grievances)

    You may omit other material depending on which state you're in. California law, for example, says that letters of reference and records relating to criminal investigations need not be kept in the employee's personal file. An attorney can tell you the specifics of your state's laws.

- *Keep files in a secure place.* Personnel files should not be readily accessible. Ideally, they should be kept locked.

- *Limit access to the files.* Even with the files locked, people who have no business looking at a file may try to do so. Access should be limited to
  - Managers, provided they have a legitimate management reason to review the file
  - Members of the HR staff
  - The employee him- or herself (under certain circumstances; see "Stay Out of Jail")

    Ideally, files should never leave the room in which they're kept. If anyone must take the file (including you), it should be "signed out." You never want a file to be missing or to inexplicably turn up in your living quarters months after it couldn't be found.

- *Don't keep a "shadow" file.* You may be tempted to keep files at your desk on the people who report to you. It may seem convenient, or a good way to keep notes private, but don't do it. Anything worth putting into writing should be kept in *the* personnel file; otherwise, it looks like you're trying to hide something (which, in effect, you are). Nothing you keep is truly private; your "shadow" files can be subpoenaed in a legal dispute.

Stay Out of Jail

- *Don't put anything in the file you wouldn't want read in court.*
- *Allow employees to see their own files.* Employees have many reasons for wanting to see their files, and in broad terms the courts have said they should be allowed to. The courts also have ruled that access shouldn't be a free-for-all, and that employers should be allowed some limits, such as

- Requiring employees to submit a written request
- Allowing employees to see their file only by appointment
- Allowing employees to see their file only during regular business hours
- Allowing inspection only on the employee's own time
- Requiring that a representative of the employer (such as you or someone from HR) be present
- Limiting the frequency of inspections

Virtually every state has laws regulating personnel files. (The Connecticut law, for example, affects both public and private sector employers, defines which records should be included and excluded from files, establishes access rights, states the procedure for correcting information, defines the requirements for disclosure to third parties, and so on.) Check with an attorney about what's required in your state.

OVERTIME/COMP TIME: HOW TO PAY PEOPLE

Know the Issue

You've seen the shell game: someone puts a small object (a walnut, perhaps) under one of three identical shells or cups and quickly rearranges them. The challenge is to watch carefully enough that you can identify which shell is hiding the object. Unless the person performing the trick cheats, nothing disappears—it may just appear to.

Paying employees is sometimes like that shell game. Employers start with a basic 40-hour work week and they shuffle the hours (using alternate schedules, comp time, and other tactics) to avoid paying overtime. But as in the shell game, the hours beyond 40 are still there and although employees or the law may be temporarily confused, the truth is that employees must be paid for that time. Anything less, no matter what euphemism you use, is cheating and ultimately results in penalties.

Take Action

- *Understand overtime law.* Federal law and the laws of most states base overtime requirements on individual workweeks. The rule is quite simple: nonexempt employees must be paid overtime (1.5 times the regular rate under federal law and most state laws) if they work more than 40 hours in a single week.

  Some states also stipulate a *daily* overtime rule. In such cases, employees must be paid overtime for working more than eight hours in a single 24-hour period. (Note: In at least one state, if an employee asks to make up time lost in the same work-week, he can do so without accruing daily overtime, provided that the employee requests the make-up time, in writing, without solicitation or encouragement from management.)

- *Forget about comp time.* Although the concept of comp time (in which employees are given time off in exchange for, or as a reward for, working overtime) is popular, in reality, there's no such thing. The law doesn't allow this exchange unless it's done in the same week as the overtime was worked. If that happens, there's no reason to call it "comp time" because the employees' time cards will show they didn't work overtime that week. If the requirement isn't met, and employees are given the time off in another week, you may think, erroneously, that you don't have to pay for the overtime actually worked.

The situation is further complicated in states with daily overtime requirements. In California, for example, to even the hours in the workweek, employees must be given 1.5 hours off in the same workweek for every daily overtime hour worked. (In addition, in California, if the time off will be taken in a different week, employers and employees must agree to it in writing. Even that could run afoul of Federal law if the employee worked more than 40 hours in the work week.)

Comp time also exposes you to the risk that how you classify employees will be challenged. Remember that exempt employees aren't eligible for overtime, but if you give them time off and call it comp time you may imply that they should be eligible for overtime and therefore they are not really exempt.

Finally, managing comp time can be a nightmare. How much time and money will you spend tracking time that's only being moved from one column to another?

- *Use time off as a reward.* You can still grant time off to reward effort or time worked. Using your discretion lets you reward exempt employees and you may improve productivity and morale.

Stay Out of Jail

- *Pay nonexempt employees overtime for any time exceeding 40 hours in a single week, and as otherwise required by state law.*

NEGLIGENT SUPERVISION: HOW WHAT YOU DON'T DO CAN COST YOU

Know the Issue

As kids, we learn there are two ways to get in trouble. We get in hot water for doing the stuff that we shouldn't do: putting crayons in the dryer with Daddy's nice shirts, giving a haircut to the dog, or filling the bean bag chair with milk to see how much it will hold. But we also face the music for *not* doing stuff we should do: for not feeding the dog, finishing our homework, or brushing our teeth before bed.

As managers we sometimes forget that we can get into substantial trouble for *not* doing something. We spend so much energy focused on what we *are* doing that we overlook the consequences of what we're *not* doing. Unfortunately, those consequences can be serious. Suppose you send an untrained employee to make a minor repair and he electrocutes himself. Or an employee threatens a co-worker, but you decide you'll deal with it when you have time. How will you explain yourself if the employee makes good on her threat before you found the time to deal with it?

These situations are examples of negligent supervision: the failure to meet accepted standards of care, resulting in harm to employees or the public. The law recognizes that supervision is serious business—lives may be at stake. Consequently, you and your firm can be held liable for damage that occurs because of negligent supervision. If you are held liable, the penalties can be substantial, but they're nothing compared to living with the knowledge that you could have prevented a tragedy.

Understand the risks. Be vigilant, and take action.

Take Action

- *Understand your exposure.* It's an exaggeration to say that anything you do (or don't do) might be seen as negligent, but several situations demand particular care:
  - Hiring (see "Negligent Hiring," pages 120–122)
  - Training
  - Permitting an employee to use a company vehicle
  - Permitting an employee to be alone with other employees or members of the public
  - Promoting an employee
  - Certifying an employee
  - Failing to fire or discipline an employee
  - Firing an employee without doing an effective investigation.

- *Don't make any assumptions about employees.* Just as you shouldn't accept at face value the accuracy of a resume, don't make assumptions *after* the hire. Employees may volunteer for additional responsibilities out of boredom, a wish to please, or to earn a higher wage. It doesn't mean they can actually do the work. Investigate their claims.

- *Don't ignore or minimize problems, actions, statements, or signs that an employee is a potential danger to himself or others.* After the tragic shootings at Columbine High School, the media was filled with evidence of the boys' troubling behavior. The nation wondered, why didn't anyone notice? Why didn't anyone do something?

  If something seems amiss, it may *be* amiss. It's better to be safe than sorry.

- *Investigate, inquire, and consult with experts—including the police.* Respect employees' privacy rights (see "Privacy," pages 382–386), but don't ignore potential problems.
- *Request training on workplace violence.* Learn the warning signs and how to respond.

Stay Out of Jail

- *Be sure employees receive all necessary training before being put in a situation that requires it.* If appropriate, verify that the employee has mastered the necessary skills. For example, as a society we don't accept completion of a driver's education course as evidence that someone can drive; we make them demonstrate their skills to get a license. If an employee has been trained to do a task that involves some risk (making an electrical repair, for example), have the employee demonstrate in a simulation that he can do it before sending him out to do the work.
- *Follow up on all allegations.* Suppose you hear of an employee's
  - Proclivity to violence
  - Threats of violence
  - Dishonesty
  - Lack of skills
  - Lack of knowledge
  - Inappropriate behavior from a co-worker, vendor, customer, former employer, or even an employee's family member

Always take such allegations seriously. Your exposure to liability of negligent supervision is greatest if you know of a situation and do nothing. Investigate the accusation immediately, and keep records of your investigation.

During the investigation, minimize the risk. If an employee tells you that a co-worker isn't following safety protocols, for example, pull the employee off the job while you investigate.

- *Take action.* If your investigation confirms a problem, *do something.* Exercise effective discipline, including termination, where necessary to protect others. For guidance, turn to your employee handbook, consult with human resources, or contact an attorney.

Real Life Example

Mona was in a no-win situation. A co-worker was stalking an employee. The employee was understandably terrified, and the stalker was unresponsive to discipline and even to a restraining order. Mona believed that she needed to fire the stalker and reassign his victim, but the stalker was a diagnosed schizophrenic and therefore protected by the Americans with Disabilities Act. Mona knew that if she fired him, she could expose the company to a wrongful termination suit.

Despite that risk, Mona fired him (and also reassigned the employee). "I was at risk either way," Mona said. "But I decided that I'd rather go to court than to a funeral."

TRAINING: HOW TO KEEP PEOPLE LEARNING AND GROWING

Know the Issue

Remember the inevitable dinnertime question? "What did you learn in school today?" When's the last time anyone asked, "What did you learn at work today?"

Somehow we get it into our heads that school is a place to learn and work is a place to use what we've learned. As a result, there's almost no focus on learning in the workplace.

That's unfortunate. If employees are really our greatest assets, it only makes sense to invest in them. Training improves employee contributions. It creates better teams.

It is also a tremendous retention tool. Employees *want* training; so much so that many cite lack of training as the reason for leaving their jobs. They want the challenge and pride of learning new skills. In today's fluid marketplace, they want the tools to compete in the job market if they have to. (Yes, there's the possibility that an ambitious employee will move on after you've invested in training and someone else will reap the rewards, but what's the alternative—to have someone with minimal skills stay on?)

What kind of training do employees want? All kinds. Some you can provide yourself (teaching an employee to use a Palm Pilot or to file an expense report, for example), but most training demands subject expertise (sexual harassment training, for instance). It may also demand expertise in adult learning, curriculum design, evaluation, and presentation skills. Training (though sometimes seen as a part of HR) is a profession with its own standards, certification, and associations. Rely on that expertise, whether you find it in your company's own training department, you contract with an outside expert, or you partner with a local community college.

Whatever expertise you rely on, put training at the top of your to-do list. The rewards are limitless.

Take Action

- *Make an inventory.* Before you offer to teach anybody anything, find out what they already know. That doesn't mean you need to put together a complicated formal inventory. Just create a simple form that asks employees to identify their

  - Computer skills (What software do they know? Are they Internet-savvy? Do they have specialized skills, such as familiarity with local area networks?)

  - Language skills (Which job-related or computer languages are they fluent in? Consider writing and reading skills as well as speaking and understanding.)

  - Equipment skills (Can they operate all the equipment in your office such as the telephone system, copier, fax machine?)

  Ask employees to note whether they have any job-related certifications (such as being certified by the American Red Cross in first aid). Also ask them to list any training courses they remember taking in their current or previous jobs.

  The goal is not to note every skill of every employee, but to get a sense of the general skill level of employees and to identify people who may be able to coach their co-workers.

- *Identify training needs.* Before you contract for training or develop a training plan, determine specifically what you'd like employees to be able to do. A lot of training fails because it isn't measurable or applicable; it's a generalized knowledge dump. Suppose you think employees need better computer skills, for example. What do you envision? Do you want them to be able to open a word processing program, write a letter and save it, print the letter, and use a mail-merge function to print an address label? Or do you want them to be able to open a spreadsheet program, create a spreadsheet to use as an expense-report form, enter the expenses of an actual trip, and save and print the report? Develop specific, measurable training goals that will serve as learning objectives. Trainers can use these goals to design the training, and employees will understand what they're expected to learn and whether they've learned it.

Employees may also have ideas of training they'd like. Solicit those ideas at staff meetings, during performance reviews, or through informal surveys. Don't feel compelled to find a way to honor every request, though. Even if you wanted to, you couldn't. There aren't enough hours in the day or dollars in your budget. And you shouldn't. Training should never be offered for training's sake; it always should support a business goal.

If you think an employee's request has merit, ask him to justify the training. The idea isn't to intimidate or discourage people, but to have them think in business terms. What's the value of the training? Do they need enhanced skills to do better in their current job? Or do they feel they need the skills to be promoted to the next job? Employees should be as specific as you are about what they'll be able to *do* after the training.

Although training can be a retention tool for your top performers, you should never offer training to people just to placate them.

- *Look for cross-training opportunities.* The receptionist is out sick and within minutes the awful truth is apparent: no one else knows how to use the phone system. Or you lay awake at night in terror that your system administrator, the person everyone turns to when they have computer problems, will resign.

  No one wants to be in those situations, and training can help you avoid them. Take time to make a list of all the skills your department needs to keep functioning. Beside each one, identify who has the skill. If only one name is beside any skill, it's time for cross training. Have employees teach each other. Then ask the employee who has just learned the skill to teach you. Teaching is often the best way to learn, so employees will reinforce the skills they just gained and you'll learn, too.

- *Offer training before you have a problem.* Don't wait until you're fighting a crisis.

- *Find out what training is readily available.* If you have an internal training department (or an HR department that offers training), become familiar with what they offer. Are there courses your staff needs? Encourage employees to sign up. If you have a handful of people who need training, but not enough to justify a whole class, find out if another department is being trained; perhaps your staff can sit in on that training.

  In addition to teaching courses themselves, a training department may be able to recommend off-the-shelf training products or may have licensed certain training programs for company use.

If nothing currently exists internally to meet your needs, see if HR or the training department will work with you to develop and test a program.

- *Investigate outside resources.* If internal training isn't feasible, pursue outside resources. If the training you need is fairly generic and widely needed (computer training, for example), you may be able to contract with a local community college. Many colleges work with businesses, and rates are usually inexpensive. For training that is highly technical or specialized, or training you'd like customized, you'll probably have to use a professional training firm. Such training can be expensive, but expertise usually is.

- *Choose a training package carefully.* The most affordable way to use a professional firm is to choose an off-the-shelf training package. Such packages, written by the training company, provide instructional materials (to train the trainer), a training script, workbooks, and other support material. Most often, no one from the firm actually does the training.

  How do you choose a training package? Find out which training programs are available by checking out *Training* or *Training & Development* magazines. You can see many of the products available and talk to training company representatives at the American Society for Training and Development's annual conference.

  - Ask for preview materials. Most training firms make material (such as videos or workbooks) available for preview.

The preview period is usually limited, and some charge a preview fee. (When they do, the fee may be applied to the purchase if you decide to use the program.) Study the materials. Did you learn anything? Are the learning objectives clear? Is the tone appropriate? Does the amount of information seem appropriate?

- Ask for references and call them.

- Ask about the development of the material. What are the author's credentials? Was the training pilot tested? If so, who was the sample audience? How old is the program? Is it current?

- Clarify costs. Are you buying the program outright to use as you like? Or are you licensing the program for a specified number of uses? Are ongoing fees paid per trainee or for materials? Are you entitled to any updates or revisions to the program?

- If your staff is large enough for it to make sense, do a pilot. Use the program to train a group and get their feedback. Did they learn anything? What did they think worked or didn't work?

- *Choose a training firm carefully.* Packages aren't always the best solution. If you need training that is technical or customized, a training firm can work with you to develop a program, and then teach people in your company to deliver the training. Or choose a firm to design *and* deliver the training on a contract basis. How do you choose a firm?

  - Review their promotional literature or visit their Internet site. What sort of work do they do?

- Ask for references and call them. Ask how well the training worked, but also ask about the client's culture. You may wish to be very involved in developing a program, for example, whereas someone else may have wanted no involvement. Or the training company's laid-back style may have worked well in the client's Silicon Valley worksite, but raise eyebrows in your buttoned-down corporate headquarters. Try to find references with a culture similar to yours.

- Ask for a preview. See if you can attend a training session at another client, or ask if the firm will do a preview session for you and other stakeholders. Get a sense of the trainer's style and how he presents material.

- Find out who'll you be working with. Large training firms are like consulting firms and have many employees. Don't assume you'll be working with the first person you meet with.

- Find out how the firm develops curriculum. What are the principal's credentials? What resources do they use? How customized to your needs will the training be?

- Explore the firm's approach to training. Will trainers lecture, or will the training be interactive? What technique does the firm use to engage people who have different learning styles?

- Ask how the firm will evaluate the training. How will they know whether the training has been effective?

- Clarify pricing. Are you paying a flat fee to develop the program or a sliding scale? What control do you have over the final cost? Once the program is complete, who owns it—the training firm or your company? For the training itself, do you pay a set fee per session or is it priced per trainee? Who will pay to produce any necessary training materials?

- *Get outside the box.* Most corporate training is methodical, highly structured, and even a bit, well, boring. It doesn't have to be. Training can be fun if you let your imagination run wild. Ken Adelman teaches management lessons by having trainees act out scenes from Shakespeare. Dick Eaton, founder of the training firm Leapfrog Innovations Inc. has asked trainees to design and construct holes for a miniature golf course. Other trainers have taught management skills using clips from classic films and by having trainees organize an assembly line to make peanut butter and jelly sandwiches.

- *Put the training in context.* Once you've chosen a course of action, explain it to employees. Tell them why you've decided to offer the training, why you selected the program or trainer you chose, and what you expect them to get out of it. Without that, employees can easily dismiss the training as the flavor of the day.

- *Apply the training.* People won't remember the training any longer than they remember a fast-food meal if they don't use what they've learned. Structure activities that give employees the chance to use their new skills. Suppose employees just received sexual harassment training, for example. Take time at a staff meeting to discuss incidents in the news or on popular television shows. If an employee has just learned a word processing program, give him the chance to create, store, and print documents.

- *Evaluate the training.* Don't ask employees how the training went and accept "fine" as a definitive answer. Write formal evaluations of any training programs. Look for commonality in the observations. Were some parts of the training confusing or especially helpful? Do people still have questions that haven't been answered?

  If you're teaching difficult skills (such as computer skills), consider a post-training test to measure whether employees met the learning objectives.

- *Accept that training isn't always the answer.* Despite training's complexity, it's often seen as an easy fix when there are productivity problems. Suppose, for example, that the hand-off from one group to another is always difficult. Each group says the other isn't meeting its commitments. Product specs differ, deadlines are missed, and tempers are short. One solution is to offer training on communication skills or project planning.

  Even if employees learn something, the training may not improve the situation at all. Perhaps communication is fine, but the groups feel their priorities are unclear. What if the groups consistently get supplies too late? Or if the sales department changes the order mid-project? What if the production schedule is simply unworkable?

  Before you offer training, talk to employees. Ask what they think the problem is. Observe the situation yourself. Do you see a skills gap? What do employees need to be able to *do* that they aren't doing? If you have an HR or training function, they can be a great resource at this stage.

Stay Out of Jail

- *Document all training performed, including who received the training, and keep records of employee training in the appropriate personnel files.*

- *Offer training based on need.* Don't offer training only to employees you like. Be particularly careful not to single out gender, racial, or other demographic groups either to receive training or not to receive it.

- *Understand that you can be held liable for negligent training if you don't offer employees the training they need to perform their jobs safely.* For example, if you put a truck driver on the road without the training to keep him from being a hazard, you could be liable if he caused an accident. Similarly, an employee could file a claim if he were injured because a co-worker hadn't been trained to properly use equipment. Believe it or not, an employee can even claim he can't be terminated because the reason he caused $10 million in damage by forgetting to set the fire alarm at night was that he was not properly trained to do so.

Get More Information

The American Society for Training and Development, 1640 King St., Box 1443, Alexandria, VA 22313-2043, 703/683-8100, www.astd.org.

Employment Law Learning Technologies, 415/677-3102.

The ASTD Handbook of Training Design and Delivery, George M. Piskurichy, Peter Beckschi and Brandon Hall, editors, McGraw-Hill, 1999.

Structured On-the-Job Training: Unleashing Employee Expertise in the Workplace, Ronald L. Jacobs and Michael J. Jones, Berrett-Koehler, 1995.

The Trainer's Handbook: The AMA Guide to Effective Training, Garry Mitchell, AMACOM, 1998.

10

Discipline and Termination

As drivers, we all know what we're *supposed* to do, but we don't always do it. That's why occasionally the police step in. They issue friendly (or not so friendly) warnings, write tickets, suspend or revoke licenses, and even send drivers to jail. We need them to do these things to protect the public safety, and state regulations ensure their actions fit the crimes.

If you set expectations and effectively manage performance, employees know what they're supposed to do, too, but, like drivers, they don't always do it. That's when *you* need to step in and take action. Your safety and liability, along with that of your company, demand it. Like the police, you have many options to choose from, and like the state, your company should have policies to help you match your action to the "crime."

DISCIPLINE: HOW TO CHANGE PROBLEM BEHAVIOR

Know the Issue

If you were ever spanked as a child, you probably heard your parents say, "This is going to hurt me more than it's going to hurt you." As you felt the sting of the swat, you probably thought, "Yeah, right."

As an adult, you may better understand what they meant. The pain they felt was emotional, not physical, and it probably *was* harder on them. None of us likes to see another person's spirit diminished, even temporarily, and none of us likes to be the bad guy.

That's part of why discipline at work is often done so poorly. Other reasons are because it's done emotionally (usually in anger), because it's applied inconsistently (different disciplinary measures for the same infraction), because the company has no discipline policy (so managers don't know what to do when an infraction occurs), and because managers forget the real purpose of discipline (which is not to punish, but to change a person's behavior).

Administering discipline is never easy, but it becomes far less difficult if you do it fairly. That means know your options. Use them appropriately. Act rationally, not emotionally. And keep your eye on the big picture—reforming the behavior, not giving the employee "the business."

Take Action

- *Use the employee handbook.* Understand the policies and procedures outlined in the employee handbook (see "The Handbook," pages 33–35). It's important that any discipline be consistent with the handbook. You don't want to discipline any employee for taking a long lunch hour on voting day, for example, if the manual says she may.

- *Listen to employees.* There's no excuse for some behavior, such as harassing a co-worker or stealing, but you must obtain the accused's side of the story *before* you take action. The employee may offer a credible denial or admit to the behavior. They may have logical explanations for apparent lapses. Was an employee late because she stopped in the parking lot to help an injured colleague? *Ask* before you assume the worst. Most jurors will consider you unfair if you don't give the employee a chance to explain.

- *Know your options.* At-will employers reserve the right to use whatever discipline, including immediate termination, they believe is appropriate. Many potential options, and combinations of options, are available, including

  - Oral admonishment, warning or instruction
  - Written admonishment, warning or instruction
  - Training
  - Suspension without pay
  - Indefinite or temporary demotion
  - Indefinite or temporary transfer
  - Indefinite or temporary loss of benefit(s)
  - Termination

  The key is to choose the option that effectively changes inappropriate behavior or poor work performance, deters or prevents unlawful conduct, and shows your concern for the rights of your employees. Sometimes an immediate termination is necessary (such as for sexual harassment or stealing) and sometimes a milder action is more appropriate. An at-will employer reserves the right to make the decision at its discretion. Nevertheless, because legal as well as management or labor relations issues lurk behind these decisions, always consider consulting with HR or your boss before imposing any discipline.

Be careful not to open the door to charges of discrimination. Be certain, for example, you know how your company has treated similar cases in the past. You aren't tied to the same discipline that was previously imposed, but if you vary from precedent, do so only for legitimate, business-related reasons. For example, the same offense can have different consequences for a 20-year employee with an unblemished record than for a six-month employee previously warned for the same behavior.

- *Discipline effectively.* Ninety percent of all the discipline you impose will be warnings. To be effective and complete, a written warning must

  - Communicate what the problem is. Describe what the employee has done that is inappropriate, against the rules, or not productive.

  - Communicate what your expectations and requirements are. Describe what the employee must do in the future.

  - Communicate the consequences of failing to meet your expectations or requirements. Describe what will happen, such as suspension without pay or termination. (Beware: You may be limited to consequences you have communicated. Was the employee fairly put on notice of the consequences?)

- Provide space for the employee to object or answer.

- Be signed by the employee.

  Extra credit is given to warnings that explain *why* the employee's behavior is a problem: "Your tardiness puts an unfair burden on other employees in the department who must not only do their own work, but who must also, unexpectedly, rearrange their responsibilities to handle the work they were expecting you to perform."

- *Exercise restraint.* No rules exist that dictate which form of discipline to use for which circumstance. (Exceptions may arise if you are governed by a collective bargaining agreement or your employee handbook limits your options.) However, certain guidelines should be considered:

  - Unless the problem is serious, start with an admonishment. If you start with harsher discipline, it could limit your options in the future if the problem persists, and the employee may feel you're unfair.

  - Don't feel you have to use every option available. In some cases (excessive tardiness, for example), there isn't any training that's likely to help. In other cases, you may need to respond to new circumstances. Suppose you overheard an employee calling a co-worker a fool. Giving the employee an oral admonishment might be appropriate. If the employee continued to call his co-workers names, a written warning would be the next logical step. But if the employee instead threatened a co-worker or even hit someone, you'd need to impose harsher discipline, such as a suspension or even termination, right away.

- Discipline usually becomes progressively harsher. It's uncommon to suspend someone and then backpedal to a warning.

- *See every step of discipline as the last one.* Some high school principals create a self-perpetuating problem. They tell certain students that they expect to see them again, and so they do. People tend to meet your expectations for them. Inappropriate behavior is more likely to stop if you expect it to stop. See every step as an opportunity to teach.

- *Meet with employees.* Meet privately. Remain calm and respectful. If necessary, take some time before the meeting to collect yourself and your thoughts. Getting angry or emotional is liable to provoke a confrontation. Allow the employee to leave if he asks to. Have a witness present so that there's no argument later about what was said.

- *Revisit the problem.* Don't discipline an employee and then forget about it. Remember, the goal is improvement. Review the situation again (30 days may be a good target); has it improved? If so, commend the employee for improving. If not, further discipline may be needed.

Stay Out of Jail

- *Be consistent.* If something is against the rules, then *all* employees who break the rule should be subject to discipline. Although other factors (such as previous infractions) can inform your actions, don't impose harsh discipline on some employees while letting others go unpunished. Be especially careful not to consistently impose harsher penalties on members of protected groups (such as older employees or racial minorities, for example).

- *Document all discipline and keep records in the appropriate file.* Always remember that documentation is a potential exhibit in a lawsuit. Draft it, read it, and read it again before you give it to the employee. In the documentation, limit yourself to legitimate, business-related issues. Don't say anything that may be construed as discriminatory or reflecting a stereotype.

- *Don't let it be personal.* Focus on work-related behavior, not personality or psychology. For example, let an employee know that he's expected to complete assembling 10 swing sets each day; don't tell him he's "lazy."

THE ACTUAL TERMINATION: HOW TO LET PEOPLE GO FAIRLY AND LEGALLY

Know the Issue

Juries, doctors, and paramedics are among those who face life-altering moments of truth: Is the defendant guilty? Is there still value in treating the patient or has the disease progressed too far? Can the accident victim be rescued in time to save her life? These are wrenching decisions that deserve the utmost care and solemnity.

Your role as a manager means that you, too, may be in a position of facing a moment of truth: Is it in the best interests of the business to terminate an employee? Deciding "yes" is one of the hardest things you will ever do as a manager. Most terminations will feel like a loss to you, to the employee, and probably to others in your

company. Even if the employee "deserves it" because of poor performance or insubordination, it is still one of the most stressful events in a manager's life. Expect to face anger, hurt, and fear, and no matter how many times you terminate someone, it doesn't get easier.

There is nothing we can offer to make terminations easy or pleasant, but doing the wrong things can certainly make terminations harder and open the door to legal challenges. There are actions you can take to preserve an employee's dignity, limit the damage to the organization, and reduce your legal exposure.

Take Action

- *Take the decision seriously.* An employee's job is her livelihood and a large part of her identity. Do her the courtesy of considering a termination decision very carefully. Never decide to terminate an employee in the heat of anger, or because you think it would be easier than trying to improve her performance, because you don't like the person, or just because you can. Any decision should be based on a legitimate business reason:

  - The employee has consistently not met performance standards and has not shown improvement despite warnings and the opportunity to do so.

  - The employee has either violated company policy consistently (such as missing too many days without a legitimate reason) and has not changed his behavior in response to any discipline offered or has violated a policy in such a serious way (attacked a co-worker, for example, or embezzled) that you are compelled to protect the company, its employees, or its assets.

- The nature of the job has substantially changed over time and the employee no longer has the skills to perform it, and there's no way you can alter the job or find another position for the employee.

- A downturn in business necessitates reducing the size of the workforce.

Just because you have an at-will employment policy and you *can* terminate an employee at any time for any reason doesn't make it a good idea.

Being fair and focusing on business concerns is how to best avoid wrongful termination claims. "Wrongful termination" is a broad term that refers to a termination a former employee contends should not have happened. The employee may claim he was terminated

- In violation of an express contract to terminate only for cause

- In violation of an implied contract to terminate only for cause

- In violation of anti-discrimination laws

- For exercising a right (such as going to the labor commissioner with a concern)

- For being a whistleblower (reporting or threatening to report the employer to the IRS or SEC or some other agency)

- For refusing to violate a law (illegal dumping, lying under oath, or illegally terminating an employee)

- For a combination of or a variation of any of these reasons Good labor relations, good documentation, good disciplinary action, good employee handbooks, and good management are your best defense against any of these charges.

- *Take steps first.* Except in some instances of a workforce reduction, a termination should never be a complete surprise. If an employee's performance does not meet standards, she should be given the opportunity to improve. The same may also be true if an employee innocently violates a policy and does not cause harm to the company or to a co-worker.

- *Tie up loose ends.* Don't terminate an employee without collecting all the data you need:

  - Find out how much sick time, vacation time, or personal leave the employee has accrued. Determine whether your employee handbook or state law requires that the employee be paid for those benefits and when. California, for example, requires that accrued vacation be paid at the time the employee is terminated.

  - Calculate how many hours they have worked during the current pay period, including any applicable overtime. People must be paid for that time.

  - Calculate any commission owed the employee.

  - Determine whether the employee is eligible for continuing benefits coverage under COBRA (see "COBRA: A Primer" pages 325–326).

- *Determine how much severance, if any, to give the employee.* You may not want to give employees being terminated for poor performance (for cause) any severance, or you may want to give two weeks salary as a good-will gesture and obtain a release against legal claims. Whatever you do, be consistent. Don't use the whim system.

If an employee is being terminated for other reasons (such as a downsizing or the elimination of a department), you'll probably want to offer severance. Whatever you decide, follow some logical rationale (such as a week's pay for each year employed with the company). (Beware: If you have a set "plan" with respect to severance, there are ERISA requirements that may apply.)

Also decide whether you'll offer any other help, such as outplacement counseling. If so, define the terms up front, put them in writing, and obtain a release in exchange.

- *Determine the employee's final date of employment.* If employees are being fired for cause, it doesn't make much sense to keep them around after they are terminated. They will likely be angry and therefore disrupt morale in the office. In addition, they will want to focus on getting a new job. It's best for them to leave the day you notify them, even if you give them severance pay for a subsequent period. People being laid off or discharged for reasons other than performance may appreciate the chance to stay while they look for other jobs. Be consistent in what you decide, particularly for all employees in the same group.

- *Consider the timing of your meeting.* If you can avoid it, don't fire employees on Friday. It's harder for them to begin looking for a new job on the weekend, which may make them feel angrier or more frustrated.

Also avoid waiting until the last hour of the day to fire people. They may have obligations they must meet, such as getting to a child care facility that will preclude them from staying to clean out their desk. Avoid the awkwardness of their having to come back in the morning to face that task in full view of the office.

- *Meet with the employee.* *Never* fire someone by e-mail or voicemail or send a not-so-subtle hint by changing the locks on their office door. Doing so is cowardly and guaranteed to make the situation worse. Meet with the employee. Respect the employee in the process:

  - Prepare exactly what you are going to say before the meeting begins, and then meet privately or with one witness. Don't fire someone in front of the whole office.

  - Give them time to collect themselves. If they cry, for example, let them calm down and dry their tears. Don't force them to walk back to their desk in their most distressed state.

  - Give the employee a copy of the termination letter (see "Termination Letters," pages 331–334). Also, give the employee a copy of the severance agreement, if there is one.

  - *Never* argue with the employee about the merits of your decision to terminate. Explain that you understand he may have a different opinion, but you are not meeting to discuss that issue at that time. (Of course, you have already investigated the reasons for the termination and you already heard the employee's position with respect to it.)

  - Never require an employee to stay in a room or building with you. Make it clear the door is being shut for the employee's privacy, but that she may leave at any time if she wants to do so.

- Remain calm and respectful at all times no matter what.

- Keep the meeting brief and to the point. Have an agenda and stick to it, but avoid being abrupt. Don't ever be rude.

- Make no admissions, asides, excuses, or remarks about the employee, the company, or your boss. This meeting should be respectful, but all business.

- If need be, debrief on the status of any pending work so you know where to find material and understand what still needs to be done.

- *Manage their departure.* Under certain circumstances (such as when an employee is being fired for embezzlement or you think that sabotage is a possibility), it makes sense for you and/or a security guard to follow the employee to his desk and watch as he packs to leave. Don't give the employee the chance to destroy evidence by deleting or altering computer files.

Except in such extreme circumstances, however, we suggest you *don't* escort employees out. Unless they actually are a criminal, they shouldn't be treated as such. That unnecessarily undermines their dignity. It's also more likely to do serious damage to overall morale because other employees will be uncomfortable.

Let them know when you expect them to have collected their things and then leave them alone to do it.

Before they go, be sure to collect any company property, such as computers, keys, or credit cards.

Ideally, you should present employees with their final check in the termination meeting. If you can't do that, let them know when they can expect it. Make it available as soon as possible and meet that commitment. (In some states, you must have the final paycheck ready and available at the time of the termination.)

Stay Out of Jail

- *If you have an HR department, review any termination and your supporting evidence with them before you act.* If you don't have an HR department, consider having an attorney evaluate the situation.

- *Keep your meeting brief and to the point.* If the employee is being terminated for a particular cause, you should have had several meetings about the situation. This is *not* the time to rehash those discussions. Don't argue with the employee about whether he deserves it. If need be, simply keep repeating calmly that you have made your decision. Generally, the less said, the better.

- *Be consistent.* Do not give some employees better severance or more notice simply because you like them. And never terminate someone simply because he has a different ethnic background or for other reasons that may be seen as discrimination.

- *Do not talk about the termination with other employees.* They do not need to know why someone was fired, how many chances she had to improve, what happened when you fired her, and so on. Simply say that anything that happened is between you and the employee, and that you would respect the same policy if they were the employee in question.

- *Be aware of your responsibilities under COBRA* (see "COBRA: A Primer," pages 325–326).
- *Explain relevant COBRA provisions to the terminated employee, but don't promise more than you need to, or can, deliver.*

Real Life Example

- One boss worked so hard at making an employee feel better that the employee came to work as usual the next day. He didn't realize he'd been fired.
- Another boss invited employees to a Christmas party and handed them envelopes as they arrived. During the party, people opened the envelopes and found pink slips. When he was confronted, the boss said he felt the party would take some of the sting out of the situation. It didn't.
- One WorkingWounded.com reader suggests that the best way to fire someone is to let him make that choice himself. The manager calls the employee into his office to discuss the issues that led to the meeting. The boss shares specific examples of the problem and outlines the behavior that the employee needs to demonstrate in a timely manner.

  Next, the boss asks the employee if she really likes her job. Most answer, "Yes." He asks the employee to think about how she can improve her performance. Then he advises her to take a paid day off to think about how to eliminate the problems. He also asks her to write down 20 ways she feels she can improve her performance. The employee is then told that if the problems continue she will be terminated.

The employee is also told that if she chooses not to return, two weeks pay plus any monies owed her will be ready upon request. "Every time I used this system, the employee chose not to return," the manager says. "Listing how they would improve their performance wasn't something anyone wanted to put on paper. The employee was given a way out with the option of retaining their dignity and having enough money to make a transition."

LAYOFFS: HOW TO CUT THE RISK OF LAWSUITS

Know the Issue

You had the winning lottery ticket, and your check is on the way. Now you can finally realize your dream house. You call the Goodwill to pick up all your furniture and head out to buy new pieces for every room. What fun!

But suppose instead that you're being asked to move to the other side of the country to accept a new job. Your new home is smaller than your present one, and there isn't enough room for all your furniture. You have to make tough choices—selling family heirlooms and antiques. Your family complains bitterly about the choices you made, and for months you miss the furniture that you gave up. The process is so painful that your excitement about the new job has been undermined.

Perhaps these emotions are familiar. If so, they offer a hint of what's in store if your company decides that layoffs are necessary. If

COBRA: A Primer

The *Consolidated Omnibus Budget Reconciliation Act* (COBRA) was designed to ensure that employees and their families would not lose their health insurance coverage when they lost their jobs. Although the concept is simple, like most laws, it's complex and challenging. For expert advice in complying with COBRA, consult with a benefit plan expert or an attorney. Here are the basic provisions of the law:

Who Is Eligible for Coverage?

All employers (except churches) with 20 or more employees must give employees the option of maintaining health care coverage under COBRA when they are terminated. (Some states have "mini-COBRA" laws that apply to employers with fewer than 20 employees.)

Employers don't have to offer COBRA to employees terminated for willful misconduct. (Because the risk of penalties for not complying with COBRA is so great, most employers ignore this option, even when an employee is terminated for stealing and confesses.)

In addition, COBRA must be offered under specific circumstances triggered by "qualifying events."

What Are Qualifying Events?

In addition to an employee's termination, other situations trigger entitlement to coverage. These include

- The death of a covered employee (his dependents must be offered COBRA coverage)
- A reduction in an employee's schedule (as when you ordinarily provide coverage only to full-time employees and an employee who has worked full time assumes a part-time schedule)
- The divorce or legal separation of the covered employee from the employee's spouse (the spouse must then be offered COBRA coverage)

continued

- A dependent child of an employee ceases to be a dependent (the child then must be offered COBRA coverage)
- An employee becomes entitled to coverage under Medicare (in which case dependents must be offered COBRA coverage)

Keep in mind that COBRA is intended to extend existing coverage; it is not intended to create new classifications of covered employees.

How Long Does COBRA Coverage Last?

Eighteen months, or 29 months for people with disabilities. However, if another qualifying event happens during that time then coverage is extended for another 18 months for a total of 36 months. For example, if a former employee died during the initial 18 months, then his dependents would be eligible for an additional 18 months.

Does Coverage Last That Long No Matter What?

No. Coverage may cease before 18 months pass if

- The employee becomes covered under another employer's plan (unless the new employer's plan has a pre-existing conditions clause that directly affects the employee)
- All employer-provided health plans are terminated (in other words, no employees receive health-care benefits)
- The covered individual doesn't pay the required premium (see the following section)
- In the case of a former spouse, the individual remarried and is then covered under another health plan.

Who Pays for COBRA Coverage?

Individuals may be required to pay a premium. The cost may not exceed 102 percent of the applicable premium paid on behalf of active employees. (The additional 2 percent theoretically offsets the employer's cost.)

we are so affected by having to make choices about furniture, imagine the feelings that are stirred up when employees lose their jobs.

In a layoff or reduction in force (RIF), the pain is particularly acute because the employees who are terminated would otherwise not be asked to leave. They often are solid performers who will be missed by their colleagues and by you.

Whatever the impetus for the layoff (a downturn in business, an upturn in expenses, a change in ownership, a change in business direction), the risk of litigation can be high. Not only do employees claim that the layoff should never have happened, but individual employees—even if they see the need for a layoff—also argue that the company was wrong to lay *them* off.

When you meet with employees, follow the guidelines outlined earlier in the chapter. Because layoffs are so charged and put the company at risk of a lawsuit, there are additional steps to take.

Take Action

- *Make certain the reasons for the layoff are obvious, documented, discussed at the highest levels of the company, and considered as a last (or near-to-last) resort.*
- *Base layoff decisions on objective, work-related criteria.*
- *Support the reasons for the layoff decision (for example, the employee refused cross-training in an important area where his skills are now needed) with reviews, disciplinary records, and personnel files.*

- *Don't take action that conflicts with the employee handbook, the collective bargaining agreement, written employment agreements, published company policies, and so on.*

- *Consider having outside experts, such as accountants, economists, business consultants, involved in the decision.* If such an expert is involved, a written recommendation, consistent with the company's eventual action, can be very helpful.

- *Make certain (or advocate) that the people (for example, the committee), or the person, deciding which employees leave and which stay, will be effective witnesses, able to explain why the layoff was necessary and why each employee was chosen for layoff.*

Stay Out of Jail

- *The WARN Act applies to employers of 100 or more full-time employees if there is a plant closing resulting in employment loss to 50 or more employees (not including part-time employees) or a mass layoff (defined as loss of employment to at least one-third of the employees, (which is at least 50 employees or 500 employees).* If WARN applies, 60 days notice of the layoff must be given to the employees' labor representative (union) or, if there is no representative, to the employees directly, and to state and local governmental entities.

- *Ask employees to sign a release waiving the right to file wrongful discharge claims in exchange for their severance.* Remember, the *Federal Age Discrimination in Employment Act* (ADEA) requires special language in the release if employees who are 40 or older are offered exit incentives or are terminated as part of an employment termination program. The special language must advise employees of their right to consider whether to agree to the release (and therefore the waiver of a Federal age claim) for 45 days, and their right to rescind the agreement within seven days after the 45-day consideration period.

- Be careful about the laws against discrimination.
- Remember that ERISA covers such benefits as severance, if given in accordance with a severance plan.

CONSTRUCTIVE TERMINATION: HOW TO PROTECT YOURSELF FROM CLAIMS PEOPLE WERE FORCED TO QUIT

Know the Issue

Hounded by the press, facing a trial in Congress, and abandoned by his own party, President Richard Nixon resigned on August 9, 1974. He remains the only U.S. President ever to resign the office.

But if Nixon had been a corporate manager instead of a public servant, he might be able to argue that he was actually fired. That's because of a little-known legal concept called *constructive termination*. In constructive termination, an employee quits her job because her working conditions have become unbearable. Although the resignation is voluntary, a court might view such a resignation as *involuntary* because by not repairing the working situation, the employer has, in effect, forced the employee to leave. An employee forced to leave under these circumstances may be able to sue her former employer successfully.

So beware. You may sometimes find yourself wishing that Bertha Bademployee "would just quit," but don't look the other way because Bertha's discomfort can become your legal problem.

Take Action

- *Encourage employees to come to you.* You don't want to face a constructive termination lawsuit over a problem you didn't even know existed. Suppose, for example, an employee feels he must quit because he can no longer face the racial epithets being left in his voicemail or e-mail. That's a problem you could have taken steps to correct if you knew about it. Make yourself accessible.

- *Investigate all claims.* If an employee comes to you with a complaint, take it seriously. Investigate to figure out, as best you can, what's really going on. Don't hope the problem will just go away.

  If you find that an employee's complaint is valid, take action to solve the problem; ignoring it may be seen as condoning the behavior. Deal with the problem directly, openly and honestly. Offer training to employees who are causing the problem or, if need be, discipline (including terminating) those responsible.

- *If an employee has a performance problem, deal with it.* Meet with the employee and counsel her for improvement or, if need be, discipline the employee. *Never* resort to giving an employee the cold shoulder, ignoring her at meetings, leaving her out of events, or otherwise passively expressing your displeasure.

Stay Out of Jail

- *Never assume that forcing an employee to quit will end all employment problems and prevent a lawsuit for wrongful termination.*

TERMINATION LETTERS: HOW TO WRITE A DOCUMENT THAT PROTECTS YOUR COMPANY

Know the Issue

There's a reason that Dear John letters are the stuff of movies and songs much more often than, say, Dear John telephone calls. Having the message in writing makes it more final and less ambiguous. Whatever it says is right there in black and white.

Termination letters are important for the same reasons. They make the finality of your decision absolutely clear. They leave no room for an employee to wonder why he was fired, and they offer a stronger defense in court should an employee file suit over his discharge. Termination letters are one of the most important pieces of documentation you must draft.

Take Action

- *Always put it in writing.* Just because a termination seems inevitable or obvious to you doesn't mean that an employee will see it that way. Even if he does, it doesn't mean that he won't seize on an ambiguity to make a case in court. *Always* give an employee a letter when he or she is terminated explaining the reasons for the termination.

The letter should include

- The employee's name and position
- The date the termination is effective
- The severance the employee will receive (including any vacation or personal leave time on the books that the employee must be paid for)
- Information about benefits coverage (how long any existing coverage will continue)

- *Explain why.* The letter also should include the reason(s) the employee is being fired. Without a clear (and substantiated) reason, the employee's attorney can argue in court that the reasons her client was fired were made up "after the fact" in response to the lawsuit, and that he was actually fired because of discrimination or whistleblowing.

  In addition, if you don't give your reasons for firing someone, you may never even get the *chance* to defend those reasons in court because some arbitrators and judges compare termination letters to an "indictment" require all "charges" to be clearly stated or they will be "lost." Think of it this way: You can't be called into court to prosecute a man for burglary if he was never charged with burglary.

- *Give the employee a copy.* During your meeting, give the employee a copy of the letter. Have the employee sign the letter to show receipt, and provide a space on the letter for the employee to respond in writing.

- *Keep a copy in the employee's personnel file.*

Stay Out of Jail

- *Stick to legitimate business reasons.* When explaining an employee's termination, stick to legitimate business reasons, such as "Because of a downturn in business, the company is reducing its workforce" or "The employee is being terminated for failure to follow a direct order on January 12, 2001, when she was ordered, with a witness present, to work on the McGraw account, but she refused to do so for no legitimate or stated reason."

- *Do* not *include anything in a termination letter based on your personal feelings* ("The employee is not well-liked," for example). Also do *not* mention anything that reflects a stereotype, such as "Like many older people, the employee cannot learn things quickly." Focus on the unacceptable outcome, *not* a supposed reason for the employee's behavior.

- *Focus on what you can prove.* Don't include claims against an employee that you can't prove. For example, don't state that the employee was fired for poor attendance if you have no records to show when and how often the employee was absent. It will be very difficult to defend any claim that you can't substantiate.

  In addition, if you can't prove one of your claims, you may lose the chance to claim any of them. Suppose, for example, you fire an employee because he was tardy, swore at a co-worker, and attempted to burn the facility down. If you can prove the employee swore at a co-worker and tried to burn the building down, but you *can't* prove that he was tardy, a judge

or arbitrator may rule that you failed to prove your case and reject your *entire* explanation.

- *If the letter doesn't make it clear that an employee's employment was at-will or that he was given prior discipline or that he gave you his promise he would never repeat his offense, you may compromise your ability to establish those facts at trial.*

- *If you have an HR department, have someone in HR review the letter before you give it to the employee.* If you don't have an HR department, consider having an attorney review the letter.

RESIGNATIONS: HOW TO GET CLOSURE WHEN PEOPLE MOVE ON

Know the Issue

Dinner was great until you realized that you were being dumped. Now you're a mass of emotions: surprise, hurt, anger, confusion, maybe even relief. You may want to bolt from the table and seek succor in a double scotch or a three-scoop hot fudge sundae. But first you probably want to know what went wrong and how the dumper can be so stupid. You'll want to know what hideous character flaw you need to hide on your next date. You'll want reassurance you aren't a total loser. In short, you'll want closure.

Surprisingly, you may feel many of these same feelings when an employee dumps *you* by resigning. No, the emotions aren't as strong. You aren't likely to build a bonfire with everything in your office that reminds you of the employee. But a resignation *is* a loss, and it's only natural to want to learn from the experience and to get some closure. Unlike even the worst dates, you also need to consider the legal issues on behalf of your employer.

Take Action

- *Get it in writing.* If an employee resigns, ask him to write a letter of resignation or, better yet, help him draft it. Be sure to include the fact that his resignation was *voluntary* and not due to anything the employer did or did not do. Doing so can help mitigate the risk of a constructive termination claim (see "Constructive Termination," pages 329–331). Assuming the reason isn't one that can be considered a constructive termination, put it in the letter: "I'm quitting to take a better position" or " . . . for family-related reasons" or " . . . to travel" or "to go back to school." The letter also should state the employee's position and the date the resignation is effective. Keep a copy of the letter in the employee's personnel file.

- *Accept the employee's resignation in writing.* Keep the letter brief and to the point. Simply acknowledge receipt and acceptance of the resignation. Include the employee's name and position, and the date the resignation is effective.

- *Consider whether you want the employee to stay after the resignation.* If the employee is leaving for personal reasons, you may want to let the employee work the last two weeks (if he's given you that notice) and put things in order during that time. If an employee quits in hostility ("I hate you and I have to get out of here!"), however, it's better to accept the resignation immediately and let them leave that day. If they offer two weeks notice, pay them for that time and tell them the notice is appreciated, but their presence isn't needed. You're better off doing that than having them poison the atmosphere in the office for two weeks.

- *Do an exit interview.* Unless you had a terrible relationship with the employee, ask for constructive feedback about the company and about you:
  - If you want her to reconsider, ask if there's anything you can do that would prompt her to change her mind.
  - What did she like best about the job and the organization?
  - What did she like least?
  - If she was the boss, what's one thing she would do differently?
  - Does she have any suggestions for improving workflow or productivity?
  - Are there any problems that she thinks you're unaware of?

    Of course, you hope employees always feel free to talk to you about these things, but sometimes employees who are leaving feel they have nothing to lose and may be more candid. You may learn a lot that no current employee would want to tell you.

- *Tie up loose ends.* Debrief with the employee about the status of pending projects. Be sure you know where to find relevant information and material. Collect any company property, including keys and credit cards. Get a number where he can be reached in the event you must call to get some information.

Stay Out of Jail

- *Meet with the employee to discuss her reasons for leaving.* If you learn something you would rather not know, you *cannot* ignore it. If you hear about sexual harassment, for example, do an investigation right away. (See "Sexual Harassment," pages 368–381) If the person quitting says she was harassed, explain to her that harassment is against company policy, that you will investigate whether she stays or not, and that you would like her to reconsider her decision to quit. Document your statements in a letter to the employee and follow through with the investigation.

  If the investigation concludes that there was harassment and effective remedial action is taken (the harasser is terminated or moved), let the employee know via letter (even if she quit months earlier) and encourage her to come back to work.

  What you are trying to do is to turn a possible constructive termination into a more positive situation. The same applies to other improper actions that bothered the employee.

- *In some states, employees who quit must be paid all wages, bonuses, vacation, and other amounts due within 72 hours of quitting or at the time of quitting if the employer was previously given 72 hours notice.* Be sure you know what your state requires.

11

Communication

When President Reagan fired the nation's air traffic controllers in the '80s, millions of passengers wondered whether it was safe to fly. Just how would all those airplanes know where to go—and how to avoid each other—without experienced professionals providing that all-important network of communication?

Within days, less experienced controllers flocked to the control towers and, in a trial by fire, rose to the task of keeping the airspace safe. As a manager, you face a similar trial by fire, because communication is no less important between you and your employees than it is in the airspace over Chicago.

Listening well and talking clearly are two of your most critical skills for keeping your employees headed in the right direction, making progress toward their destinations, and not on collision courses with each other. Without effective communication, your department is as doomed as an airborne plane that's lost contact with the ground.

Although there aren't as many rules for workplace communication as there are for jet-to-tower exchanges, you can follow certain guidelines to improve communication and keep your department aloft.

LISTENING SKILLS: HOW TO HEAR WHAT PEOPLE REALLY HAVE TO SAY

Know the Issue

"Stop. Look. Listen." Classic advice to help children cross the street safely.

Good advice for managers, too. Employees want to be heard, and a big part of your job is to listen. As the boss, you'll hear complaints, concerns, and fears. People will want rumors confirmed or denied, conflict resolved, and questions answered. They'll need to vent, worry, and even cry. They'll also want you to understand that they are hard-working, smart, and creative, or that their co-workers are not.

All of which, believe it or not, shapes how you're perceived as a manager. If employees feel you're a good listener, you'll be seen as confident, compassionate, aware, and fair. If you're seen as a poor listener, employees will describe you as arrogant, mean, out of touch, and unfair.

Beyond that, if employees believe you're a poor listener, they'll stop talking to you. On some days, that might be a very appealing idea, but in the long-term, it's not what you want. You need information to manage, and if employees don't talk to you, you'll never have enough.

So what does it mean to be a good listener? Here are some basics.

Take Action

- *Give employees your full attention.* You're busy. Your own boss is breathing down your neck. So when employees come with a question or concern, it's tempting to sort through your mail or sign checks or approve expense reports while you listen. Resist the temptation. Set aside whatever you're doing and give the employee your undivided attention. It's important for the employee to *see* you listening:
  - Focus on asking questions instead of giving answers.
  - Focus on what they're saying, not what you'll say next.
  - Focus on what you can learn instead of what you can teach.
  - Focus on giving them the benefit of the doubt instead of doubting their benefit.

  If you're caught at a time when you can't be interrupted, make an appointment with the employee for the earliest available time.

- *Notice body language.* Watch employees when they talk. Is their body language consistent with what they're saying? For example, suppose you ask an employee if he knows anything about why the shipment didn't go out on time. If he looks straight at you, makes eye contact and says that he knows nothing about it, what does that tell you? Is the message the same if he looks at the ground and shuffles his feet while making the same assertion? Be careful about jumping to conclusions, especially if the employee has different cultural values from the American business norm (see "Cultural Values: How To Get Past Race and Ethnicity" Chapter 8, page 188). But if what you hear and what you see don't correlate, that's your prompt to ask more questions.

- *Remember that silence is golden.* Yes, employees usually want advice or information when they come to you, but they also want to be heard, so don't feel compelled to fill every pause in the conversation. Some people simply need more time to formulate a thought or to process what they've heard.

- *Keep tissues handy.* Sooner or later, someone *will* cry. It's a natural expression of feeling. Nonetheless, it may be embarrassing for the employee, and you may feel very uncomfortable. When it happens, don't feel you need to *do* anything. Just reassure the employee that it's OK and hand her a tissue.

- *Repeat what you hear.* We all hear through the filter of our experience and viewpoint. It's important to be sure that what you hear is what the employee really intended. To do that, pause occasionally and repeat back to the employee what you believe you heard. Say, "I want to be sure I understand what you're saying. What I heard is . . . ," and then ask the employee whether you have it right. That gives the employee the chance to fix any misunderstandings or to add information. It also shows the employee that you're listening.

- *Think before responding.* Be sure you really want to say what you say before you say it. If an employee is critical, argumentative, or accusatory, it's natural to defend yourself or refute the exaggeration. Choose your words carefully so you don't say something you'll regret.

- *Address the employee's expectations.* Occasionally, employees will talk to you with no expectation that you *do* anything. Usually, however, they expect some outcome from the discussion. Once you've heard what the employee has to say, decide what you're going to do. It may be that you'll do nothing. Either way, tell the employee what you're going to do and why. At the end of the conversation, he should have some sense of closure. Without it, he'll just be frustrated.

- *Make notes.* You don't need a record of every conversation. If an employee simply wants clarification about a procedure or a request you've made, then there's probably no need to note it. There's also no need to document conversations in which employees share information about their personal lives, but you should make notes of some conversations:

  - Discussions of employee performance problems
  - Requests for training, promotions, or other career-related matters
  - Accusations of misconduct (such as charges that another employee is stealing or harassing others)
  - Requests for leave (particularly FMLA leave)
  - Requests for an ADA-covered accommodation

  In these cases, make notes (see "Documenting Performance," Chapter 9, page 271) and put the notes in the appropriate file.

Stay Out of Jail

- Unless something an employee tells you requires you to take action (such as investigating a complaint, for example) it's best to keep it to yourself. If you're unsure what to do about a situation, you may seek advice from HR, your boss, or another manager, but *never* gossip about employees or violate a trust.

Real Life Example

- The new manager, Juanita, had been told that one of the store's employees was "difficult," that Lisa was short-tempered, bossy, and often in conflict with other employees. So she met with Lisa to address the problem.

  But it wasn't long before Alex, another employee, was in Juanita's office to complain about Lisa again. Juanita pumped Alex for information, but as she did so she sensed that Alex knew more than he was telling. Eventually, with a lot of prodding, Alex admitted that Juanita, herself, was part of the problem.

  Shocked, Juanita asked Alex to explain. He acknowledged that Lisa was difficult and prone to outbursts, but he said that Lisa's behavior had been aggravated by the perception that she and others thought Juanita was apathetic and didn't really understand what went on in the shop.

  Juanita was angry and hurt, but she kept her feelings to herself and simply asked if Alex knew why people felt that way. He offered examples of miscommunication and of issues that people felt weren't being addressed.

  Juanita listened carefully. She thanked Alex for his candor, admitted that she was surprised and disappointed, and promised to think about what he had said.

  The next day, Juanita took Alex aside and shared some of the specific steps she was taking to improve. As a result, Juanita earned Alex's respect. He became her advocate to other employees and helped improve morale.

- A manager received a threatening telephone call. He was very concerned, and told a co-worker what happened. The company decided that the matter would be dealt with confidentially. Unfortunately, the manager's secretary overheard enough of the manager's conversation with his co-worker to know that there was the potential for a serious problem.

After two sleepless nights, the secretary decided to confront a vice president. By watching and listening, it was clear to the vice president that the secretary was concerned about the manager, concerned for her own safety, and concerned about what she didn't know. The vice president asked the secretary to promise confidentiality, and she complied. He then told the secretary the nature of the threat and generally what the company was doing to protect the manager. He reassured her that the threat was not directed at the company or at anyone other than the manager, and offered her time off.

The secretary was appreciative, informed, empowered, and fully willing to face the known risk. She did not take any time off because of the situation.

Manage Up

- *Use your best listening skills with your boss.* Make a point of repeating back what you think you've heard to be sure you have it right.

Get More Information

Listening: The Forgotten Skill, Madelyn Burley-Allen, John Wiley & Sons, 1995.

The Zen of Listening, Rebecca Z. Shafir, Quest Books, 2000.

KEEP EMPLOYEES IN THE LOOP: HOW TO FILL THE INFORMATION VACUUM

Know the Issue

The flight was scheduled to leave at 8:20. The sign at the ticket counter shows that the flight is on time, but it's now 9:10 and the flight hasn't even boarded. Why? Is the weather bad? Are passengers waiting for new safety instruction cards to arrive from the printer? Are the pilots drunk? No one knows. As the minutes pass, passengers grumble. Tempers flare. Shouts are exchanged. "Are we boarding in two minutes, or can I go eat?" one passenger fumes. "I wish they'd tell us what the hell is going on."

Your employees are the passengers on your airline. They want to know what's going on. If they don't know, morale stays firmly earthbound. They aren't quiet about it, either. Do you want *your* employees venting to customers, "Management never tells us anything"?

Now, a dose of reality: It isn't possible to keep all the people happy all the time. (In fact, it's not even a sensible goal.) There always will be people who claim they didn't know, or didn't know soon enough, or found out the "wrong" way. Some employees will seek information, while others remain passive and expect to be spoon-fed. A few will claim they didn't know, even if they really did.

So why bother to keep employees in the loop? Because *most* employees will appreciate it, because keeping employees in the loop is too important to ignore, and because it's a big part of your job.

Take Action

- *Remember, it's about* them. Listen to the questions that employees ask when they get new information. Almost all of them will be some variation of, "What does that mean to me?" Employees naturally want to know what to expect and what's expected of them. Does it mean longer hours? A bigger bonus? No bonus? More responsibility? Different tasks? Focus on how employees will be most affected and be straight with them about it.

- *Provide context.* According to the polls we've taken in organizations, most employees say that management's decisions are arbitrary and poorly considered. That belief reflects the fact that employees are rarely given any context for the information they get. As abstractions, many decisions *do* seem arbitrary. Employees are more likely to reward you with patience and support if they understand the thinking behind decisions. Take a page from Journalism 101 and tell them:
  - *Who* made the decision and *who* will be affected by it
  - *What* the decision is and what it means
  - *When* it will happen
  - *Where* the company is going and how the decision contributes to progress
  - *Why* the decision was made
  - *How* the plan will be implemented

- *Don't sweat the small stuff.* Keep in mind that what employees *want* to know and what they *need* to know are two different things. Some employees want to know everything

about everything, even if it isn't any of their business. Does everyone need an announcement that Linda is moving to a different cubicle?

Employees really only need information about things that affect the whole company (mergers, downsizing, purchases, product launches, key management changes, new policies) and those that affect their specific jobs.

- *Don't rely on one format.* People learn and process information differently. Some people learn by hearing, others by reading, and still others through action. Meet those needs, and take some pressure off yourself to do all communicating face to face, by sharing information several ways:

  - Hold meetings
  - Send e-mail
  - Leave "broadcast" voicemail
  - Post information in break rooms or other gathering spots
  - Post information on the company intranet

  Don't use every media to convey every piece of information. Use more "active" media (such as e-mail) for more urgent or important information, and more "passive" media (such as an intranet) for less urgent information. Experiment to see which media your employees respond to best.

- *Ask for feedback.* You've put the information out there, but did anyone notice or care? One way to find out is to ask for feedback. Are employees confused? Frustrated? Mad as hell? Indifferent? Asking the question increases the odds that employees will pay attention, and the responses can tell you whether you need to communicate more.

Let employees know what you're going to do with the feedback. Share it? Act on it? Ignore it? Set realistic expectations.

- *Be proactive.* Don't wait to be asked before sharing information.

- *Get help.* You don't have to do all the communicating yourself. Ask employees working on specific projects or responsible for specific functions to communicate with their coworkers. Review their initial efforts before they share them to be sure they're complete and helpful. Offer coaching or training if employees need help with their communication skills.

- *Review the union contract.* If a union represents your employees, be sure you're familiar with the terms of the contract. Are you required to give specific notice of work assignment changes, changes in shifts, or other job matters?

- *Cut yourself some slack.* If every employee knew everything all the time, it would be a miracle. Feel good if *most* employees know *most* of what they need to know *most* of the time.

Stay Out of Jail

- *Be sure that employees are aware of any policy changes.*

Real Life Examples

- Laura Janke became the manager of 13 people who were dispirited and wary after working with an unsuccessful manager. To get things back on track, she implemented weekly meetings to discuss everything and anything. At first, no one knew quite what to expect and sometimes the meetings were little more than gripe fests. Ultimately, they became an effective tool.

The meetings were a forum to discuss changes, deadlines, and activities in other departments that might have bearing on Janke's department. Janke also used the meetings for training, praise, and thanks. At the end of each meeting, everyone attending had a chance to share news.

Janke says the meetings were a success in part because they happened consistently. The meetings were held at the same time each week, and Janke had a sign in her office as a reminder. Employees reminded Janke if she got busy or forgot; only twice in a year did she cancel the meeting.

"The meetings helped build a truly cohesive department that was fragmented and in disarray when I stepped in," Janke says.

- Chris was in a foul mood, and everyone knew it. After what seemed like a very long morning, a co-worker took him aside and asked if everything was OK. It was not.

Chris had met the new manager the day before, and he was not happy. Oh, he had nothing against the woman, at least yet. He was just fuming because there *was* a new manager. After all, she was the fourth one in six months.

"I just figured out how to work with the last one, and now she's gone," he complained. "How long will this one be here?" True, the company was in the midst of change, but Chris was far from alone in his frustration. The entire department was up in arms. Each new manager had been introduced as the "new manager," only to be reassigned elsewhere after a few weeks.

The staff spent a lot of time commiserating about the changes and speculating about the next one. Morale had dropped; people had begun grumbling about leaving. "Why can't they just tell us what's going on?" Chris asked.

- "I left on vacation for three weeks to go on a long camping trip that everyone in my work group knew about," one software engineer said. "After I returned, I was at work for four days before my boss had any contact with me at all. No email. No phone call. No visit to my office. No questions about the trip. No updates about what had happened while I was gone. No direction about what I should be doing. It left me feeling rather insignificant and unimportant."

WALK THE TALK: HOW TO ALIGN WHAT YOU SAY AND WHAT YOU DO

Know the Issue

"It's too late for me to quit," the father says to his son, lighting a cigarette, "but you're young. Don't you start."

What are the odds this son won't take up the habit?

Unfortunately, *do as I say, not as I do* isn't very credible parenting—or managing. If you consistently say one thing and do another, your employees are guaranteed to follow your *actions.*

Granted, you can't always follow your own advice. Occasionally, you get new information, or change your mind, or forget. (As Ralph Waldo Emerson observed, "A foolish inconsistency is the hobgoblin of litle minds.") But if you can walk your talk *most* of the time, you'll be out ahead of the pack.

- *Follow the rules.* You're looking for trouble if you believe that there is one set of rules for you and a different set for your employees. If you insist on punctuality, for example, don't show up for work whenever you want to without explanation. If you ask people not to eat at their desks, don't let people catch you dropping sandwich crumbs into your keyboard. If you don't respect the rules, others won't either. They'll just break them behind your back.

- *Make decisions based on core values, not expediency.* Business gurus James C. Collins and Jerry I. Porras have built their careers on the simple premise that the companies that do best over the long haul are those that formulate core values, such as honesty, ethics, or continual improvement, and stick to them, even when it would be easier not to. Their book, *Built to Last,* cites examples that range from Procter and Gamble to Wal-Mart.

  This is good advice for individual managers, too. If you say you value honesty, for example, then be honest, even if it means admitting that your competitor's product might better serve a client's need. If you say you value creativity, don't postpone your decisions so long that every new idea dies on the vine. Employees know that values are tested when times are tough, and they'll look to you to pass the test. If you do, they'll know they can count on you to support them when they rely on those values to make a decision.

- *Don't be careless*. Months have passed, and you can barely remember that you had to make this decision once before. You certainly can't remember what you decided. And if you can't, no one else will either, right? Wrong. You can count on at least one employee recalling *exactly* what you decided.

  Before you make a decision, stop and consider the precedent you've set. Then follow the precedent unless you have a really good reason not to. If you can't remember the precedent, ask.

- *When you don't walk the talk, explain why*. Times will occur when you'll have to do something that appears inconsistent with what you've said. For instance, suppose a core value is to ensure customer satisfaction. That may be a great overall philosophy, but you may have a customer who is never happy, one who demands endless corrections, custom options, and special treatment. Suppose you run the numbers and realize that the time invested in this customer is so great that you can't make a profit on his jobs.

  It would be a smart decision to decline further business from him. To your employees, however, that might seem like you've abandoned your values and that all the work they did to satisfy the customer was a waste of time. Save the situation by explaining *why* you've decided to walk away from his business. Employees may not agree with every decision, but they'll respect your integrity and the fact that you were open about your reasoning.

- *Face the music*. If you articulate values and then act in a way that contradicts them, it's only reasonable to expect employees to call you on it. When they do, pay attention. Strength will come from rethinking your actions and apologizing if need be. Don't be "right" just because you're the boss.

Stay Out of Jail

- *Enforce the rules.* You don't want to find yourself in court listening to evidence proving that you enforced the rules inconsistently or didn't enforce them at all. Don't ignore the rules that are inconvenient or that you don't agree with.

Real Life Example

"They *say* we should provide the best possible customer service," says Charles, an employee of a retail store that promotes its excellent service. "Service is the whole focus of the training we get. We hear the mantra every day, and they include examples of what they want in every employee newsletter. But they don't really mean it."

Charles points out that employees were docked pay if they were so much as a minute late from their break, even if a manager could see that they had stopped on the way to answer a customer's question. "You can imagine how many questions we answer now," he says.

He cites other examples, too. "We spent months developing a relationship with one of our customers, and he bought thousands of dollars in merchandise. It got to the point where he gave us his credit card number and trusted us to buy on his behalf. When we introduced a series of prints, he bought the whole set, with the understanding that he'd get one each month. Then, when it was time to ship him the last one, the manager decided to sell the print to a customer who was in the shop that day. So our best customer missed out on the last one. He returned the whole set, and we all felt like idiots. We felt that we violated his trust, and we won't be put in that situation again.

"We're going to the CEO," says Charles. "We want the manager fired."

Manage Up

- *Never agree to something with your boss and then do something different.*
- *Never disregard something your boss says and then nail your employees for ignoring it.*

APOLOGIZING: WHY MANAGING OFTEN MEANS HAVING TO SAY YOU'RE SORRY

Know the Issue

"Love means never having to say you're sorry." In case you're too young to remember, that phrase comes from Erich Segal's best-selling schmaltzfest, *Love Story.* No one understood what it meant, but that didn't keep it from becoming one of the catch phrases of the '70s.

Today the catch phrase might be, "Managing means never having to say you're sorry." It makes no more sense than Segal's phrase, but that doesn't stop managers from following its prescription—into trouble. Because even though some managers believe that apologizing is a sign of weakness and weakens their stature in the eyes of employees, the opposite is true. As novelist Jessamyn West observed, "It is easy to forgive others their mistakes; it takes more grit and gumption to forgive them for having witnessed your own."

Managers who never apologize are diminished. Employees know that no one is perfect and lose respect for managers who can't accept that. "Is it that he doesn't care when he screws up, that he's too dumb to know, or that he's too big a coward to admit it?" one

employee asked about her boss. "Either way, I have no confidence that he's going to notice a problem and do something to fix it. And it's hard to respect someone who shows no respect for you."

Hardly a recipe for a happy, healthy workplace is it? Now, we're not asking you to whip yourself with a wet noodle or to go on "Oprah" to atone for your sins, but we are asking that when you blow it, you admit it and offer a sincere apology.

Take Action

- *Accept that you aren't perfect.* Yes, you're the boss. That doesn't make you infallible. In fact, as a boss you have more chances to goof up than anyone. Don't you feel better already?

- *'fess Up.* No screw up is worse than the mess you can get into pretending it didn't happen. (Nixon. Watergate. Clinton. Monica. Point made.) If you dropped the ball, *say so* and apologize. And when you apologize, do it sincerely.

- *Listen to your inner voice.* Adding numbers incorrectly is one kind of mistake; setting unrealistic deadlines is another. And then there are situations that just don't *feel* right, such as when you lose it in a meeting, snap at a colleague because you have the headache from hell, or stoop to sarcasm when you run out of patience. The little voice in your head will squawk enough to call your attention to most transgressions. When you hear it, heed it and apologize.

- *Don't wait to be asked for an apology.* Times will occur when you really don't know you blew it. When that happens and people call you on it, offer an apology with grace. More often, you'll know you made a mistake. Don't make people come to you and ask for an apology; that's more than a little manipulative.

- *Accept your role as apologist-in-chief.* You're the boss, which to your employees makes you the voice of the company. That means you'll be called upon to apologize for things you may have had nothing to do with. If an employee is shown to have been sexually harassed, for example, extend an apology on behalf of the company. Be sensitive to such situations. Your employees will feel like you're supporting them against the bureaucracy.

- *Don't play the blame game.* Finding blame is highly overrated. It has only one possible outcome, which is to make everyone afraid of making mistakes. It's better not to blame anyone. Instead, see mistakes as learning opportunities.

- *Be honest with yourself.* When mistakes happen, you should first ask yourself what you may have done to contribute to the problem. Perhaps you've done nothing. Ask anyway. It's a good exercise to keep yourself honest. When you've blown it, admit it to yourself.

Stay Out of Jail

- *Don't make promises you can't keep.* Apologize for what's happened, but resist the urge to assure employees that "it will never happen again." You intend that it'll never happen again, but life is unpredictable.

- *If legal issues are involved, talk with an attorney before you say something that could come back to haunt you.*

Real Life Examples

- The employees of a particular business report to work each morning two hours before the shop opens. That way, they have time to reconcile the cash registers, clean the shop, and put away stock. One morning, they walked in to find so much new stock that they knew it would be a challenge to get it all put away. The situation was further complicated when the boss asked them to attend a morning meeting. One of the employees explained the situation and offered that if they attended the meeting the shop might not open on time. The manager agreed that that was all right.

  But after the meeting the boss gave them only a few minutes before he popped in and asked when the shop would open. The employees assured him that they were doing their best. A few minutes later he was back. The third time he appeared he stayed in the shop and began looking in the cases at the merchandise. Around him, employees put stock away and then opened the shop.

  Afterward, one of the employees went to the boss. "I told him I didn't appreciate how things had gone," he said. "We had discussed the shop opening and agreed it would be late. Having him keep asking about it, and then stand around doing nothing, didn't help. I suggested that it would have been better if he had helped, or at least sent some other people in to help.

  "He looked at me, and then he agreed. He said that we seemed so organized that he hadn't seen anything he could do, but he said he should have asked. And then he apologized. His apology went such a long way toward defusing the tension. It just stopped right then. Otherwise, we probably would have stewed about it all day."

- The CEO was having a monthly meeting with the management team. As usual, there was a long agenda. When it came time for new business, one manager, a newcomer to the team, shared some ideas she had for employee recognition.

  She wasn't prepared for the response she got. The CEO flew into a rage, screaming at the manager, pounding the table and shaking paper. She shouted that she had *been* recognizing employees, and that it was no longer up to her to do it. When the manager said quietly that she hadn't intended that the CEO implement her ideas, she was greeted with more screaming. Everyone at the table was shell-shocked.

  Later, the CEO paid a visit to the manager. She explained that recognition had been an ongoing struggle, and that the discussion had touched a raw nerve, but she didn't apologize. Nor did she apologize to any of the other managers who had been at the meeting.

  The manager was appalled. "It was so inappropriate," she said. "I just felt abused. When there was no apology, I felt the CEO had no respect for us at all."

  She and another manager at the meeting later cited the meeting as a turning point in their decisions to leave the company.

Manage Up

- *If you make a mistake, bring it to your boss's attention. And then apologize.*

E-MAIL: HOW TO USE ELECTRONIC COMMUNICATION WISELY

Know the Issue

Technology is a wonderful thing. Thanks to microwave ovens we can overcook food faster than ever. ATMs let us empty our checking accounts in record time, and email revs miscommunication to lightning speed.

At least on the email front, it doesn't have to be that way. E-mail can be a valuable tool, but many email boxes are jammed with more excess than Imelda Marcos' shoe closet. They're stuffed with junk mail, jokes, love letters, and sometimes with incendiary material that makes the secret files of the tobacco giants pale in comparison. Then there's the superfluous stuff we send just because it's easy. (One manager never cured an employee of her habit of sending him e-mail asking him to check voicemail that directed him to notes left on his desk.) That leaves only a fraction of material that's actually useful. But you can help turn the tide.

Take Action

- *Don't hide behind email.* Some managers rely on e-mail in lieu of face-to-face conversation. It's especially tempting when people are off-site, such as telecommuters, vendors, or independent contractors.

  But using e-mail for everything makes about as much sense as hoping your doctor can make a diagnosis without ever seeing you. Unless you're the Marion Jones of typing, e-mail is too time-consuming. Email is more easily misinterpreted because it doesn't allow for give-and-take discussion and people aren't guided by facial expressions and vocal intonations. And the more dependent you are on e-mail, the more mysterious you become. Even the Wizard of Oz learned that being the man behind the curtain only gets you so far. Go down the hall, hang out in the lunchroom, or pick up the phone at least some of the time.

- *Use email intelligently.* Just because you *can* use e-mail doesn't mean you should. Limit your use to concise messages:

  - Request, confirm, or change appointments.
  - Remind people of deadlines.
  - Make announcements (such as which days the office will be closed for holidays).
  - Let people know when you'll be out of the office (and how to reach you).

  You can also use e-mail to forward documents that you expect people to file electronically for further reference, such as meeting minutes or budget reports.

  Do *not* use email to

  - Ruminate on strategy.
  - Announce changes in strategy.
  - Announce major changes (such as mergers, acquisitions, reorganizations, or downsizing).
  - Announce major policy changes (such as vacation time or benefits coverage).
  - Send information likely to generate questions.

  Now that we've said the rule is never, remember that rules are made to be broken. You can use email occasionally for more complex communication, but don't let it become a crutch.

- *Don't let e-mail become a tennis match.* We've all known email debates that have volleyed back and forth more times than a tennis ball at Wimbledon. If an e-mail goes back and forth more than three times, and especially if the distribution list gets bigger, that's a sure sign that the discussion is bigger than email. Call a halt and bring people together to resolve the issue.

- *Think twice before you click send.* E-mail will not protect you from yourself. Be careful that you are sending what you intended to send, and that you are sending it to the right person. One employee read a general e-mail from the boss and found it insulting. In the heat of the moment, she typed an angry comment to her colleague that ended, "Does she think we're stupid?" Imagine her red face when she received another e-mail from the boss that said simply, "Yes, I do." If you can't e-mail something nice . . . .

- *Don't become dependent.* It's hard to believe, but people actually worked for centuries without e-mail. That means they didn't check e-mail from home or while they were on vacation, and they didn't send it during those times either. Don't expect people to be chained to e-mail 24 hours a day, 52 weeks a year. Hardly anything is really *that* important.

- *Focus on your own e-mail.* Snooping through other people's e-mail is a risky activity. For more information, see "Privacy," Chapter 12, page 382.

- *Establish an e-mail policy.* Without guidelines, every member of your team is likely to use e-mail differently, and some people may use it inappropriately. If your organization does-n't have an email policy, draft one. To get started, see the dis-cussion of Internet policies on page 409.

Stay Out of Jail

- *Don't put anything in email that you don't want to see in the newspaper or hear in court.* Now that organizations as diverse as Microsoft and the White House have found their internal email printed in newspapers and read in court, you know that even "private" email is *not* really private. Nor can it be eas-ily deleted. Don't put *anything* confidential in e-mail. That includes

  - Salaries

  - Comments about employee performance or discipline

  - Information about job candidates, and the reasons they are or aren't hired

  - Personal opinions about employees

  - Proprietary information (such as passwords)

  - Anything that may be construed as interfering with union business or union organizing activities

    Remember, e-mail is a document, and not even a note on scrap paper that might get lost or destroyed. Look at every-thing you write with the idea that it could be found and used against you. That includes personal email sent or received at work. More than one couple involved in an office romance has found their most intimate thoughts broadcast to the entire company.

- *Be careful about humor.* Just because you think something is funny doesn't mean that others will. Although e-mail has become almost as popular a source of humor as late-night TV, sending jokes at the office is risky, especially if the humor is based on race, ethnicity, gender, age, or sexual orientation. Something you thought was hilarious could end up being used as evidence in a sexual harassment or discrimination suit. Chevron, for example, was forced to pay $2.2 million to settle a harassment case based in part on e-mails with such titles as "Why beer is better than women." If in doubt, don't send it.

- *Keep e-mail that may be evidence of employee performance problems.* Hang on to e-mail that shows an employee is stealing, engaging in unethical behavior, underperforming, harassing employees or customers, or otherwise violating company policy or standards. Ideally, print it and keep the hard copy. Yes, experts can often retrieve e-mail, even if it's been "deleted," but it's easier to find if you've kept it.

Real Life Example

Employees from all over the company were inquiring about exactly how much time they had accrued for personal use, such as vacation or sick leave. The HR department charged with answering the questions spent so much time answering the questions that it was becoming a productivity drain. Finally, someone decided to send an e-mail broadcast to employees so that everyone would have current information.

It's easy to see why the idea seemed a good one, but it all went terribly wrong when the person sending the email didn't notice that salary information was being sent along with the leave data. Within moments, everyone in the company knew exactly how much everyone else was making, and within weeks, 20 percent of the work force was gone. The HR employee who sent the e-mail was probably among them.

Manage Up

- *Be as smart about using e-mail to your boss as you are to your employees. Keep e-mail brief, focused, and professional. Keep it clean and don't send confidential information.*

12

And Then There's Real Life

We all know that Cinderella got her prince, Rapunzel was rescued from her tower, Jack came down the beanstalk with his treasures, and Little Red Riding Hood got out of the woods.

But when Stephen Sondheim and James Lapine used those stories as the springboard for their musical *Into the Woods*, the stories didn't end there. Although the characters end Act I singing that they are "happy ever after," in Act II things aren't so rosy. The giant comes back for revenge, Cinderella and Rapunzel face infidelity, and Red Riding Hood is lonely—so much for happily ever after.

Though Sondheim and Lapine didn't intend it that way, their show can be seen as a parable for management. We all seek the happy ending, and we hope that if we do what seems to be the right thing, we'll find it. However, despite our best intentions and efforts, real life intrudes. People do things they aren't supposed to; they make mistakes; they get sick.

No magic potion can prevent these problems, but you can take steps to respond in ways that are effective, compassionate, and minimize the risk of getting into legal trouble. In management, that *is* happily ever after.

SEXUAL HARASSMENT: HOW TO RECOGNIZE AND PREVENT INAPPROPRIATE BEHAVIOR

Know the Issue

Which of the following true incidents do you believe are sexual harassment?

- A co-worker keeps his wife's picture on his desk. The picture was taken on their Hawaiian honeymoon, and she's wearing a bikini. The picture is visible to anyone who enters his office.
- An older man in the office refers to the younger women in the office as "the girls." When addressing them, he calls them "honey" or "sweetheart." Sometimes he puts an arm around their shoulder, and tells them that "pretty girls keep this old guy going."
- As they walked out of a restaurant following a business lunch, the boss dropped a handful of M&M's into his secretary's breast pocket and squeezed her breast.
- A newly hired employee leaves his wife and two children at home when he accepts a job on an offshore oil rig. On the rig, he's taunted by other employees and supervisors. One day a co-worker holds him in a shower stall while another co-

worker shoves a bar of soap between his buttocks and threatens to rape him.

Perhaps you find all these incidents offensive; or perhaps you find the photo harmless, the older man lacking in judgment, and the M&M's and soap incidents repugnant. Therein is the challenge of sexual harassment—what's hostile or offensive is, to a large extent, in the eye of the beholder, which makes it hard to define.

Officially, the *Equal Employment Opportunity Commission* (EEOC) says that *sexual harassment* includes "unwelcome sexual advances, requests for sexual favors, and other verbal or physical conduct of a sexual nature." Specifically, such requests, advances, or sexual conduct constitute harassment when

- Submission to such conduct is made a term or condition of employment, or submission to or rejection of such conduct is used as a basis for employment decisions affecting the individual (these are often referred to as *quid pro quo* or economic harassment).

- Such conduct has the purpose or effect of unreasonably interfering with an employee's work performance or creating an intimidating, hostile, or offensive working environment (commonly known as *hostile work environment* or environmental harassment).

This polite legalese covers, if you'll pardon the phrase, a multitude of sins: pressure for sex, touching, groping, suggestive behavior, provocative clothing, sexual humor, sexually explicit or suggestive photos, Internet porn, a *Sports Illustrated* swimsuit issue, a Victoria's Secret catalog, and much more.

Are all those examples of sexual harassment under any circumstances? No. The courts have generally determined that something is harassment by using the standard of a "reasonable person." (Some courts have held that if the alleged victim is a woman, then the standard is what a reasonable woman—not person—considers unwelcome and sexual.) That legalese certainly sounds, well, reasonable, but it hasn't kept sexual harassment from becoming the most controversial, divisive issue in the workplace.

That's because it's proven surprisingly difficult to reach a consensus about what's "reasonable." Cultural changes—including the greater prevalence of sexual images, language, and discussion throughout society, a backlash against ideas seen by some as "politically correct," the use of false allegations of sexual harassment to retaliate, and an increase in workplace dating—have complicated the picture.

So what's a boss to do? Look the other way and hope for the best? Or clamp down on workplace behavior with more rules and policies to make sure that no one is ever offended? Both approaches have been tried without much success. Ignoring the issue can lead to class-action suits and multimillion dollar judgments, as Mitsubishi Motor Manufacturing discovered. More policies led down an Orwellian path to "love contracts," in which employers require dating colleagues to sign a document stating they wouldn't claim sexual harassment if the relationship goes sour. (Don't misunderstand: we agree such a contract may be legally desirable under certain circumstances.)

The prudent approach is to take the middle road. State clearly that you take sexual harassment seriously and that you'll investigate all complaints promptly. Then follow these guidelines. The guidelines won't guarantee that no one will ever be offended. Indeed, sexual harassment law is so complex that we can't help you through every possible scenario, but the guidelines can help you through most situations.

Take Action

- *Foster a climate of respect.* Sexual harassment is usually *not* about sex; it is about power. Harassment reflects a misguided sense of superiority (particularly over the person being harassed), and it's therefore more likely to happen when disrespect of any kind is tolerated. Don't allow employees to post sexually explicit photos, even in locker rooms or restrooms. Don't tolerate inappropriate humor, language, or familiarity at work. For example, don't permit jokes or cartoons based on racial, ethnic, or gender stereotypes to circulate. Don't allow employees to use profanity. Be sure that employees refer to one another by name, rather than using nicknames or terms of endearment ("sweetheart," for instance).

- *Look for warning signs.* If you create a positive environment, employees usually step forward when a problem arises, but this is not always the case. It helps to be aware of the signs that may indicate a problem. Parallax Education, a Santa Monica, California-based firm that specializes in sexual harassment issues, suggests watching for

  - A noticeable change in the behavior of an employee, including, but not limited to, tardiness, absenteeism, and mood swings

  - An employee who avoids another employee or shrinks from another employee's physical proximity

- Openly sexual behavior between employees, even if it seems welcome (for example, one employee sitting in another's lap)
- Frequent after-work partying or heavy drinking
- Unprofessional behavior during business trips or conventions

  If you observe any of this behavior, don't assume that there's a sexual harassment problem. You should, however, counsel employees not to engage in any openly sexual behavior at work, and remind them to act professionally when they represent the company, even if it's outside the office. If individual employees seem troubled, don't ask if they're being harassed, but do ask if you can help with anything.

- *Take seven steps to fight harassment.* In a 1998 ruling on sexual harassment, the Supreme Court said that employers may be able to avoid liability or limit damages if they can establish that

  - They exercised reasonable care to prevent and promptly correct any harassing behavior.
  - An employee unreasonably failed to take advantage of any preventive or corrective opportunities provided by the employer, or he or she otherwise failed to take reasonable steps to avoid harm.

    There are seven steps you can take to demonstrate a good faith effort in preventing and correcting the problem, and encouraging employees to step forward if a problem arises. (For the seven steps, see "Stay Out of Jail," page 375.)

- *Take all complaints seriously, but don't assume guilt.* Any charge of sexual harassment should be taken seriously and investigated promptly (see "Stay Out of Jail" for more information), but don't assume that all accusations have merit. Employees may charge they've been harassed if a consensual relationship ends to settle a score or to express anger. (One employee, for example, filed a sexual harassment complaint within hours of being disciplined for excessive absenteeism.) In each case, look at the evidence presented by the witnesses and do your best to reach an impartial conclusion. (The disciplined employee, for example, provided a list of witnesses to the alleged harassment, but in the investigation none of them corroborated the incidents.)

- *Be sure that you don't take action without sufficient grounds to do so.* In an effort to stop sexual harassment immediately, some supervisors have stepped in to solve problems that didn't exist. It's possible, for example, to overhear a conversation or to hear something out of context and assume that sexual harassment has occurred, when the employee in question views the situation differently. But *always* investigate if you have reason to believe harassment has occurred or a complaint is filed, and take action when it is warranted.

- *Keep sexual harassment complaints and investigations confidential.* You won't accomplish anything good by letting the whole office know about a sexual harassment investigation, and you could do a lot of damage. For example, if an employee is accused of harassment and later found innocent, the employee could argue that he was defamed if word of the charges is spread. Generally, limit any conversation to

  - The employee who claims to have been harassed
  - The person accused of the harassment

- Representatives in your HR department
- An attorney representing your employer in the case
- Any people who are witnesses or possible witnesses to the alleged harassment or similar conduct by the alleged harasser or witnesses who the alleged harasser says will support his denial

  Caution everyone involved to respect an employee's confidentiality and not to talk about the situation or the investigation.

- *Come to a conclusion.* The investigation's purpose is to determine whether sexual harassment occurred and, if it did, to swiftly punish the conduct so it doesn't happen again. If you fail to take swift and effective action to prevent sexual harassment, you stand to lose all credibility in the eyes of your employees, the EEOC, and the courts. It can also result in punitive damages. Remember, whether you took effective action to prevent sexual harassment will probably be judged in hindsight and be based, at least in part, on whether sexual harassment occurs again under your watch.

- *Track complaints.* Keep confidential records of all harassment complaints. Without records, you could be unaware of a pattern of harassment by the same person. Such a pattern could be relevant in determining someone's credibility or in disciplining an employee.

- *Don't ignore the aftermath.* Sexual harassment investigations are painful, especially if the allegations prove true. Even when the investigation is complete and you've taken action, it will take time for the wounds to heal. Take these steps:

- Do not answer questions about the case from other employees; the details should be confidential. You can answer questions about the company's policy on harassment or about how claims are addressed.

- Put a copy of the conclusion reached following the investigation in both employees' personnel file.

- An employee who's been harassed may feel uncomfortable continuing to work alongside the harasser. If the employee who was harassed asks to be separated from the harasser, consider honoring the request by moving the harasser. Doing this shows good faith on your part. It isn't always reasonable to honor such requests. It is generally a bad idea, however, even to consider reassigning an employee who was harassed; if she is unhappy with the new assignment, you may face complaints that you made the assignment in retaliation for the harassment claim.

- If you have an *employee assistance program* (EAP), remind the employee who was harassed about the program. If you don't have an EAP, consider paying for a limited number of sessions with a professional therapist. Counseling is the compassionate thing to do and can help the employee be more productive at work.

Stay Out of Jail

- *Understand the legal landscape of harassment.* Sexual harassment takes many forms. It can happen at work or offsite. It may involve employees, customers, or vendors. Very few people are truly an expert on harassment law, but you should know the basics.

- *Follow these seven steps to fight harassment.*

    1. *Make sure your company has a written (and legally satisfactory) anti-harassment policy:* Work with an expert, such as an attorney, to develop a policy on sexual harassment. The policy should be easy to understand. Be sure it includes specificsabout the procedures for making a complaint. The procedure should give employees options for making a complaint to more than one person.

    2. *Distribute the policy:* Having a policy in a three-ring binder somewhere is not enough. Make sure *all* employees have a copy. Review it with employees, and have them sign a statement that they received it and understand it.

    3. *Conduct training:* All managers and supervisors (yes, that means you) should have training on sexual harassment regularly (we recommend annually). One of the best ways to prevent harassment is to teach *all* employees about specific prohibited behavior and tell them they will be held accountable for such behavior.

    4. *Audit employment decisions:* Be sure that all employment decisions (such as promotions or terminations) are handled appropriately and consistently, and that no decisions are made outside the system. Otherwise, for example, employees might be unfairly punished for resisting a supervisor's advances. If you work in a large organization, ask HR for help.

5. *Conduct prompt and thorough investigations:* Take every complaint seriously and investigate promptly. If your firm has an HR department, work with HR to conduct the investigation. If you don't have an HR department, consider bringing in an outside expert (such as an attorney or a consultant with expertise in sexual harassment). That's because a thorough investigation is critical and an incomplete, inaccurate, or biased investigation can make the situation worse. The investigation should include

- Interviews of the employee making the complaint
- Interviews of the person charged with the complaint
- Interviews with witnesses (usually identified by the employee who was harassed or by the person charged with the harassment)
- Review of any evidence presented by either side (such as notes, e-mail, voice mail messages, photographs, and so on)

Document each step of the process and any findings.

6. *Take prompt and effective remedial action:* If you conclude that harassment has occured, take swift action to stop it and prevent its recurrence. Depending on the situation, that action might include

- Oral or written warning or reprimand
- Transfer or reassignment
- Demotion
- Reduction of wages
- Suspension

- Discharge
- Training or counseling of harasser to ensure that he or she understands why the conduct violated the employer's anti-harassment policy
- Monitoring the harasser to ensure that harassment stops

Ascertain what the complainant believes would be appropriate discipline. Although it's important to consider the complainant's opinion, keep in kind that her suggestions may be too punitive or too lenient. The discipline meted out should reflect the seriousness of the offense. If the harassment was minor, such as a few crude remarks by someone with no history of misconduct, then counseling and an oral warning may be all that's needed. If the harassment was severe or persistent, however, suspension or discharge may be necessary. Remember, it's up to you to take swift and effective action to prevent a recurrence.

In most cases, it may also be necessary for the company to rectify the consequences suffered by an employee who was harassed. This may include

- Restoring leave taken because of the harassment
- Expunging negative evaluation(s) in an employee's personnel file that arose because of the harassment
- Reinstating a fired employee
- Asking the harasser to apologize
- Monitoring treatment of the employee to ensure that he or she is not subjected to retaliation by the harasser or others in the workplace because of the complaint

- Correcting any monetary harm caused by the harassment (for example, compensation for losses, including emotional distress and lost wages or salary)

7. *Follow up on remedial measures:* Check back with the employee who made the complaint to be sure that your action has been effective. Document any follow-up interviews, including the employee's comments.

Real Life Examples

- Rena Weeks was employed as a secretary by the legal firm of Baker & McKenzie for just 70 days. During that time, she was assigned to work with attorney Martin Greenstein for less than a month. But shortly after leaving the firm, Weeks filed suit, claiming that Greenstein had sexually harassed her. Her claim resulted in a judgement against the firm of $3.5 million in punitive damages and $50,000 in compensatory damages. Greenstein personally was ordered to pay $225,000 in punitive damages.

  This case underscores how seriously you should take sexual harassment because those judgments were rendered despite the facts that Weeks worked in the firm such a short time and worked for Greenstein an even shorter time. Beyond that, the incidents that Weeks defined as harassment happened over a two-week period and were, compared to many incidents of harassment, relatively tame. Weeks accused Greenstein of

  - Dropping a handful of M&M's into her breast pocket and squeezing her breast following a business lunch

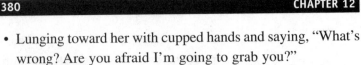

- Lunging toward her with cupped hands and saying, "What's wrong? Are you afraid I'm going to grab you?"

- Repeatedly asking her during lunch, "What's the wildest thing you've ever done?"

- Grabbing her buttocks as they were packing items into a van

  But Weeks didn't win her case alone. The jury heard testimony from seven other women who claimed that Greenstein also harassed them and it decided that the firm had not made sufficient effort to stop the harassment. The jury initially awarded damages of $6.9 million, but the judge later reduced this figure.

- The doctor felt an immediate affinity for the new lab technician, and as they talked he learned that they had a lot in common. He was particularly struck by how similar their backgrounds were: Both had been born in Africa and raised in France before immigrating to the U.S. Consequently, they shared many cultural values and perspectives.

  The doctor made a point of saying hello to the technician, and eventually began asking for her by name. He tried to arrange it so she could do the lab work he required.

  One day the technician mentioned the doctor's visits to her supervisor and shared some of his comments. Days later, she was called into the supervisor's office. There, she was greeted by her supervisor and by the officer for medical affairs. They wanted details about the sexual harassment she had experienced from the doctor. They talked to her at some length about what had happened and assured her that the matter would be resolved.

The following day, the technician called the medical affairs officer from her home. She said that she had been surprised and upset by the meeting. She didn't feel the doctor had harassed her and didn't want his reputation to suffer. She said that she hadn't complained to the supervisor and didn't understand how the situation had spiraled out of control.

Ultimately, the investigation was dropped and the supervisor was coached by HR for taking aggressive steps without a complaint or any evidence that there was a problem.

Do at Least the Minimum

- *Insist that employees treat each other with respect.*
- *There are no shortcuts when it comes to sexual harassment.* Follow the seven-step plan outlined above. Investigate complaints promptly, confidentially, and thoroughly *every* time.

Get More Information

The First Line of Defense: A Guide to Preventing Sexual Harassment, Wanda Dobrich and Steven Dranoff, John Wiley & Sons, 2000.

The Manager's Pocket Guide to Preventing Sexual Harassment, Terry Fitzwater, Human Resource Development Press, 1999.

What Every Manager Needs to Know About Sexual Harassment, Darlene Orlov and Michael T. Roumell, AMACOM, 1999.

PRIVACY: HOW TO BALANCE THE RIGHTS OF YOUR EMPLOYEES AND YOUR COMPANY

Know the Issue

While doing the laundry, you find a note in your son's pocket that suggests he may be using drugs. Do you ignore it? Do you ask him about it when he gets home? Or do you rush to his room and search for evidence? What if instead of a note you find a permit to buy a gun?

The answers aren't easy. If you ignore the evidence someone could get hurt or worse. Your son's grades, reputation, and health are at risk. On the other hand, if you search his room, you risk shattering his trust in you and undercutting any willingness he might have to discuss difficult topics with you. Unfortunately, these are dilemmas faced by parents every day.

Managers face them, too. On the one hand, you have a responsibility to protect employees and company property, including equipment, data, and money. But getting results demands communication, and employees are less likely to talk with someone they don't trust.

The issue is further complicated by the fact that the workplace privacy issue is far from crystal clear. All of us struggle with where the right to privacy begins and where it ends because there is no single authority on the topic. There isn't a single word in the U.S. Constitution about privacy, yet the Supreme Court has ruled that there is a "penumbra" of rights that address the issue. Yet because the U.S. Constitution restricts government action, decisions on privacy rights in the workplace involving the U.S. Constitution apply mostly to federal employees. That hasn't stopped many states (including California) from including guarantees to privacy in *their* constitutions that apply to private employers. Privacy standards have been shaped by state and federal statutes and regulations and by court decisions.

By now that may sound like enough to send you running from the room, but stay with us; there are ways to balance employees' right to privacy with your right to protect people and your company's assets.

Take Action

- *Establish expectations.* Ironically, the less your employees *expect* privacy, the less likely you are to have a problem. Practically speaking, low expectations mean employees are not disappointed or surprised by their employer's actions. Low expectations also provide the legal defense often needed if there is a lawsuit. Employee handbooks, job application forms, written policies, and contracts should all carefully set forth your right to inspect, search, test, and check for illegal substances and objects, illegal activity, and the improper use of company equipment (including computers, telephones, desks, lockers, locks, and e-mail) consistent with applicable laws.

- *Focus on business reasons.* Just because you *can* search an employee's desk doesn't make it a good idea. If employees feel their privacy is invaded, they may feel distrusted and angry, and morale may suffer.

  Therefore, don't even think about conducting a search unless you have evidence or a strong, verifiable reason to believe that

  - An employee is stealing.
  - An employee is using company equipment improperly.

- An employee is engaged in illegal activity (such as selling or possessing illegal drugs).

- An employee's safety may be at risk.

  Don't mistake suspicion for a reason based on objective fact. You should always have a compelling reason based on objective fact to jeopardize an environment of trust.

- *Consider doing a search only as a last resort.* First, try old-fashioned detective work and simple questioning of employees; that's often enough to "crack the case."

- *Stay out of employees' private lives.* Don't ask employees about their marital status, the health of their personal relationships, or other issues unrelated to work performance.

  In addition, it's usually best not to try to regulate employees' off-duty activities. Some employers, for example, have tried to dissuade employees from parachuting or bungee jumping (for fear of injury and therefore expensive medical claims). Others have sought to keep employees from moonlighting or from participating in events that the employer feels may cast the company in a negative light (marching in a political protest, for example). But 28 states now limit such restrictions, and four (California, Colorado, New York, and North Dakota) ban any employer restrictions on lawful activities after hours.

Stay Out of Jail

- *Because so many jurisdictions govern privacy law, be sure you know and understand the law that applies to you.* Consult with your HR department or with an attorney. A mis-step can result in a lawsuit involving emotional distress damages and punitive damages, as well as poor public relations. Jurors take privacy issues seriously. You should, too.

- *Be very careful about searching anything that isn't company property, such as purses, briefcases, or pockets.* Such action should always be discussed with an attorney *first,* should never be done without an objective reason for suspecting an individual, and should be supported by "airtight" language (such as in your handbook).

- *Consult your policies and follow them.* Don't make up the rules as you go along.

- *If an employee does not voluntarily open her purse or desk, or otherwise doesn't cooperate with an investigation, the last thing you should do is touch the employee.* Do not physically detain, push, grab, grab at, or move an employee or her purse or other belongings. Assuming the employee was obligated to assist in the search, it's better to consider the employee's evasion as an implied admission of guilt and try to get the information some other way.

- *Never conduct a search or inspection with respect to an employee because he or she is a member of a group (for example, a minority or a political group).*

- *Don't overreact or react emotionally.* Drugs in the workplace, pornography, and illegal gambling are serious offenses and you can't ignore them. But whatever you do should reflect reality. The fact that there may be (or is) a problem on the manufacturing floor does not mean that employees' rights may be ignored.

- *If an employee shares personal information with you, keep it to yourself.*

Do at Least the Minimum

- *Be sure your employee handbook and other key documents accurately clarify expectations of privacy consistent with the applicable law.*

- *Do not conduct a search or investigation without having a compelling business reason.*

MEDICAL PROBLEMS AND THE FMLA: HOW TO HELP AN EMPLOYEE THROUGH A PERSONAL OR FAMILY MEDICAL CRISIS

Know the Issue

A star athlete pulls a hamstring and there's no question: He goes out on the disabled list, he gets the best treatment, and, unless the injury is exceptionally severe, *he comes back.* No one—coaches, fans, team-mates, or sports writers—questions any of it.

What a contrast to what sometimes happens when the average employee gets sick or injured. She begs for time off to get treatment. She gets demoted to lesser jobs. Behind closed doors managers won-der, "How do we get rid of her?" To her face they make it clear that her illness better not get in the way of her job performance.

Why this ugly disparity? It's simple: Sports teams understand that players are their greatest assets; the focus is on getting the player back because losing him or her is expensive and painful. Many employers *don't* understand that employees are their greatest assets, so they believe it's easier and cheaper to replace someone than to face lost productivity or take a hit on their medical insurance premiums. They are wrong on both counts.

Because of this mistaken thinking, the problems faced by sick and injured employees have become so prevalent that Congress has taken action to protect them. The 1993 *Family and Medical Leave Act* (FMLA) gives about 70 percent of the workforce basic protections when they or their loved ones face a serious medical problem.

However, the law is so complex that many people—employers and employees alike—don't understand it; therefore, it's often used incorrectly or not at all. Almost a third of the workforce isn't covered by the FMLA. Many aspects of managing an ill or injured employee aren't addressed by the law.

Employees *will* get sick and injured, so this isn't an issue to ignore. Understanding the basics of the FMLA helps (and, if you're in a company with 50 or more employees, it's a necessity), but it isn't enough. Go beyond the FMLA and imagine that all your employees are star players and the Super Bowl is approaching. Think about how you can help them get well and come back.

Take Action

- *Encourage employees to stay healthy.* There's no magic wand to keep employees from getting sick, but encouraging healthful behavior can significantly reduce the risk. If you work for a large company that has a wellness program, encourage employees to use it. If you don't have that resource, think about other things you can do such as
  - Brown-bag lunch programs or training on nutrition, exercise, CPR, first aid, pre-natal care, HIV, and even defensive driving
  - Smoking cessation programs

- Partial or total reimbursement of gym memberships
- Encouraging before- or after-work walking programs

  These efforts needn't be expensive. Classes are available from many non-profit organizations that charge nominal fees. Even training by professionals is less expensive than paying a claim after something happens.

- *Don't encourage people to work when they're sick.* Do you see every cough, sniffle, and wrenched back as a personal affront or a sign of weakness? Do you make employees feel guilty for taking time off? If so, you prolong symptoms, impair productivity, and spread germs throughout the office. You also send a signal that employees are only cogs in the machine, not people.

  Keeping top people is easier if you let them take care of themselves. If your company has a sick or personal leave policy, encourage employees to use it. If your firm doesn't have a policy, advocate for one. If people come to work a hacking, sneezing mess, encourage them to go home, and then deploy other resources to make sure the work gets done. If you're sick, do everyone a favor—model the right behavior and stay home.

- *Keep medical information confidential.* The nature of an employee's illness isn't anyone's business—not even yours. You need to know only two things: that an employee is too ill to come to work, and that he or she is well enough to return. You don't need to know why and you don't want to know. If you have medical information about an employee, you run the risk of a discrimination charge if you take any action the employee feels is negative, even if you know your action is unrelated. You also carry the burden of protecting the employee's privacy. If you don't know, you can't tell.

Many companies have a policy requiring a doctor's note for an employee to return after an absence of a specified period (more than two days, for example). The policy is reasonable, but advise employees that the doctor needn't put a diagnosis on the note.

Any medical information about employees should be kept in a confidential file separate from their personnel file.

- *Respect employees' wishes.* Employees may choose to share medical information with you. (Studies have shown that when people are diagnosed with a serious illness, someone at work is often the first person they choose to tell.) If that happens

  - Ask why the employee is telling you (Does he simply need someone to listen? Is she requesting an FMLA leave? Does he need a reasonable accommodation? Is the employee offering an explanation for what he may feel is diminished performance?)

  - Find out what the employee would like you to say, if anything.

    Some employees may want to keep the diagnosis private; others may want to share it with co-workers; still others may want co-workers to know, but want *you* to tell them. If the employee asks for privacy, do *not* talk to others. If the employee asks you to share the news, ask her to make the request in writing and keep a copy in her medical file.

- *Be sure employees understand their benefits.* Employees often don't think about their benefits until they are ill and need them. However, they don't always think clearly under stress. If you have an HR department, set up an appointment for the employee to meet with someone who can explain his coverage. If you don't have an HR function, contact the insurance carrier and ask for someone who can help the employee understand the plan. Employees need to understand their coverage, their rights, and their responsibilities.

- *Understand the Americans with Disabilities Act (ADA).* Some illnesses and injuries are serious enough that employees become disabled. If that happens, they may be protected by the ADA and entitled to reasonable accommodation. (See "Disabilities," Chapter 8, page 225)

- *Understand the Family and Medical Leave Act (FMLA).* Depending on the severity of an illness or injury, employees may need time off to recover. If you're in an organization with 50 or more employees, your company is subject to the FMLA. (See "The FMLA: A Primer," page 394) If you have fewer than 50 employees, you may still choose to follow FMLA guidelines. Doing so is good for morale and retention (and may be required by a state law). Just be consistent; don't pick and choose who can take leave on any basis other than a legitimate business reason.

- *Don't discriminate based on pregnancy.* Until fairly recently, it was common for companies to refuse to hire pregnant women, to fire women during their pregnancies, or to refuse to allow a woman to return to work after giving birth. All of these practices are illegal. A woman's pregnancy tells you *nothing* about her ability to do the job, so assume it's not relevant in any hiring, promotion, work assignment, or termination decision. Beyond that

- View a disability caused by pregnancy or a related condition just as you would any temporary, physical disability. (In California, leaves may have to be more generous than those provided for other temporary disabilities.)

- Don't attempt to practice medicine; rely on actual medical observation and opinion.

- *Recognize that employees aren't the only ones who get sick or injured.* Employees may face a crisis at home if a spouse, child, parent, or partner is ill or injured. They may even need time off to be a caregiver. The FMLA provides for employees to take leave as a caregiver for a spouse, parent, or child in certain situations. (See "The FMLA: A Primer.") Some companies also give leave to employees who must care for a domestic partner.

Stay Out of Jail

- *Don't make decisions about hiring, promotion, work assignments, termination, or other work activities based on an employee's actual or perceived illness, injury, or other medical condition.* (The exception to the rule is when an employee brings medical evidence justifying, for example, a transfer.)

- *Don't permit jokes, remarks, comments, or inappropriate statements relating to any employee's illness, injury, pregnancy, or related conditions.*

- *Don't decide yourself when an employee's condition merits a leave or transfer.* Rely on a doctor's opinion.

Real Life Examples

- The manager's secretary was diagnosed with a serious illness and needed to take time off. Because the manager liked the woman, and in fact found her indispensable, he told her that she should take whatever time she needed and that her job would always be there. A few weeks later, another employee needed a medical leave. This time, the manager gave the employee notice that she was being put on a 12-week FMLA leave and gave her paperwork explaining her rights.

  Ultimately, one of the employees sued the company. Which one? The first employee to go out on leave. While she was out, her manager left the company. Without him, no record of the arrangement was made and the company terminated her employment. She claimed, unsuccessfully, that a promise had been broken.

- An employee was a young mother fighting a rare kind of cancer. Traditional therapies didn't work, and doctors wanted to try experimental treatment. The treatment would require her to spend a day every two months as a hospital outpatient, and would leave her weak and tired. Nonetheless, she wanted to keep working, and she didn't want anyone's pity.

  With her manager's approval, she decided to use her personal days for treatment. Together, they shuffled deadlines and work schedules so that her absences wouldn't coincide with crunch times. The employee also offered cross training to some of her colleagues so they could help if need be when she was out.

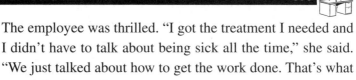

The employee was thrilled. "I got the treatment I needed and I didn't have to talk about being sick all the time," she said. "We just talked about how to get the work done. That's what was right for me."

- The star employee hadn't been himself, and then he started calling in sick. The CEO asked the HR director what was wrong, but she refused to tell him. One Friday, he cornered her, threatening her job if she wouldn't tell. Reluctantly, she acknowledged that the employee had AIDS. She made the CEO promise not to tell anyone else.

The next morning, the employee did his usual weekend errands at the post office, the cleaners, and the grocery. Everywhere he went he was treated differently than how he'd been treated before and not in a way that made him feel loved.

He had told only one person his diagnosis, so on Monday he went to the HR director. She admitted telling the CEO, and apologized. After the employee left, she went to the CEO. "You promised not to tell anyone," she said.

"I only told my wife," the CEO said, but his wife had decided that people in town "needed to know, to protect themselves."

Several weeks later, the man resigned his job and left town, his life in ruins. The company began fighting an expensive lawsuit that it was destined to lose.

The FMLA: A Primer

The FMLA applies to all private organizations with 50 or more employees. Those firms must comply with all the statute's requirements if 50 employees are within a 75-mile radius. Smaller firms may also want to comply in the interest of recruiting and retention. The law is complex, but here are the basics:

What's the Point of the FMLA?

The law says that the FMLA is intended "to balance the demands of the workplace with the needs of families, to promote the stability and economic security of families, and to promote national interest in preserving family integrity."

Which Employees Are Eligible?

All employees who have worked for your company for at least 12 months and have worked at least 1,250 hours during that time are eligible. (The law assumes that exempt employees who do not keep time records have worked the requisite hours unless the employer can prove otherwise.)

When May Employees Take Leave?

Employees are entitled to take leave

- Following the birth of a child
- After adopting a child or assuming responsibility for a foster child
- To provide care for a child, spouse, or parent who has a serious health condition
- Because of their own serious health condition that prevents them from working

continued

Within that framework, the law broadly defines *child* to include employees' own children, as well as stepchildren, adopted children, foster children, and legal wards. It also includes children age 18 and older if they are unable to care for themselves. *Parents* are defined as biological parents only. *Spouse* refers to husbands and wives only, including common-law married couples. The law does not require that employers grant leaves to care for domestic partners or significant others.

What Does the FMLA Mean by "Serious Health Condition"?

The law isn't meant to apply to every case of flu or sprained ankle. It applies to any condition requiring in-patient care or continuing treatment by a healthcare provider. Continuing treatment by a healthcare provider includes

- Incapacity of more than three straight days
- Treatment for that incapacity that involves two or more visits to the doctor or ongoing treatment under the doctor's care (such as taking prescription drugs or receiving oxygen). Taking over-the-counter drugs and resting, even under doctors' orders, are *not* sufficient to constitute a regimen of continuing treatment.
- Incapacity due to pregnancy (pregnancy by itself is *not* sufficient reason) or for prenatal care
- Incapacity or treatment related to a chronic condition (such as asthma or epilepsy)
- Permanent or long-term incapacity due to a condition that can't be treated (such as Alzheimer's disease or a stroke)
- Absence to receive multiple treatments (such as kidney dialysis, chemotherapy for cancer, or physical therapy following an injury)
- Treatment for substance abuse (though an employee's absence because of using illegal drugs is not covered)

continued

- Offering comfort or reassurance that would benefit a child, spouse, or parent who is receiving inpatient or home care

Finally, the courts have ruled that conditions that don't by themselves qualify an employee for leave (severe headaches or a sore throat, for example) may qualify him for leave if he has several of them at once and together they leave him incapacitated. In all cases, however, to qualify for leave, employees must prove that they were *required* by a doctor not to work. Employees can't decide to take leave because they don't feel well.

What Information Can Employers Request from Doctors?

Employers may ask for a doctor's statement that states

- That the employee or family member has a serious medical condition
- The date the condition began
- The probable duration of the condition
- That the eligible employee is needed to care for child, spouse, or parent and for approximately how long
- That the employee is unable to perform the functions of his or her job

    For intermittent leave or a reduced schedule, employers can also ask for

- The dates when treatment is scheduled and the expected duration of the treatment
- A statement of the medical necessity for the intermittent leave or reduced schedule and its expected duration

continued

Can an Employer Get a Second Opinion?

Yes. If employers question the legitimacy of a leave, they may require a second opinion. If the original opinion and the second opinion are different, employers may require a third opinion by a doctor approved by both parties. The third opinion is final and binding. Employers must pay for the second and third opinions. Employees who fail to cooperate can lose FMLA protections.

How Much Time Can Employees Take?

Employees are entitled to as much as 12 weeks of FMLA leave per 12-month period. In determining the 12 months, employers may choose

- The calendar year
- Any fixed 12-month period, such as a fiscal year or a year dating from an employee's anniversary
- The 12 months measured from the date an employee first takes FMLA leave
- A rolling 12-month period measured backward from the date an employee uses an FMLA leave

Any option is fine, provided that employers apply it consistently. If holidays occur during the leave, leave doesn't have to be extended by equivalent time.

Does the Leave Have to Be Taken All at Once?

No. Leave may be taken in blocks of time as needed, ranging from an hour or less to several weeks. Leave may also be taken in the form of a reduced schedule (for example, an employee is too weak to return to work full-time and works part-time while recovering). Employers and employees must cooperate in determining a leave schedule. An intermittent leave or reduced schedule must be medically necessary.

continued

Can Employees Just Stay Home and Call Later to Claim an FMLA Leave?

No. Employees asking for leave don't have to mention the FMLA, but they do have to give their employers reasonable time—ideally, at least 30 days. In case of a medical emergency, notice should be provided as soon as possible—preferably within two business days of taking the leave. When they give notice, employees can't simply say they "don't feel well." They must be prepared to provide documentation that they have a "serious medical condition," as noted above. Employees are not permitted to provide false information or to withhold notice that they have a serious medical condition.

Who Decides a Leave Is an FMLA Leave?

Initially, employers, with "oversight" by the courts. If an employer designates a leave as an FMLA leave, the employee must be told so within two business days from the time he requests leave.

Do Employees Get Paid During Their Leave?

No. However, employees may choose to use accrued vacation or personal leave time for any part of the FMLA leave. Employers also may require employees to use accrued leave, provided that employees have written notice that they must do so. Employers also may require employees to use accrued sick time when taking leave because of their own health condition. Employers are required to maintain an employee's coverage under its group health plan for the duration of the leave. Employees are also entitled to any general raises given during their absence (such as a company-wide cost-of-living increase). Some state laws provide employees with additional rights.

DRUG AND ALCOHOL ABUSE: HOW TO CONFRONT THE ADDICTED EMPLOYEE

Know the Issue

When the Exxon *Valdez* ran aground and spilled millions of gallons of oil into Alaska's pristine offshore waters, it was an ecological disaster. It was also a high-profile example of what can happen when employees abuse drugs or alcohol on the job. Exxon spent years slogging through the aftermath.

Drug abuse is a serious problem. The Research Triangle Institute says it costs U.S. business $26 billion a year. That's why many employers carefully screen applicants to help keep users of illegal drugs off their payrolls (see "Pre-Employment Drug Screening," Chapter 5, page 97).

But what if drug users slip through the screening and get hired? Or existing employees begin using illegal drugs? You can still take steps to protect your employees and your business.

Take Action

- *Know your organization's policy.* Review your employee handbook. Most organizations have a stated policy about drug testing and illegal drug use. Whatever the policy, follow it. Don't be the only manager to require drug tests *unless,* for example, you manage the only department in which employees directly affect public safety.

- *Don't keep the policy a secret.* If your policy requires employees to pass drug tests as a condition of employment, remind employees of that. You might post notices of the policy in work areas, for example.

- *If no company policy exists, develop one for your department.* Don't do drug testing using the whim system. Determine why and when you'll test for drug use. When hiring, focus your attention on employees whose jobs involve safety or security. Once employees are hired, you also want to be able to test if you have a reasonable suspicion or evidence of drug use. The policy also should expressly prohibit the sale or possession of illegal drugs. Make sure the legal department or an attorney approves it.

- *Know the law or consult with someone who does.* Drug testing, like many employment issues, pits two competing sets of rights squarely against one another: the employee's right to privacy and the employer's right to a safe, productive work environment. Given this conflict, it isn't surprising that federal and state legislatures and courts have enacted laws or expressed opinions on the subject. Your options must be evaluated within the limitations of the states and court decisions that apply to you and your company's employees.

- *Know your options for testing.* You can't discipline an employee for drug use merely on the suspicion of drug use. You need to have evidence of drug use, which is why testing is so important. (Of course, you can discipline an employee for poor performance, violation of company rules, insubordination, and so forth whether or not the infractions are drug-related.) You have six different potential options for testing, and there are appropriate uses for each:

- *Periodic testing* is conducted, as the name suggests, periodically, in conjunction with an annual physical, for example. But periodic testing also may include unannounced tests for a group of employees (such as people in jobs in which safety or security are at issue) when random testing is impractical because of the number of employees involved. Periodic testing can be controversial because it is unrelated to any suspicion or evidence of drug use and therefore unlawful in some states. Controversy is mitigated if the physicals are job-related and consistent with business necessity, if employees are told before being hired that they'll be tested, and if employees are told they're subject to discipline if they fail the test or refuse to take the test.

- *Reasonable suspicion testing* may be done if you have direct, specific, and immediate observations of behavior, appearance, odors, and/or speech that suggest drug use or that your substance abuse prevention policy has been violated. (Symptoms of drug withdrawal also may be grounds for testing.) It's best to have another member of management confirm your observations.

- *Postaccident testing* assesses employees who have had an on-the-job accident that caused a fatality, a serious injury, or significant property damage (scarring the Alaskan coastline counts). Such testing may also be done after near-accidents, such as when an employee loses control of a vehicle but manages to stop without hitting anything. Unfortunately, in many states the fact that an accident occurred is not sufficient grounds for creating the suspicion that drugs or alcohol were involved. Check with an attorney about the laws in your state.

- *Random drug testing* refers to selecting employees for testing at random and without notice. It may also refer to testing of the entire workforce on a date selected at random and not announced. (Note: Employers in some industries, including trucking, shipping, airline, and nuclear power, are required to do random testing of some employees.) As a legal matter, this is the most risky type of drug testing you can require. There are fewer justifications for it, and employees are not warned. Random testing is illegal in Rhode Island, Vermont, and other states.

- *Return-to-work testing* is used after an employee has tested positive for drug use or otherwise violated a company's drug policy, after rehabilitation and before returning to work. *Follow-up testing* is designed to encourage recovering addicts to stay clean. Testing is done after rehabilitation at pre-determined regular intervals. Before doing either of these kinds of testing, check the law. It's also a good idea to draft a written contract that addresses the terms and conditions for return-to-work and for follow-up testing.

- *Choose a methodology.* There are several methods of drug testing. The accuracy, legality, and expense of the tests vary, so review your options and choose what's best for your company. (See "Pre-Employment Drug Screening," Chapter 5, page 97.)

- *Choose a vendor.* If your HR department already has identified a testing vendor, use that one. If not, be sure to select a reputable and reliable vendor. (see "Pre-Employment Drug Screening," page 97).

- *Encourage employees to seek treatment.* Even if you are not required by law to give employees leave to seek treatment (see "Stay Out of Jail"), consider allowing such leaves if employees request them. (Usually, policies allow employees to take leaves without disciplinary consequences if employees volunteer for them before employers find they have violated policies.) There are good reasons to do so:
  - Drug-abuse prevention programs that include employee assistance or rehabilitation are most effective at achieving drug-free workplaces.
  - Employees have incentive to seek treatment earlier.

Stay Out of Jail

- *Know the law in your state or seek legal advice before taking action.*
- *Don't subject an employee to a drug test merely because he associates with another employee known to use drugs.* Base your decision to test strictly on observable job-related behavior.
- *Be consistent in asking employees to be tested for drug use.* Be careful, for example, that you are not singling out only employees of a particular racial or ethnic background.
- *The Americans with Disabilities Act (ADA) is complex legislation (see "Disabilities," Chapter 8, page 225) that has some implications for drug testing:*

- Current use of an illegal drug is *not* protected by the ADA.

- Addicts who are participating in or have completed a supervised drug rehabilitation program and are no longer "current users" *are* protected.

- Those wrongly perceived as using illegal drugs are protected.

- Employees taking drugs under a physician's care are protected. Therefore, give employees who test positive for drugs the chance to provide medical documentation to explain the results. Do not require employees to reveal prescription drugs they are taking.

- Current users of alcohol may be disabled under terms of the ADA even though current drug users are not. However, even a current user of alcohol is not covered *if* the alcohol is affecting the employee's job performance or conduct.

- *Keep the results of drug tests confidential.* Keep the results in medical files separate from an employee's standard personnel file.

- *The Family and Medical Leave Act (FMLA) is another federal law (see "FMLA," page 394) with provisions that relate to drug and alcohol use.* If your firm is subject to the FMLA, you must allow qualifying employees to take leave for treatment of drug addiction or alcoholism.

- *Where practical, use the same lab to assure uniformity of testing.*

- *Employees who test positive for illegal drugs may claim that they are not users.* In such cases, they may ask for another test to confirm the results. (Normal protocols for testing stipulate that labs test only one-third of the sample provided. That means that they can conduct another test without getting another sample.) You are not obligated to pay for the second test. However, false positives are possible. Many employers choose to pay for the second test as a matter both of fairness and precaution.

Get More Information

Center for Substance Abuse Prevention Hotline, 800/843-4971

The AMA Handbook for Employee Recruitment and Retention, Mary Cook, Ed. The American Management Association, New York, 1992.

THE INTERNET: HOW TO NAVIGATE THE ONLINE FRONTIER

Know the Issue

If only Pandora had never opened the box the gods gave her. But curiosity got the better of her, and she lifted the lid enough to release a swarm of all things evil. Poor Pandora slammed the lid shut, but it was too late. We've had to live with evil ever since, a state mitigated only by the gods' foresight to place hope among the dark contents of the box.

Today's employees face similar temptation. The techno-gods have given them a box that also contains all things evil, and they have been asked not to open it. But many "Pandoras" *have* opened it, and used the Internet at work to view pornography, gamble, buy illegal drugs, and harass one another. That lid can't be closed again; the Internet is here to stay.

Although Pandora had only hope to offset the evil, the techno-gods have given us much more. The benefits unleashed—communication, learning, research, shopping—are so plentiful that we don't *want* to close the lid. We simply want to control what we allow to escape.

Gaining that control is not simple, popular, or perfect, but it is necessary. Rely on a combination of software, rules, and diligence.

Take Action

- *Know the risks.* Internet porn gets all the press, and it's ugly. It's also only the tip of the iceberg. Employees have found more ways to misuse the Net than Baskin-Robbins has flavors. You need to know what you're up against:

  - *Harassment and cyberstalking*: Under a cloak of presumed anonymity, employees can send each other sexual propositions, racial epithets, attacks on religion, and threats of violence ("I have a gun and I know where you are"). E-mail messages, postings on message boards, and discussions in Internet chat rooms can all be used. If the messages persist, it becomes stalking. The stalking extends beyond the virtual. One stalker posed as his victim and used the Internet to post "her" fantasies of being raped; six men showed up at her home.

- *Cyberlibel*: Disgruntled employees vent their anger by making false and harmful statements about their employers and disseminate them using the Internet. A former CFO was accused of posting messages that his employer's future was "uncertain and unstable" on an investment message board. An Internet post falsely claimed that electronic greeting cards made by Blue Mountain Arts contain a virus that destroys the recipient's computer system when they're opened.

- *Possible trademark infringement*: Employees can use your company's name in ways you wish they wouldn't. Most commonly, this takes the form of Internet sites created as gathering spots for employees and customers to diss you; U-Hell and netscapesucks.com are examples. These sites are never fun, but they become even less fun when they're used for blackmail. An ex-employee might agree to shut down a complaint site in exchange for a more lucrative settlement to a lawsuit, for example.

- *Posting personal information*: An angry consumer posted the home addresses, phone numbers, Social Security numbers, and other data of several employees at a collection agency that he felt had wronged him.

- *E-mail abuse*: E-mail is a cheap method of mass distribution. A former employee sent regular mass e-mails to thousands of current employees warning them of pending layoffs and urging them to distrust management.

- *Disclosure of trade secrets*: Employees can wittingly or unwittingly reveal trade secrets while chatting online or posting to message boards.

- *Fraud and misrepresentation*: Employees and applicants can use the Internet to transmit false documents because their authenticity is harder to discern. Applicants may supply false transcripts, for example, during the hiring process.

- *Excessive Internet use*: Employees may spend 80 percent of their day (or more) surfing the Net. Psychiatrists assert that addiction to the Internet is a serious problem; they label the disorder *Internetomania, computer addiction, Internet addictive disorder,* and *cyberaddiction.*

- *Train employees to use the Internet.* Employees are routinely offered training in how to use various software programs, but rarely get training on Web surfing. If you're currently offering computer training, add an Internet component. If not, offer stand-alone training. Be sure to present your Internet policy (see "Stay Out of Jail") at the training, and demonstrate how to navigate the Internet to reach specific sites and to avoid others.

- *Block access to inappropriate sites.* Software is available that blocks access to sexually explicit and other inappropriate sites; use it.

- *Monitor use.* Work with your Information Systems (IS) department or an independent consultant to be sure that you can track Internet use. Do random checks of how much time employees spend on the Web and where they go. Employees should be on notice that such checks will occur.

- *Set a good example.* Monitor your own Internet use at work. Limit the time you spend online, and don't visit inappropriate sites.

Stay Out of Jail

- *Have an Internet policy.* Be sure the policy is thorough:
  - Warn employees that e-mail and messages posted on the Internet are formal communication. Remind them that e-mail messages are *not* easily deleted and may be retrieved.
  - Outline acceptable uses of the Internet, such as for research, communication, or ordering supplies.
  - Delineate unacceptable uses, including using the Internet for personal gain or to advance individual views; soliciting for any non-company business; sending e-mail anonymously or under an alias; using another employee's password; and sending, saving, or viewing offensive material.
  - Advise employees that the company has the right to review employees' Internet use, including any information, email, or files transmitted or stored through the company's computer.
  - Remind employees that e-mail and Internet access are not entirely secure.
  - Counsel employees not to copy or distribute copyrighted material.

    Also remind employees that activities otherwise prohibited (such as harassing a co-worker) are prohibited online as well. Tell employees that violating the rules will result in discipline, including possible termination.

- *Have an attorney review the policy.*
- *Distribute the policy to all employees.* Have them sign a doc-ument stating that they received the policy, understand it, and agree to abide by it.
- *Enforce the policy consistently.* Take steps to monitor Internet use and discipline employees if need be. Don't neglect disci-plining an employee because you like him or because an employee's Internet use doesn't appear to interfere with his work. Match the punishment to the crime: a verbal warning may be enough if an employee simply spends too much time online, but more is called for if an employee is harassing oth-ers or circulating offensive material.

Real Life Example

An employee complained to HR that a co-worker was sending her sexually explicit images using the company's e-mail system. HR investigated her complaint and was stunned to discover thousands of pornographic images stored on the company's intranet. The pictures had been downloaded from Web sites by dozens of employees, who in turn circulated them among themselves and with employees of other companies.

Working with the IS department, HR monitored Internet use for several days and catalogued the images as evidence. Before the dust settled, dozens of employees were terminated and others disciplined. HR was particularly shocked to find that some managers had been participating.

"I thought it wasn't right," one employee told HR when he was fired. "But when my manager did it, I was confused."

13

POST-SCRIPT

Eric Moussambani, a swimmer from Equitorial Guinea, was in over his head. Moussambani was at the Sydney Olympics, swimming a heat in the 100-meter freestyle. Through a series of weird circumstances, all the other swimmers in his heat had dropped out or been disqualified; Moussambani was alone in the pool. Not only had he never won a race of that distance, Moussambani had never swum that far before. Ever. With almost half the race to go, he was exhausted—gasping for air and doubting he'd make it to the wall.

Moussambani was in Sydney through an outreach program to help athletes from disadvantaged countries. Unlike the other competitors, he had no coach, no corporate sponsors—he didn't even practice in an olympic-size pool. Now he was swimming alone watched by a stadium full of spectators and the television eyes of the world. He had no chance of winning a medal, or even of qualifying for the final. The best he could hope for was to finish the heat. It was more

likely that his reward for flying halfway around the world was to be laughed at.

As a manager, you may sometimes feel like Moussambani felt in that pool. You haven't been fully prepared for the experience. You're exhausted and struggling to get through the day, and everyone is watching. You suspect people are laughing, and you know there's no way you can do everything right.

When you have those days, think about Eric Moussambani. He willed himself to the finish of the heat. He had an Olympic experience that no one who saw the heat will ever forget. When he climbed out of the pool, the crowd in the stadium was cheering. Moussambani knows what he can do now, and he'll swim another day. There's glory in doing the best you can.

Get More Information

- *Sign up for our free weekly newsletter at*
  http://RetentionEvangelist.listbot.com
- *Opportunities to network with other bosses*
  visit **http://BossSurvivalGuide.com**
- Legal Advice:
  Alan Levins
  Littler Mendelson
  650 California Street, 20th Floor
  San Francisco, California 94108

- *About "12 Steps to Better Bossing," The Boss's Survival Guide presentation:*

Contact us for information on our keynotes, seminars, and corporate training programs at **http://RetentionEvangelist.com**.

About Working Wounded: Visit **http://WorkingWounded.com**.

Also visit **www.thepositiveworkplace.com**

Index

Symbols

12 steps for better management
abusing employees, 11
customer focused, 13
don't follow Golden Rule, 12
energy in workplace, 15
feast attitude during famine, 10
get out of way, 12
measure, evaluate, reward, 14
mother flame, 16
ready, aim, fire management, 11
recruiting atttudes, 10
revealing waterline, 14
what will it take to keep
employee, 15
90-day reviews, 179–183

A

abusing employees, 11
acceptance letters, 164
access to resources, managing
performance, 253
accidents and drug testing, 401

accomodations for disabled
employees, 233
accomplishments
recognizing formally, 266
recognizing informally, 260
ADA (Americans with Disabilities
Act), 225, 230–232, 390
adaptability, emotional
intelligence, 201
ADEA (Age Discrimination in
Employment Act), 328
administrative exempt
employees, 49
affiliative management style, 249
Affirmative Action, 241
aftermath of harassment
complaints, 375
agencies for hiring employees, 61
contingency search firms, 66
credentials, 62
employment placement
agencies, 65
making offers, 67
monitoring progress, 64
retained search firms, 66